LAND OF BEAUTIFUL VISION

Topics in Contemporary Buddhism
GEORGE G. TANABE, EDITOR

TOPICS IN
CONTEMPORARY
BUDDHISM

LAND OF
BEAUTIFUL VISION

Making a Buddhist Sacred
Place in New Zealand

SALLY McARA

University of Hawai'i Press
Honolulu

**Library of Congress Cataloging-in-
Publication Data**
McAra, Sally, 1967–
Land of beautiful vision : making a
Buddhist sacred place in New Zealand /
Sally McAra.
p. cm. — (Topics in contemporary Buddhism)
Includes bibliographical references and index.
ISBN-13: 978-0-8248-2996-4 (hardcover : alk. paper)
ISBN-10: 0-8248-2996-4 (hardcover : alk. paper)
1. Sudarshanaloka Retreat Centre. 2. Buddhism—
New Zealand—Thames Region. 3. Buddhist
converts—New Zealand—Thames Region.
4. Western Buddhist Order. Friends. I. Title.
BQ6387.S83M33 2007
294.30993'323—dc22
2006031475

University of Hawai'i Press books are
printed on acid-free paper and meet the
guidelines for permanence and durability
of the Council on Library Resources

Designed by Elsa Carl, Clarence Lee Design
Printed by The Maple-Vail Book Manufacturing Group

In memory of my grandfather,
Ed McAra (1906–1941)

Contents

Series Editor's Preface

In telling and analyzing the story of a Buddhist retreat center in New Zealand, Sally McAra delves into major issues of contemporary transculturality. Affiliated with the British-based Friends of the Western Buddhist Order, the Anglo-European founders brought a distinctive and sensitive approach to exploring their relationship as settlers to local spiritual forces and to their own inherited and adopted traditions. The mix is complex, and McAra uses carefully defined analytical tools to elucidate this intriguing case of European, Asian, and Polynesian interactions.

This is an important contribution to this series, which is dedicated to the examination of the contemporary developments of Buddhism in traditional places like Taiwan and Japan, but also its remarkable passages to countries such as Brazil and New Zealand.

George J. Tanabe, Jr.
Series Editor

Acknowledgments

First and foremost I wish to express my gratitude to Christine Dureau and Karen Nero, who supervised the MA thesis from which this book originated and patiently helped me to give shape to my research findings. Christine, especially, has read and commented on endless reworkings of the book manuscript. I would also like to thank two anonymous readers: my external thesis examiner and the first reviewer of an early draft of the manuscript gave helpful feedback; the second reviewer, Franz Metcalf, also gave especially detailed feedback and kind encouragement.

When I embarked on this research, I made contact with people through e-mail after reading their work in the online *Journal of Global Buddhism* and other Internet sources. Although I never met them in person, Sandra Bell, Michelle Spuler, Martin Baumann, and Daniel Capper all took the time to read my early writings and share their work with me. Kitsiri Malalgoda, Michael Radich, and Adrian Croucher have all read and given invaluable feedback on different drafts of the manuscript, while Tracey McIntosh and Cristina Rocha provided guidance on specific chapters.

I wish to thank the many people in the Friends of the Western Buddhist Order (FWBO) who have allowed me to look over their shoulders, engaged in lengthy discussions about their activities, and provided practical help. There are three Western Buddhist Order members who have been most vital to my book: Prajñalila, who compiled the photograph albums and newsletters that have been so important to this study and made helpful comments on two different drafts; Taranatha, who provided examples of his own writing about Sudarshanaloka Buddhist Retreat Centre and commented on sections of the book; and Satyananda, the manager of Sudarshanaloka, who answered many questions and commented on my writing. I should mention that the excellent FWBO resources such as newsletters, photograph albums, and literature disseminated through books and Web sites greatly enriched the research. Purna, Jayarava, and others helped me locate facts and figures on the FWBO. I warmly acknowledge the encouragement and help of others in the FWBO in New Zealand, especially Akasamati. Among Order members in Britain, I thank Vishvapani and Vajrasara of the FWBO communications office in London, as well as Vessantara and Nagabodhi, who provided invaluable information; special thanks to Lokapala for tape-recording and mailing to me an all-important talk that Satyananda gave at the North London Buddhist Centre. The photographs reproduced in this book are a mixture of my own and those of various unnamed photographers who gave their pictures for the Sudarshanaloka albums.

I would also like to thank the staff and graduate students of the anthropology department at The University of Auckland for engaging discussions and feedback and for technical support provided by the Department of Anthropology, Library and Student Learning Centre. This book would not have been possible without the financial support I received in 1999–2000 when researching and writing my MA thesis: The University of Auckland Faculty of Arts Masters scholarship, the Anthropological Society of Aotearoa/New Zealand's Kakano fund, and Anthropology Department Grants-in-Aid. I was fortunate enough to have the support of my department to finish the manuscript while also working on a doctorate in a related area, and I am especially thankful for a departmental PBRF Funding Award, which helped offset costs involved in producing the manuscript. My apologies if I have omitted anyone.

Over the years I have been fortunate to receive endless support from friends and family. Besides acting as a copy editor, providing feedback on writing strategies, and producing excellent renderings of my diagrams and maps for this book, Adrian has also been a wonderful support person to come home to throughout the nine-year journey that became this book. I especially wish to thank my parents for instilling in me a love of learning.

This book is dedicated to the memory of my grandfather Ed McAra, whose calling as a writer was cut short by his death in Crete in 1941. My grandmother's typescript of his beautifully written wartime letters to her is the only way I know him.

A Note on Spelling and Transliteration

The fact that many terms come from across cultural and linguistic boundaries and thus can be transliterated, pronounced, and understood in different ways is pertinent to the larger theme of transcultural interpretation in this book. FWBO publications adopt a range of approaches with regard to Buddhist terms from languages such as Tibetan, Sanskrit, Japanese, and Pāli; while generally they anglicize the spelling, a number of their publications follow partial or full academic transliteration systems. Transliterating each of the source languages has its own orthographical complexities to manage, and I have found it impossible to devise a single coherent system.

Instead, I have three tiers of transliteration. For the Sanskrit and Pāli names of Western Buddhist Order members, FWBO-named places, and direct quotes I have followed the general FWBO tendency to anglicize the words. However, frequently used terms such as "stūpa" have been diacritically marked throughout the book, even in quotes. For Buddhist words found in English-language dictionaries and common FWBO parlance, including names of bodhisattvas, I use diacritical markings but not italics. I use italics *and* diacritics for specialized terms that do not appear in English-language dictionaries. The FWBO uses Pāli and Sanskrit terms almost interchangeably. In the glossary I have provided both where necessary, but otherwise I have used the term that is most favored in the movement or relevant to my discussion.

Sangharakshita and his followers often capitalize the initial letter of certain nouns when they want to place a special emphasis or nuance on them—for instance, when using such terms as "compassion" in their most perfected, archetypal states. I have followed this convention in direct quotes from the FWBO to retain the flavor this brings but otherwise reserve capitals for conventional proper nouns; apart from this I have standardized punctuation and spellings in quotations.

Since I began this study, some of the people featured in it have taken Buddhist names, and of course Tararu was transformed into Sudarshanaloka. In trying to develop a consistent way to refer to them, I use the Buddhist name of people who have become Order members and thus taken new names before or during the time period I am discussing (up until 2000). With those who were ordained after

2000, I have retained their former names but give their ordination names at least once in the text and in the glossary.

Because the terms will be unfamiliar to many readers, I italicize and diacritically mark Māori words, despite the fact that the terms I use have become adopted into New Zealand English.

Introduction

In August 1993, a group of convert[1] Buddhists purchased a steep section of land in the enclosed, forested Tararu Valley, around 120 kilometers (75 miles) from New Zealand's largest city, Auckland. The purchase was the culmination of a decade-long search for a suitable place to build facilities for solitary and group meditation retreats. One summer weekend in 1997, I made my first visit to the property, arriving on the Friday evening before two days of rituals for their newly built stūpa. The glimpses I caught of the stūpa spire as I traveled on the winding dirt road up the valley and the colorful banners on bamboo poles near the entrance to the property hinted that this was no ordinary part of the New Zealand landscape.

From the old farmhouse near the creek I walked up the hill for my first full view of the seven-meter-high (twenty-two feet) concrete-and-steel structure. Its whiteness and its geometric, sharp-edged lines and curves contrasted starkly with the ragged scrub and dark green ridge behind. In preparing the site, a digger had cut into the hillside, exposing rough banks of ocher clay. On either side of the muddy path leading to the monument two clusters of tall bamboo poles flew banner-style prayer flags that fluttered in the breeze. Shaped like a big white bell, the stūpa seemed almost to hover above the freshly disturbed soil on the rough, grassy slope.

The next morning I visited the stūpa again. Final preparations had now been made for the weekend's ceremonies. Strings of flags and colored ribbon ran up from stakes in the ground to meet at the stūpa's spire (Fig. I.1). It seemed to me that these additions somehow helped integrate the structure's stark shapes with the broken ground and bright sky around it.

Representing the enlightened mind, stūpas often contain relics of the Buddha or other revered teachers and are traditionally objects of devotion. A stūpa generally consists of a dome sitting on a base and topped with a spire, and variants on this style are a familiar part of the landscape in many parts of Buddhist Asia. However, they are not a familiar sight in New Zealand, and in 1997 there were, as far as I was aware, only three or four others at Buddhist venues around the country.

The people who designed, built, and dedicated the stūpa in the Tararu Valley were of Anglo-European cultural origins and affiliated with the British-based

FIGURE I.1.
Stūpa with flags, immediately prior to dedication ceremony. (Photographed by S. McAra in 1997.)

international movement known as the Friends of the Western Buddhist Order (FWBO). Their decision to construct the stūpa at all may seem something of a puzzle to people familiar with the literature on Buddhism's modern and Western interpretations. The FWBO had initially purchased the 86-hectare (214 acre) property with the intention of building a retreat center, a place where people, alone or in groups, from near or far, could spend quiet time in a natural setting, undertaking meditative practices and seeking stillness. What they most needed in a practical sense to bring about this vision was accommodation: a large facility that could host up to fifty retreatants, with a shrine room, kitchen and dining space, bunkrooms and chalets, and an ablutions block. While they had fulfilled part of this vision by constructing four self-contained cabins for solitary retreat and were able to accommodate group retreats of less than fifteen people in the old farmhouse, they had continued to defer the construction of the purpose-built retreat facilities. When they needed facilities for larger gatherings they either hired larger venues or used tents and other temporary shelters. Indeed, when they constructed their stūpa in the southern summer of 1996–1997, the lack of facilities meant that people volunteering on the project stayed in bunkrooms in the house or in old caravans set in clearings around the property, and on the weekend of the dedication ceremony, the overnight visitors slept under canvas.

By early 2006, the first stage of the retreat facility was in fact under construction. The delay was the result of a significant shift in priorities in which participants began talking about developing a new relationship with what they had come to regard as a damaged piece of land, and this took precedence over the pragmatic aim of fund-raising for and construction of retreat facilities. The narratives that people wove around this transformation entailed re-imagining their relationship to the land. These stories, and the themes that they evoke, provide the basis of this book.

TRANSFORMING A LOCALE/A TRANSFORMATIVE LOCALE

Until the stūpa dedication, the FWBO referred to the property as Tararu, the established Māori name for the valley and its main creek. After this they adopted the name Sudarshanaloka, which translates from Sanskrit as "Land of Beautiful Vision."[2] They also conducted a ritual aimed at making peace with and befriending the unseen spirit entities they felt were present in the land. The stūpa, the spirits, and the renaming of the land constitute important elements in my account of the unexpected twists and turns entailed by the creation (or conversion) of a sacred place far beyond the original Buddhist homeland (cf. Granoff and Shinohara 2003, 2–3).

The literature on Western Buddhism, which I discuss in chapter 1, highlights the FWBO's reformist stance that seeks to discard the supposed cultural accretions of the previous two and a half millennia and return to the essence of the Buddha's teachings. Somewhat controversially, theologian Phillip Mellor (1991, 1989, 1992) has applied the term "Protestant" to the FWBO in an attempt to theorize their British translation of Buddhism. While FWBO *literature* often takes a reformist approach that fits Mellor's characterization, FWBO *practice* has aspects that complicate it, as will become clear in this book. If Western Buddhists took such an approach, would a stūpa take precedence over the more apparently practical need for a retreat venue? Would nature spirits play a role, or would the notion of their existence be rejected as the animist cultural baggage of localized Buddhist traditions? These questions supply the basis of my investigation of the processes and strategies involved in the vernacularization of Buddhism. Theorization about material culture, in particular the study of the biographies of things (Kopytoff 1986) and, indeed, the social agency of the land itself, provides a medium for negotiations between the abstract universalist ideals of Buddhism and the mundane social actuality in the establishment of FWBO Buddhism in a new cultural and physical landscape.

The FWBO's utopianist vision of creating a New Society inspired by Buddhist ethics speaks to the theme of alternate religious critiques of contemporary, postindustrial society. FWBO literature has often made strong social critiques, identifying and seeking to address what it portrays as the ills of our time, such as environmental destruction, social injustice, and violence. FWBO members hope that by developing spiritual insight and transforming their own way of being in the world, they will have a transformational effect on society.[3] Through attention to members' stories, I explore how the discourses of personal and social transformation that Sandra Bell (1996) identifies in the movement in Britain inform the way New Zealand-based members of the FWBO (hereafter FWBO/NZ members) talk about transformation of the land itself. I also inquire into how emerging settler identities interact with an adopted Buddhist identity, thus tying my research to issues of place and belonging. The relationships between Pākehā (i.e., settlers of European [primarily British] ancestry), the land, and unseen forces perceived in it all play a part in the story of Western Buddhism in a new land. The fraught history of the relationship between Pākehā and the indigenous Māori has influenced how these Buddhists conceptualized their project, so I provide a discussion of this in chapter 3, with the remaining chapters entailing an exploration of the ways that FWBO members involved with Sudarshanaloka engaged with these issues and attempted to redress what they regarded as past harm done to the land.

I draw all of these apparently disparate themes together through the notion of the conjuncture, which is useful for examining the period of intersecting influences that converge during the establishment of Sudarshanaloka. Marshall Sahlins (1981), from whom I borrow the concept, is concerned with the reproduction and transformation of cultural structures in a very different contact episode, that is, the visits of Captain Cook to Hawai'i, which ended with Cook's death in 1779. In reflecting on the interpretations and responses of Hawaiians to their European visitors, Sahlins contends that the challenge to historical anthropology "is not merely to know how events are ordered by culture, but how, in that process, the culture is reordered" (8). People's cultural presuppositions, he says, affect how they respond to situations. But there are occasions in which events fall outside of preexisting categories, and this creates a process of sedimentation of "new functional values on old categories. These new values are likewise resumed within the cultural structure, as Hawaiians incorporated breaches of tabu by the logic of tabu"

(67–68; quote on 68). I, too, am concerned with what Sahlins calls "the clash of cultural understandings and interests" (68) in a period of contact and how both reproduction and transformation of the existing cultural structures ensue.

The conjuncture I am concerned with is very different, however. During the early period in the history of Tararu/Sudarshanaloka, members encountered obstacles while undertaking activities on the land that culminated in a reevaluation of their purpose. Four events illustrate key moments in the transformation: the sudden death of a man who was deeply involved with Sudarshanaloka; a tale of an unsettling encounter with hostile spirit presences on the land (both discussed in chap. 4); the dedication of the stūpa (chap. 5); and a ritual of redress that attempted to heal past wrongdoings (chap. 6). These pivotal events entailed both continuation and, in some ways, transformation of the sociocultural milieu of participants, influencing ongoing conjunctures: Māori-Pākehā, Pākehā-land, and New Zealand in relation to global Buddhism. The human participants are not the only characters in my account; key sites play important roles in the events I discuss, as does the land itself. These landmarks act as both "summarizing" and "elaborating" symbols encapsulating the "cultural schema" (Ortner 1973, 1990) at Sudarshanaloka.

In chapter 6 I also discuss the role of the key symbolic landmarks and the stories woven around them in the creation of a sense of place. This may seem to be a tidy interpretation, but the final chapter, in discussing developments in the decade following the stūpa dedication, shows that its cohesion is fleeting. The conjuncture, an idea that I have developed further since my earlier interpretation (McAra 2000), begins a new process of reconfiguration: for those who would create typologies depicting adaptive phases of cross-cultural religious transmission, this is an apposite reminder that we are concerned with processes that are living, contingent, and fluid.

TRANSCULTURAL RELIGIOUS BRICOLAGE

The concept of "transculturality"[4] is an umbrella term that helps to explain how contemporary cultures permeate one another and intermix, encompassing the competing processes of globalization and particularization and allowing for the complex conditions of cultures where both internal differentiation and external networking take place (Welsch 1999, 204–205). Concepts such as synthesis, syncretism, creolization, and bricolage are useful for thinking about these "dynamic intercultural and intracultural transactions" (Stewart 1999, 55). I take the term "syncretism" and its synonyms to refer to the ongoing dynamic transmission of ideas, practices, and material culture, characterized by the creative appropriation of hitherto alien forms of knowledge from other cultural milieus. This syncretism entails translation into indigenous terms of reference, and its outcome is a trans-cultural religious bricolage:[5] a synthesis of apparently disparate material-cultural elements that people continually weave into a coherent, albeit shimmering and mutable, fabric.

Scholars of Buddhism (e.g., Baumann 1997b, 205–206; Lewis 1997, 345–349) have called for more detailed research into the domestication of Buddhism in new environments beyond Asia. Cristina Rocha's exploration of *Zen in Brazil* (2006) is one of the first books to bring anthropological analysis to bear on the intermixture that this entails, using the trope of creolization. Members of the FWBO in New Zealand constitute a religious minority belonging to the majority settler group, and they are involved in "settling" or establishing their religious community in a new sociocultural and physical landscape (cf. Bouma 1997). They are therefore, in two senses of the word, an instance of "settler Buddhism." Fusions of "native" and adopted forms, symbols, and practices occur creatively, sometimes with full awareness, sometimes not, but in the FWBO there is a conscious attempt to create a locally appropriate expression of Buddhism that retains dynamic connections with its wider international Buddhist network. All religions have "composite origins and are continually reconstructed through ongoing processes of synthesis and erasure" (Shaw and Stewart 1994, 7), so rather than focusing on syncretism as a "category," it is more useful to investigate "*processes* of religious synthesis and . . . *discourses* of syncretism" (emphases in original). Recasting syncretism as "the politics of religious synthesis," Shaw and Stewart acknowledge that people defending specific religious boundaries often perceive academic discussion of syncretism as an accusation of inauthenticity and impurity. The term "syncretism" is often limited to religious and ritual phenomena "where elements of two different historical 'traditions' interact or combine" (10, citing Werbner 1992). In contrast, "bricolage" is used to describe "the formation of new cultural forms from bits and pieces of cultural practice of diverse origins" (10). The term was first introduced into anthropology by Claude Lévi-Strauss (1966). It is based on the metaphor of *bricoleurs*, that is, people who adapt resources at their disposal rather than obtain specialized materials. Lévi-Strauss is particularly concerned with distinguishing scientific from mythical thought. He regards the latter as expressing itself through a "heterogeneous repertoire" that can be thought of as "a kind of intellectual 'bricolage'" (1966, 17). While Lévi-Strauss's structuralist approach has been criticized (e.g., MacCormack and Strathern 1980), his concept of bricolage has taken on a new life in the growth of works on cultural hybridity and syncretism in recent years. Along with the term "synthesis," bricolage is particularly useful for referring to the strategies and processes of drawing on diverse materials and concepts that play a major part in the vernacularization of FWBO Buddhism, and I choose this term among the many possible metaphors because it fits well with my focus on material culture.

The FWBO makes a conscious attempt to render an adopted universalist religion locally meaningful, because of its explicit emphasis on creativity and innovation. Christian missionary efforts have been based on a premise that their spiritual truth, despite being "transcendental, timeless and transcultural," is "adaptable into local [temporal] idioms and symbolic repertoires" (Shaw and Stewart 1994, 11). For such missionary work, "proper enculturation" or "indigenization" is good and "illegitimate syncretism" is not, despite the impossibility of defining where the boundaries between the two lie (11, citing Hastings 1989). For Buddhists, too, there is always a question of how far a doctrine can be indigenized without losing its fundamental truths. From my own observations, different Buddhist teachers and organizations have vastly different concepts of where the boundaries lie. My analysis suggests that the FWBO provides a particularly marked instance of the strategies and processes of synthesis; many of its members draw on forms and practices of diverse origin in the manner of bricolage, whereby practitioners selectively and consciously draw upon their particular sociocultural environments.

Much of the anthropological literature on religious syncretism focuses on colonized peoples, while the domestication of Buddhism in the West is taking place in very different political circumstances. Many of the activities I describe in this book are consistent with numerous other instances of domestication or indigenization that have occurred in the 2,500-year history of the diverse religious expressions that derive their core doctrinal content from the vast body of teachings attributed to the Buddha. At the same time, the conjuncture of people, events, things, and places that I discuss here provides an opportunity to investigate how members of a settler culture explore issues of belonging. Thus the wider sociocultural setting and the land, the particular place, come to play an active role in shaping the imported religion, informed by the rich narratives of key members about the creation of the "myth of Sudarshanaloka."

WHY STUDY THE FWBO IN NEW ZEALAND?

One of the main themes of this book is how people are re-imagining their identities and connections with particular places as a response to an era of increasing mobility. As Akhil Gupta and James Ferguson observe,

> [t]he irony of these times . . . is that as actual places and localities become ever more blurred and indeterminate, *ideas* of culturally and ethnically distinct places become perhaps even more salient. It is here that it becomes most visible how imagined communities (Anderson 1983) come to be attached to imagined places, as displaced peoples cluster around remembered or imagined homelands, places, or communities in a world that seems increasingly to deny such firm territorial anchors in their actuality (1992, 10–11).

This quote sets the scene for the ways that contemporary, transcultural Buddhist movements are putting down roots. The FWBO as an *international* movement draws from an enormous diversity of Buddhist and non-Buddhist sources to constitute and, through its media, imagine itself as a global Buddhist community. At the same time, New Zealand-based members of the movement engage in the creation of a new *local* Buddhist, spiritual homeland in a difficult-to-access, rough, and bush-clad valley. In this book I investigate the question, Does Sudarshana-loka serve as a "territorial anchor" in which FWBO members create a re-imagined place, and if so, how?

Anthropological literature on intercultural religious conversion and the vernacularization of foreign religions has focused on power relations in the context of colonization. The spread of Buddhism into new sociocultural settings provides an opportunity to investigate the manner of adaptation to the new locale in distinct political circumstances.[6] Increasingly in the last two decades, researchers are writing about Buddhism in various strata of society in national and international contexts, investigating the kinds of transformations taking place in Buddhist practice.[7] My book contributes to this literature, while also speaking to other themes, including the role of material culture in religious transplantation, combined with settler identities.

APPROACH

According to an outdated archetype that persists in popular representations of the discipline, the anthropologist undergoes a period of immersion in fieldwork in some distant, exotic location, returning to produce an authoritative monograph detailing such matters as kinship structures and modes of subsistence in his or her chosen society. However, this approach was based on an assumption that "different cultures inhere in discrete and separate places" (Gupta and Ferguson 1997, 35) and cannot speak to contemporary conditions. The outdated methods do not allow for research in "spatially dispersed phenomena" (34) or processes of transculturation. In the last two decades, cultural anthropology has entered a new phase, entailing an increasingly reflexive and self-critical approach (Brettell 1993, 1). Further, it is no longer appropriate to adopt the authoritative, omniscient stance that Edward Said (1978) and others associate with imperialism. Rather, ethnographies are fictions "in the sense of something made or fashioned" (Clifford 1986, 6), and they are "partial" in the senses of being incomplete and of being inextricably shaped by the observer's worldview.

In the last decade I have attended meetings, talks, classes, and study groups at the Auckland Buddhist Centre and retreats at Sudarshanaloka and hired venues. In 2004 I joined the committee that manages the business of Sudarshanaloka, both to keep in touch with developments there and to contribute to the retreat center project. My approach is participatory: my earliest visits to Sudarshanaloka were part of my personal exploration of Buddhism, and, even after deciding to undertake this research in 1999, I attended retreats and talks more as participant than observer, albeit with both an openness to research-related ideas and an awareness of the need for respecting others' privacy and confidentiality in personal matters. However, I should also stress that I am wary of homogenizing terms such as "insider," since research relationships usually entail multiple complexities and ambiguities (Narayan 1993). I acknowledge that the "multiplicity of perspectives" (Northcote 2004, 94) does not get full coverage due to the fact that my focus was on a small, core group's narratives and I did not seek views of those less involved and that ultimately the work remains in my overall control, so the "dialogue" is weighted in favor of my views. I participate in a dialectic between personal and academic involvement, having sometimes engaged in FWBO activities as part of my own personal search, at other times feeling as if I was a somewhat distanced and skeptical observer. As I discuss in chapter 1, my personal exploration of Buddhism led to my participation in events that ultimately provided the inspiration for this research, which has important consequences for this book.

In 1999–2000 I undertook in-depth audiotaped interviews with six individuals closely associated with Sudarshanaloka and had numerous informal conversations with members from various parts of the FWBO.[8] I was also privileged to be able to access a wealth of written materials, including books, personal musings, newsletters, Web sites, and magazine articles. Many FWBO talks, including transcripts and audio and video recordings, are readily accessible at FWBO centers. Further, photograph albums provide a visual record of Sudarshanaloka that supplemented my visits there and provided invaluable help for my analysis of the material culture of the retreat center.

During the time period I focus on in my research, my key interlocutors were members of the Friends of Tararu team, the group most closely involved with projects at Sudarshanaloka. Their purpose, as the name indicates, was to be friends to the land—that is, to keep in touch with the overall vision of creating a place of healing. I have focused on their stories because it is they who have been most actively and consciously involved in Sudarshanaloka. In referring to Tararu/Sudarshanaloka's visionaries and key people I have struggled to find a suitable collective word. I have chosen to use the terms "Friends of Tararu" and "the trustees" and occasionally "FWBO/NZ members" in a fairly loose sense, rather than aiming for absolute accuracy, because the membership of groups of people associating with Sudarshanaloka in various ways has changed over time.

I have not used pseudonyms and retain actual place and personal names. In considering this I asked my interlocutors for their views. Taranatha said that the names and places "are part of our history," and he continued that he did not think publishing them would do any harm, "because the people who matter don't care for their own sake, and the posterity will want to know who those people are; that brings life and personality to it" (27 August 1999). I have also discussed my research, as it has evolved over the last six years, with several of the Sudarshanaloka trustees, and they have read earlier drafts of this book. I have attempted to work with their responses, highlighting where necessary the differences between my anthropological approach and their spiritual focus.

THE SLIPPERINESS OF WORDS

The complexities of terms like "the West," "convert," "Buddhist," "religion," and "culture" all have ramifications for this research. Such terms act as a shorthand, but we need to avoid the trap of believing that any cultural phenomenon possesses some homogeneous, unitary essence. Words are no more than a set of necessary glosses or abstractions, which are always inadequate and ambiguous, evoking ideal types that do not exist empirically. Still, it is unfortunate that words often have the effect of simplifying and freezing complex concepts, and it is all too easy to fall into using them in ways that do not allow for difference. Abu-Lughod (1991, 149–152) complains that generalization is a "language of power," hiding behind a "professional discourse of 'objectivity,'" although it can also be a language of resistance. This facilitates detached abstraction and reification and allows the ethnographer to impose a false sense of coherence, flattening out differences among community members.

The term "West," then, as a term denoting a form of culture should be used with extreme caution. Just as Said cautions with regard to representations of the

"East," we should be wary of making the "West" into a "mythically unitary culture" (Okely 1996, 5). The term, often used interchangeably with the equally problematic "First World," encompasses aspects of life in Western Europe, Britain, North America, Australia, and New Zealand but socioeconomically incorporates the wealthier strata of capitalist societies around the world. In this book, then, I use the word "West" as a generalized reference to a particular transnational cultural context with secular, post-industrial features, but also distinctive Judeo-Christian influences.[9] The very idea of the West does convey something about the FWBO as an institution shaped by its English and Western countercultural origins. While the label "Western Buddhism" fails to adequately categorize one recognizable cultural form, I have a further reason to use it, in order to be consistent with the term that FWBO and other Buddhist Westerners have adopted. Because the movement has centers in places that are not widely considered Western, members recognize that the term is problematic (see, e.g., Sangharakshita 1992b, 21–27; Subhuti n.d.), and indeed the Indian wing of the movement adopted another name: Trailokya Bauddha Mahasangha Sahayaka Gana (TBMSG). Sangharakshita, the FWBO's founder, notes the complexities of the term, suggesting that FWBO centers around the world "are united by a common spirit" (1992b, 23) rather than by being Western.

In looking at the nexus of phenomena frequently referred to as Western Buddhism, we should also acknowledge that on its own "Buddhism" remains a problematic category, having been created "as an object of western knowledge" by nineteenth-century European Orientalists (Lopez 1995b, 2). Scholars of Buddhism also note the problems of such terms. For example, Rick Fields argues that the term "Western Buddhism" does not "distinguish between the very different national styles of, say, British and French Buddhist groups" (1998, 127), to which I would add that it also fails to distinguish the many different adaptations of Buddhism that transcend national styles, often following particular international networks such as the FWBO, where centers in diverse countries have a similar overall style.[10] By Western Buddhism I mean the phenomenon of Buddhism as adopted by converts who can be considered "Westerners" in terms of their cultural baggage. Following many Buddhists (e.g., Sangharakshita 1992b, 48–49), I use the term "Buddhism" to include cultural aspects of the various Buddhist traditions and "Dharma" to refer to the doctrinal aspects (see glossary).

LAND OF THE STŪPA AND SACRED *PŪRIRI*

Taranatha, Satyananda, and Prajñalila are the three main characters in this book whose stories about Sudarshanaloka I draw upon. All three, despite the impression given by their Sanskrit ordination names, are Pākehā New Zealanders. Satyananda was ordained in 1984 and so is the most senior Order member of the three, although in years he is younger. He has long been involved in social and environmental issues; he worked with Greenpeace and some Auckland low-income housing projects, and his path to Buddhism came via his countercultural interests. Diane Quin (ordained as Prajñalila in 1999) came from a farming family, has been interested in Buddhism since the early 1980s, and studied social sciences at university. After she encountered the FWBO she went to Britain and worked as a production manager at the FWBO's publishing house, Windhorse, in Glasgow for three years. She returned to New Zealand in 1993 to complete a Master of Fine Arts degree at Elam, the fine arts school at The University of Auckland (from which she graduated in 1998), and because, having heard that the Tararu Valley property had been bought, she wanted to be involved.

Prior to his 1992 ordination Taranatha had worked as a general practitioner; he was raised on a farm in Taranaki. It was not until he was close to retirement that he encountered Buddhism, after which he became involved with establishing the retreat center, undertaking solitary retreats, and providing vital support in terms of finances (loans and donations) and various voluntary activities such as teaching meditation at the Auckland Buddhist Centre and helping with activities at Sudarshanaloka. He wrote about his reasons for being involved with Sudarshanaloka.

> It is not the home of my childhood consciousness, responding animal-like to the beauty of sight, sound and smell, and hardening itself to the birth, exploitation and death that is the battle for human survival in the bush. The home I come to is the land of the Stūpa and of the Sacred Pūriri; the land of transformation of abundant, wild energy and beauty into devotion, love and understanding (Taranatha 1997, 3).

I take his story of transforming his way of relating to the land in tandem with his journey of personal transformation, Satyananda's aspiration to create a spiritual home, and Prajñalila's vivid engagement in creating and documenting stories and rituals at Sudarshanaloka as the central narratives of this book. Other people's stories are no less valid, but these accounts provide the most telling insight into how personal engagement with the land became an essential part of the story of transforming self and place.

1   A New Tradition

A Buddhist *movement* that doesn't change would be a contradiction
in terms.
—Sangharakshita, as quoted by Buddhadasa, a senior member of
the Western Buddhist Order (emphasis added)

From the time the Buddha gathered a sangha (community of disciples), Buddhist
institutions have emerged in various forms and spread through many parts of Asia
and beyond. With the hypermobility of the jet age, there has been an ever greater
proliferation of Buddhist sects and centers. Throughout the twentieth century,
such teachers as Ajahn Chah, Shunryu Suzuki, Thich Nhat Hanh, and the four-
teenth Dalai Lama (to note some of the more famous examples) have gathered
followings that have become large enough to require formal organizational structures. These international Buddhist networks have varying degrees of centraliza-
tion and autonomy, but they tend to develop a distinct sense of fellowship and
shared understanding that extends throughout the network. Buddhist teachings
are promoted as available to everyone regardless of where they were born, and generally Buddhists in the religion's heartland areas view Western interest positively;
the political situation of the Tibetans means that the creation of a global network
of sympathizers may also be an impetus to offer teachings.

Outside of Asia, some of these Buddhist organizations serve Asian refugee or
immigrant communities;[1] some consist primarily of Western converts, while others
are mixed. The FWBO consists of a network of affiliated centers radiating from a
hub in Britain. It has centers in several European countries, as well as the United
States, Australia, and India,[2] and is primarily an organization of converts. The
following discussion focuses on the spread of Buddhism into Western, and more
particularly Anglo-European, sociocultural settings. Generally, FWBO members[3]
come from cultural backgrounds strongly shaped by European and Euro-American
influences. There is a certain pan-FWBO ethos, but at the same time, local centers make conscious attempts to incorporate aspects of the local culture, a theme
I explore in this book.

In this chapter I situate the FWBO in the broader context of contemporary and historical Buddhism. I draw upon studies investigating the transcultural

processes involved in the adaptation of Buddhism by people from non-Buddhist sociocultural contexts. Following this, I introduce the movement itself and situate this research in terms of my own relationship to a movement that has a history of engaging with and participating in academic scholarship.

SITUATING THE FWBO

According to FWBO accounts of the origins of Buddhism, Siddhartha Gautama was born a prince of the Śākya clan and lived in the sixth century BCE in what is now the border region of northern India and southern Nepal. He left a comfortable householder's life to go on a quest to solve the problem of human suffering. Some years later, while meditating under a tree, he realized enlightenment, thus earning the title of "Buddha," which can be translated as "one who is awake." He spent the rest of his life teaching others and died at around eighty years of age.[4]

This brief sketch of the Buddha's life exemplifies the pragmatic dimension of the FWBO's approach to Buddhism in that it draws upon accounts depicting the Buddha's life as one of a human being who attained spiritual perfection, as an example of how we too might aspire to be. Indeed, like many reformist-minded Buddhists, FWBO members tend to discount the miraculous deeds that appear in some stories associated with the Buddha's life as embellishments that are not to be taken literally, but rather seen as either cultural baggage or in terms of its poetic dimension. This poetic or mythic approach is important in understanding events at Sudarshanaloka, but for now I introduce the movement and its founder, Sangharakshita.

Dennis Lingwood (Sangharakshita) was born in 1925 in London. According to an FWBO-derived biography, he discovered Buddhism while still a teenager, through the English translations of two Mahāyāna Buddhist texts: the *Diamond Sutra* and the *Sutra of Hui Neng*. During World War II he was conscripted into the army and served as a signalman in the Royal Corps of Signals in India, Sri Lanka, and Singapore. He then spent twenty years in India, during which time he renounced worldly ties; he received novice ordination and his Buddhist name in May 1949 from the Burmese monk U Chandramani and full ordination the following year with U Kawinda as preceptor and Bhikkhu Jagdish Kashyap as his teacher (with whom he studied Pāli, logic, and the Abhidhamma). At Kashyap's direction he went to Kalimpong, in the foothills of the Himalayas, which remained his base for the next fourteen years. There he founded a "Young Men's Buddhist Association" and a *vihāra* (monastery) and began writing books and giving lectures on Buddhism. During this period he also received initiations and teachings from

Tibetan *lamas* Chetul Sangye Dorje (spelled Chattrul Samye Dorje in some FWBO sources), Jamyang Khyentse Rimpoche, Dilgo Khyentse Rimpoche, Dudjom Rimpoche, and Khachu Rimpoche. Dhardo Rimpoche (1917–1990) gave Sangharakshita the bodhisattva ordination and the two became close friends. "Yogi Chen," a Chinese hermit living near Kalimpong, introduced Sangharakshita to Ch'an, the Chinese form of Buddhism from which Zen derives. In the 1950s, Sangharakshita was involved in teaching the Dalits (ex-untouchables) who had become Buddhists after the example of Dr. B. R. Ambedkar (1891–1956).[5] Building on this work, in 1979 the Indian wing of the FWBO, Trailokya Bauddha Mahasangha Sahayak Gana (TBMSG), was established, and by the turn of the millennium there were nearly two hundred ordained TBMSG members (Vishvapani 2000).

In 1964, Sangharakshita returned to England and was based for a time at the Hampstead Buddhist Vihāra, lecturing on aspects of Buddhism and teaching meditation, but his approach, which drew on Mahāyāna as well as Theravāda Buddhism, antagonized some of the trustees, who preferred to observe the latter form alone, and they excluded him from the Hampstead Vihāra in 1967 (Subhuti 1994, 34). At this point Sangharakshita decided that a new movement was needed, and the same year he founded the FWBO, which was, according to his disciple and biographer Subhuti, "based on the fundamental principles of the Dharma and open to the entire Buddhist tradition" (35). A year later he ordained the first members of the Western Buddhist Order. By the 1990s, the FWBO was among the three largest Buddhist organizations in Britain, along with the New Kadampa Tradition (NKT) and Soka Gakkai International-United Kingdom (SGI-UK) (Kay 2004, 25).

Like many other Buddhist organizations, the FWBO has centers in many British cities where meditation classes and Dharma talks, study groups, and other related activities are held. The centers in other countries follow these models, with some local adaptations. People refer to such centers as "Buddhist centers" or "Dharma centers." Either way, these are places established for the purposes of communicating the Buddha's teachings and developing a sangha or community of practitioners of those teachings, whether based in the city or in remote areas intended for retreat.

The FWBO was a closely bounded organization during its first three decades, with clearly delineated hierarchies and institutional structures (S. Bell 2000, 398). Its centers do not, as a general rule, host guest speakers from other Buddhist groups, and it has tended to discourage committed members from "shopping around," that is, tasting and sampling spiritual guidance from an array of sources in a way that precludes experiencing one approach in depth. Where the movement has established flourishing centers, some of the more committed members live in single-sex residential communities at least for a few years, often taking jobs in the movement's "Team-Based Right Livelihood" businesses.[6] This means that it is possible, in some situations, for FWBO members to live and work within the bounds of the movement and reduce contact with the world outside.

Like many international Buddhist networks finding favor in the West, FWBO members consider meditation to be an important tool for cultivating the qualities of wisdom and compassion. Dharma study and an ethical way of life (see below and appendix 2) are equally vital. The two principal meditation techniques taught to newcomers at the FWBO, which I learned at an introductory course at the Auckland Buddhist Centre in 1996, are the mindfulness of breathing (Pāli ānāpāna sati), a technique that develops increased awareness, and the mettā bhāvana (cultivation of loving-kindness towards all beings). Both of these are associated with Theravāda Buddhism, while other techniques draw on Mahāyāna and Vajrayāna sources. Deity-visualization practices (an aspect of Vajrayāna) require initiation, which is regarded as a lifelong commitment and taken only upon joining the Order.[7] Beyond this, individuals adopt practices according to their inclinations. The Zen-inspired practice of "just sitting" and the Tibetan Buddhist practice of Dzogchen, glossed as "Pure Awareness," are often the focal practice on FWBO retreats.

On regular occasions at FWBO centers, members perform a devotional practice called the sevenfold pūjā (or a shorter variant, the threefold pūjā). This involves reciting selected scriptures, chanting mantras, and making offerings such as candles, flowers, and incense before the Buddhist shrine, with the aim of inspiring feelings of commitment and devotion. The sevenfold pūjā draws strongly from Śāntideva's classic text on the bodhisattva ideal,[8] while the Refuges and Precepts section (recited in Pāli and English) are adapted from Theravādin forms.[9] An English translation of the Heart Sūtra by Zen master Philip Kapleau also features.

In many contemporary Western Buddhist organizations, the role of monks and nuns and the centrality of the Vinaya in monastic practice have been questioned, revised, or eliminated (Prebish and Baumann 2002). In the FWBO, Sangharakshita emphasizes the centrality of "Going for Refuge to the Three Jewels"[10] (the Buddha, Dharma, and sangha). Sangharakshita (1992a, 19) says that he found that some Buddhists were adhering rigidly to rules such as those in the Vinaya without understanding what he felt was the spirit of Buddhist teachings. Thus he says that the commitment to going for refuge is the "central or definitive act of the Buddhist life and as such the fundamental basis of unity and union among Buddhists." His statement that "commitment [to the spiritual life] is primary, life-style is secondary" (e.g., Subhuti 1994, 145–146) has become an FWBO aphorism.

The Sanskrit term adapted for Order members has been, since 1982, Dharmachari (male) and Dharmacharini (female), meaning "Dharma-farer," chosen because this term did not distinguish between monastics and laity (Subhuti 1994, 126), instead emphasizing the orientation towards the Dharma. The English term "Order member" is more widespread in the movement, with the Sanskrit term serving primarily as a title before an Order member's name. Order members may choose to take vows of celibacy, in which case they are known by the title of Anagarika. Some Buddhists use the word "sangha" primarily with regard to ordained monks and nuns, but in the FWBO it refers to the community of people who follow the Buddha's teachings, and more specifically to one's local network of spiritual friends and acquaintances. There is a particularly pronounced emphasis in the FWBO on the spiritually beneficial role of carefully cultivated friendships, a topic I return to in the next chapter.

Ordained men and women run FWBO centers, teaching meditation classes and holding study groups. People interested in finding out about meditation and Buddhism can attend night classes at FWBO centers, where they are referred to as "newcomers." A "Friend" is someone who has attended the basic courses in meditation and continues to be involved in FWBO activities. The conventional (and, to some extent, expected) career of a newcomer is that after a period of meditating and attending FWBO events as a Friend, one asks to become a *mitra*, which is the Sanskrit term for "friend." *Mitras* spend more time developing friendships and helping with FWBO activities, and some choose to ask for ordination. This can entail years of training, retreats, and study. When the preceptor, in consultation with other Order members, decides an ordinand is ready to be ordained, he or she joins other ordinands of the same sex to undertake a specialized ordination-training retreat. In the actual ordination ceremony the preceptor "formally witnesses [the ordinand's] going for refuge" (Buddhadasa 2006) and initiates the ordinand into a visualization practice. In recognition of the life-changing transformation that all of this represents, the ordinands take a Sanskrit or Pāli name. Some of these are well-known Buddhist names that have been used at various times in Buddhist history, while others have been coined to describe spiritual qualities that the ordinand aspires to develop. Order members are free to choose how widely they will use their Buddhist name: some use it only in FWBO circles, while others change their name by deed poll.

In the Western Buddhist Order worldwide in 1982 there were 187 Order members; by 1990 there were around 450, and by 2002 they had reached 1,000. The FWBO's register of Order members gives a figure of 1,335 by mid-2006. So the period from 1982 to 2006 shows an average growth rate of around 8 percent per year. By 2006 there were about 65 urban centers and 15 retreat centers, as well as local groups, Team-Based Right Livelihood enterprises, and communities (FWBO 2005b). In mid 2006, of the more than 1,330 Order members, 742 (over half) were resident in Britain, 294 in India, and 50 in New Zealand (for more detail see chap. 2 and appendix 1). The numbers of Order members in proportion to the overall population indicate a similar proportion in Britain and New Zealand (Jayarava 2006); it should also be noted that a number of New Zealanders who are Order members reside overseas, particularly in Britain.

The numbers of *mitra*s and others in the wider movement are harder to depict accurately. The FWBO Communications Office (Vishvapani 2000) provided rough estimates of over 2,000 Friends in Britain, another 1,000 worldwide, and tens of thousands in India; the office suggested the number of *mitra*s in Britain in 2000 was around 1,300. Martin Baumann estimates the number of "supporters and Friends" worldwide to be around 100,000, with most of them in India (2000, 378). According to FWBO records in 2000 there were around 90 "ex-Order members," meaning members who had resigned, lapsed, or died. For a range of historic reasons beyond the scope of this book, the rate of ordination is higher among males than females, and in 2006 the proportion of Order members was 68 percent male to 32 percent female, although in New Zealand the gender gap was smaller.

RE-EXPRESSING THE DHARMA

The FWBO seeks to be inclusive, but most of the members are of liberal, middle-class origins and most likely to be of an Anglo-European extraction. There are exceptions: for example, an Order member named Viveka (2002, 24) writes about "the irony of being a Chinese western Buddhist." Homosexuals and transsexuals find ready acceptance. As with many international Buddhist networks consisting of Western converts, some of the long-term FWBO members also participated in the countercultural movements of the late 1960s and early 1970s, which exposed many people to Hindu- and Buddhist-derived religious movements. As Sandra Bell observes, FWBO members are also a colorful bunch with diverse backgrounds; they are critical of the "perceived flaws in contemporary society" such as "crass materialism, alienation and ecological disorder" (1991, 128).

In her review of various scholarly analyses of Western Buddhism, Helen Waterhouse notes that the FWBO is typically situated towards the dynamic or adaptive end in contrast with more traditionalist groups such as the Thai Theravāda Forest Tradition (1997, 20–27).[11] Despite the FWBO's history of discouraging "shopping around," Sangharakshita's corpus of teachings is indeed ecumenical, a result of his decision to distill what he believed was the essence from "whatever source was available to him, according to his unfolding spiritual needs" (Subhuti 1994, 29) during his time in India. Subhuti describes Sangharakshita as a "translator between principles and practice" of Buddhism who has "striven to discern the fundamental Buddhist experience behind [the many Buddhist schools] and to communicate it to the modern world" (1994, 12). Given the influence of all three *yānas*, some commentators categorize the FWBO as *"triyāna."*[12] However, one FWBO document rejects this label, asserting that the movement "seeks to return to the core teachings that underlie the Buddhist tradition as a whole, and, in doing so, to draw inspiration from its various manifestations" (Vishvapani and Cittapala 1999). The authors then suggest, in a bold claim characteristic of the movement, that this approach "might be described as the 'Buddhayāna.'"

Theologian Philip Mellor remarks on the innovative and ecumenical aspects of the FWBO's approach, which, he says, is particularly creative, "synthesizing various Buddhist traditions into its characteristically modern outlook" (1992, 104). Indeed, FWBO literature emphasizes the importance of creativity and innovation, referring to the movement as "a re-expression of the Dharma" that eschews the practices of older Buddhist movements because they arose in different sociocultural settings. The preferred alternative, as Vishvapani (n.d.) asserts, is "to interpret the teachings that express general truths," applying these "to our own situation." This entails drawing on diverse sources of inspiration, a feature of the movement that I return to throughout this book.

The movement attempts to balance its claim to being innovative with the notion that it remains true to the original teachings of the Buddha. For example, the FWBO Web site states,

> The FWBO is an international network dedicated to communicating Buddhist truths in ways appropriate to the modern world. The *essence* of Buddhism is timeless and universal. But the forms it takes always *adapt* according to context. Now that Buddhism has come to the West, the task is to *create new Buddhist traditions* relevant to the 21st century (FWBO n.d.-b; my emphases).

Elsewhere Subhuti says that Buddhism "must express itself through the culture in the midst of which it finds itself—neither compromising with it nor ignoring it" (1983, 5–6). The claim that the FWBO is recapturing the essence of the Buddha's teachings while Asian Buddhists are trapped in an age-old degeneration of Buddhism is not atypical of Western Buddhism, but it can be problematic. Buddhist-studies scholars have begun looking critically at this kind of approach, because it does imply that Westerners are now the true "curators of the Buddha" (Lopez 1995a).

CREATING A WESTERN BUDDHIST CULTURE

Not all of the material upon which FWBO members draw comes from Buddhist sources. FWBO literature often expresses a desire to see the movement as consisting of not just Westerners who do Buddhism, but also reformers undertaking something unprecedented within the West, challenging existing Western ways of doing things. Thus Subhuti writes that "Western Buddhists have, as yet, effectively no culture of their own. They must therefore create one for themselves—a culture that will truly support the Higher Evolution of the individual" (1994, 286). Perhaps addressing concerns about appropriation of knowledge, he reassures readers that we should not be troubled that we are borrowing and digesting some aspects of "oriental culture" (287), because "[c]ultures have always influenced one another." Sangharakshita (1992b, 144–145) thinks that a "distinctively Western Buddhist culture" is yet to emerge, but when it does it will have three main sources: "traditional Eastern Buddhist cultures," "elements of Western folk and high culture," and inspiration derived from personal experience.

The FWBO's core of self-styled pioneers also draws intellectual influences and creative elements from diverse sources, including two areas of emphasis: their conscious incorporation of psychological discourse about self-transformation (S. Bell 1996) and exploration of how Buddhism can be re-expressed using Western "culture" (the arts) such as the literary, philosophical, artistic, and musical traditions. The movement also explores Western Europe's imagined pre-Christian roots through nature-centered spirituality, and I explore the implications of this for Sudarshanaloka in later chapters.

Sangharakshita distinguishes between a rational or scientific truth and a mythic or poetic truth, both of which he deems necessary to society. The problem, he suggests, is that Western society has become overly reliant on the former, alienating us from a very important dimension of life. Poetic or mythic truth manifests in "myths and legends, as well as in works of art, in symbolic ritual, and also quite importantly in dreams" (Subhuti 1994, 274–275). Sangharakshita has written several volumes of poetry, and his enthusiasm for European literary arts and philosophy[13] has influenced the literary tastes of many FWBO members, too, and inspired the founding of the FWBO Arts magazine *Urthona*.

Sangharakshita's practice of using models from Western sources to interpret such concepts as the bodhisattva ideal has come to flavor much of the FWBO's core literature. The Bodhisattva Vow is a significant dimension of Mahāyāna Buddhism; it is a vow to attain enlightenment so as to be able to work effectively for the benefit of all sentient beings in this and all future lifetimes, until every one of them has reached enlightenment. Arguing that in practice it is impossible to live up to the vow to save an infinite number of beings, Sangharakshita presents the bodhisattva ideal as a Jungian-flavored archetypal "myth" rather than a "practicable spiritual ideal for the individual" (Subhuti 1994, 96). Instead of being an individual undertaking, he suggests that the spirit of these vows should pervade the whole of the Western Buddhist Order and envisages the Order as an embodiment of the thousand-armed Avalokiteśvara, the archetypal Bodhisattva of Compassion (97), with every Order member being one of his hands.

The FWBO borrows Jungian-inspired discourses about archetypes (see Subhuti 1994, 278–279) and Joseph Campbell's interpretation of the "mythic quest" and "mythic dimension" (e.g., J. Campbell 1968, Campbell and Moyers 1988, Campbell and Van Couvering 1997). Taranatha, one of the main interlocutors in this book, describes myth as "an explanation in familiar terms of a transcendental truth" that is incomprehensible in "earthly" terms; thus myths can never be fully explained. He gives a Buddhist analogy: "The finger pointing at the moon is not the moon," an often-quoted Buddhist reminder that words and concepts "can only indicate a higher truth that they can never fully capture" (Subhuti 1994, 28), and so one should not become overly attached to them. In this case, though, the finger is the "myth," that is, the way people tell stories, and the moon is the underlying meaning that cannot be defined. This distinction helps members to accommodate this paradox.

CHANGE IN THE FWBO

As the epigraph at the opening of this chapter suggests, in a Buddhist movement change is inevitable, and even desirable. Indeed, the FWBO is very much in a fluid state, and one of the risks in writing about it is that my snapshot of Sudarshanaloka could give the misleading impression of something other than a place in motion. This is a problem of language that cannot be entirely avoided, and I use the word "movement" with reference to the FWBO as many members do, in part because it can be used as a reminder of this state of change. Even allowing for this state of change, the FWBO has been undergoing a particularly significant time of reorientation in recent years. As the movement grew, it became too large for Sangharakshita alone to conduct the large number of ordinations, so he appointed other preceptors. Sangharakshita had long pondered how the FWBO could operate after his death, and in August 2000, at the age of seventy-five, he withdrew from active leadership roles in the movement. While he handed his responsibilities to the Preceptors' College and appointed a senior disciple, Subhuti, to be the chairman for a five-year term, he intentionally left the movement without a "head" or appointed leader. The chair of the college is a short-term position, and the preceptors elected their first replacement chairperson in 2005. Since Sangharakshita's effective retirement, the Preceptors' College has worked to devolve authority and administration to the local centers, with the administrative council of the Preceptors' College being dissolved altogether. Local chapters of Order members maintain regular contact and have regional and national meetings, and every two years there is an international Order convention. The numbers of public and private preceptors are increasing, but they now are primarily spiritual guardians of the Order, with their main role being to conduct ordinations. Buddhadasa, a senior Order member who lives in New Zealand, stressed that the job of the Preceptor's College is not to issue edicts about the running of the FWBO, but to ensure that the ordination training is the same worldwide (2005). The FWBO is aiming to create a more intensive environment for spiritual practice in the Order and a more relaxed and flexible approach for the wider movement. The FWBO also participates in inter-Buddhist networks such as the European Buddhist Union and the Network of Buddhist Organisations (UK).

As it has grown in size, the FWBO has undergone many changes, sometimes in response to criticism. Indeed, the movement received negative media coverage in England after an ex-member made accusations of sexual misconduct, and it has been branded a cult on the Web site www.ex-cult.org. These issues are similar to those that have shaken several other large Buddhist organizations (S. Bell 1998, 2002). The matter was first aired publicly in 1997 via a Web site (The FWBO Files n.d.) and in an article titled "The Dark Side of Enlightenment" in *The Guardian* (Bunting 1997). One of the allegations in the FWBO Files involves coercive "conversion" of heterosexuals to homosexuality. The FWBO published a response on the Internet, to which the anonymous authors of the Files then published their own counter-response. In 2003 the matter resurfaced within the movement when an Order member named Yashomitra wrote an open letter to the wider movement. In it, he outlined his experience of what he now believes was sexual abuse by Sangharakshita and another male Order member when he attended a men's retreat in 1980 at the age of seventeen.[14] The subject is beyond the scope of this work, since it had no significant repercussions at Sudarshanaloka.

The FWBO continues to provide a support network for people with some affinity to Sangharakshita's style of teaching. The movement is now less exclusivist than in its first two decades, and indeed, some Order members, *mitras*, and Friends now choose to follow teachers outside the Western Buddhist Order while retaining affiliations with the movement. This is something that Sangharakshita himself did, in that he had teachers in India from a range of backgrounds. Nonetheless, to have the Order members taking teachings outside the Western Buddhist Order would have been unthinkable in the movement's early days. When Sangharakshita founded the FWBO, his students knew very little about Buddhism, and those who were attracted to it were often also the same people who dabbled in various forms of spiritualism or the hippie counterculture. Sangharakshita felt that if these people were to learn about Buddhism they needed structure and commitment, and this helps to explain why the FWBO operated in a somewhat exclusivist manner and why meditation was taught in a very structured way. Today people in the movement are exploring more free-form approaches to meditation. Another relatively new development that accords with the movement's countercultural strand is the Buddhafield festivals (see chap. 3).

Another factor that may explain why people are taking teachers outside the movement is that the movement is now so large that it can be difficult for people to maintain close relationships with their Western Buddhist Order mentors. One teacher with whom some New Zealand-based FWBO and Western Buddhist Order members now take teachings is Canadian-born Tarchin Hearn, a disciple of the late Namgyal Rimpoche (1931–2003),[15] who is based at the Wangapeka Retreat Centre in the South Island. The response to this broadening of practice varies, with its Western Buddhist Order critics saying they find all the inspiration they need within the Order. While this more open approach allows for a broadening of the movement's horizons, it is also possible that over time the FWBO will become more diffuse and its boundaries ever fainter.

ORIGINAL BUDDHISM?

As Diane Austin-Broos notes, one reason why people adopt a new religion is that it apparently corresponds with concepts and desires arising in an existing context (2003, 179). Intentionally or unintentionally, the convert filters the adopted ideology, concepts, and practices through his or her own prior associations, accepting some practices and rejecting others. Thus it is inevitable that as Buddhism is established in Western settings it will be influenced by them.

Buddhism has a history of over twenty-five hundred years of movement between some very diverse cultural milieus. Its diversity contradicts the frequent proclamations of a distinct and unitary "Western" or "American" or even "World" Buddhism.[16] The history of interest in Buddhism in regions with a strong European or Euro-American influence, especially among the elite and middle classes, dates back well over a century—for example, through the Theosophy movement (e.g., Almond 1988, Croucher 1989, Tweed 2000 [1992]). During the late 1960s Buddhism found many new sympathizers via the countercultural movement, which, alongside its rejection of much of Western modernity, was becoming disenchanted with conventional Christianity. Among other factors, the growth of interest in meditative forms derived from Buddhism and Hinduism was facilitated by an era of affluence (leading to people having more time to contemplate their lives if they so chose and also, according to Buddhist accounts, because they found that material comforts did not guarantee personal happiness). There are many other issues that facilitated the countercultural exploration of Buddhist and Hindu thought, including increased accessibility to Buddhist teachers in Asia through affordable jet travel, experimentation with mind-altering drugs, and the increased number of publications relating to such topics.

Martin Baumann categorizes expressions of Buddhism in Europe based on religious ideology and practice, with a focus on Buddhist groups in new sociocultural contexts beyond Asia (2002b, 51). As an alternative to the focus on nationality and ethnic origins that has dominated scholarly attempts to analyze Buddhism beyond Asia (e.g., Prebish and Tanaka 1998, Williams and Queen 1999), Baumann proposes focusing on religious ideologies and practices and identifying two predominant strands, which he glosses as traditionalist and modernist (2002b). He suggests that we consider Buddhism's developments in Asia as well as in the West, since these were prerequisites for later transmission; he references the "two Buddhisms" typology of Prebish (1979) that differentiates immigrant or "ethnic" Buddhists and converts (who are usually white). Baumann suggests shifting from an emphasis on ancestry to "*religious concepts* and *practices followed* . . . in shaping the predominant strands of Buddhism in the West*" (Baumann 2002b, 52; his emphasis). This is a useful approach, because the variety of forms of Buddhist practice does not entirely correspond to ancestry and ethnic identities. The division of immigrant or ethnic versus convert is problematic in other ways, too, such as the fact that the term "immigrant" is not appropriate when referring to the grandchildren of immigrants who may identify more with their country of birth than that of their grandparents (Baumann 2001, 24). Further, many so-called "Asian" Buddhists are as critical of so-called "superstition" in Buddhism as are many converts. Baumann writes of these two strands,

> Whereas traditionalist Buddhists strive to acquire "merit" and aim for good conditions in this and the next life, in contrast most Western modernist Buddhists have abandoned the idea of rebirth. They do not share concepts

such as accruing "merit," but rather endeavor to reach "enlightenment" or "awakening" in this life (27).

He suggests that the "cosmological views and religious goals" (27) of the two strands differ: the former approach emphasizes "devotion, ritual, and specific cosmological concepts" (27), while the latter emphasizes meditation, the study of Buddhist texts, and the development of rational understanding. Baumann also suggests a third category: a "global" or "postmodernist" (60) Buddhism that secularizes and psychologizes modernist Buddhism, just as modernist Buddhism demythologized and rationalized the traditionalist strand. He cautions that all three are Weberian ideal types rather than all-encompassing, bounded categories, and elsewhere he signals the distinct orientations by using the catchphrases "protective amulets" for traditionalist Buddhism and "awareness techniques" (2002b) to gloss the modern and postmodern expressions of Buddhism.

Many forms of contemporary Buddhism are shaped by modernization and religious reform.[17] In literature on such revitalizations, the terms "Protestant," "reformist," and "modernist" have been widely adopted (Seneviratne 1999, 13). The term "Protestant Buddhism" is associated with post-independence revivals of Sinhalese Buddhism and the "dissemination of Victorian-Protestant ethical ideals into the culture of the elite Buddhists" (Obeyesekere 1970, 46). However, John Holt contests the term's original usage with regard to Sinhalese Buddhism as a "misnomer for the revival and modernization of missionary and militant Buddhism" (1991, 307). While this reformed Buddhism was, in part, a protest against Christianity and Western political dominance prior to independence, it was, ironically, shaped by norms and organizational forms derived from the Protestant Christianity of the former colonizers. During their time in Ceylon, the founders of the Theosophical Society, Madame Helena P. Blavatsky (1831–1891) and Henry Steel Olcott (1832–1907), took the five Buddhist precepts and encouraged Buddhist leaders to debate with Christian missionaries (Sharf 1995, 253). In the process, these new leaders began espousing a form of Buddhism shaped by the Christian institutions such as Western-style education, as well as urbanization and modernization (251). A major factor in the shaping of Protestant Buddhism was the tendency of Orientalist scholars, through translating selected Pāli and Sanskrit texts into European languages, to invent "what might be called a Euro-Buddhist canon by portraying a rationalized and sanitized Buddhism in keeping with the imperatives of the sociology of their own intellectual life" (Seneviratne 1999, 2). This new canon had a profound influence on "the religio-nationalist resurgence" in the parts of South and Southeast Asia that Western powers had colonized. For example, in what was then Ceylon, the "Original Buddhism" that Anagarika Dharmapala (also known as David Hewavitarne, 1864–1933) expounded at the World Parliament of Religions in Chicago was already shaped by indigenous appropriations of colonial institutions and the influence of Olcott.[18]

Scholars have discussed the term "Protestant Buddhism" with regard to European and Euro-American situations, applying it somewhat differently (e.g., Mellor 1991, Prothero 1995). Philip Mellor (1989) investigates the FWBO and the English Sangha Trust at the level of public discourse and argues that rather than simply being a product of the transplantation of Buddhism into a new context, numerous non-Buddhist—including liberal Protestant—influences have shaped and continue to shape the FWBO's expression of Buddhism far more than the English Sangha, which attempts to adhere to Thai Theravādin traditions. He is interested in how these influences lead to the creation of specifically English forms of Buddhism and suggests that

> [t]he adoption of Buddhist religious forms by English people does not entail such a radical break with western structures and influences as has often been envisaged. Individuals may take personal decisions to become Buddhists, but Christian discourses and forms of life continue to have an observable effect on English Buddhism (1991, 73).

In discussing how early English Buddhists such as Ananda Metteya (Allan Bennett) and Alan Watts wrote about Christianity, Mellor notes that they contrasted "irrational" aspects of Christianity against "rational" aspects of Buddhism, portraying Christianity as institutionalized, dogmatic, irrational, and degenerate. "Christian ideas and beliefs are not discussed in detail as its function for English Buddhism is one of opposition and definition rather than serious inter-religious debate." Mellor suggests that the kinds of criticisms English Buddhists made against Christianity strongly resemble Protestant criticism of Catholicism (1989, 136–138; quote on 137). Certainly from a sociological perspective the FWBO does not stand independently of Western traditions, and his basic argument is congruent with sociological and anthropological assumptions that all cultural translations are syncretic. Helen Waterhouse suggests that among people who are "culturally British" (1997, 1), richly diverse expressions of Buddhism are evident, but she, too, suggests that Buddhism in Britain cannot be "characterized beyond its broadly Protestant tendencies" (240).

Several scholars call for caution in applying the term to British or European Buddhism. Martin Baumann draws on a threefold typology (romantic, esoteric, and rationalist) developed by Thomas Tweed (2000 [1992]) for his study of Euro-American Buddhist sympathizers and adherents in the late nineteenth and early twentieth centuries. Baumann suggests that early German Buddhists took a rationalist interpretation of Buddhism, regarding it as "a scientific and analytical religion which . . . reconciled science, philosophy and religion" (1997a, 279). Further, like the post-independence Sinhalese Buddhists, the Germans used Buddhism as a means of protest against the dominance of Christianity, while unwittingly perpetuating some of the Protestant attributes they most explicitly criticized. But rather than using the term to categorize what he is discussing, Baumann modifies the term to "Buddhism in Protestant shape," concluding that his findings are less about Buddhism per se and instead primarily illuminate "basic cultural values in Germany and in Europe in general" (1997a, 287). Similarly, while Sandra Bell accepts Mellor's portrayal of the movement as "in tune with high modernity" (1996, 89), she expresses reservations about his representation of the FWBO as strongly shaped by Protestant Christian discourse. David Kay cautions about the use of the term with regard to the Zen-derived Order of Buddhist Contemplatives in Britain, because elements that many scholars identify as Protestant, including "the mystical, demythologizing and anti-ritual interpretations of modern Zen apologists all have deeply traditional precedents" (2004, 221). With regard to the FWBO, too, I would argue that the characteristics in Western Buddhist discourse and practice that are referred to as "Protestant" might more usefully be called exercises in religious revitalization, reform, and renewal that constitute attempts to recover a religion's founding ideals when they have become obscured through processes of "churching" (Matsudo 2000, 64). Although some influences might resemble Protestant Christianity, it is not the most useful way to classify them; but since the label has been widely used, I think it best to simply qualify the use of the term. I regard this entire book as presenting a more nuanced discussion of Western Buddhism than simple typologies can do.

Devised in an attempt to make sense of the diversity of Buddhism among adherents and sympathizers in late-Victorian America, Tweed's esoteric, rationalist, and romantic types apply in certain respects to Western Buddhism today. The esoteric or occult type tended to be "spiritually eclectic" (2000 [1992], 54) and believed in the existence of a "spiritual or nonmaterial realm that is populated by a plurality of nonhuman or suprahuman realities that can be contacted through one or another practices or extraordinary states of consciousness" (51). The romantic type, shaped by European and American Romanticism, has also played a vital role in Westerners' enchantment with Buddhist arts, literature, languages, and so on; "[f]urther, supranormal access to hidden sources of religious truth interested them

less than the ordinary workings of the human aesthetic faculties" (69). The rationalist type was most influenced by "Enlightenment rationalism" (61) and "focused
on rational-discursive means of attaining religious truth and meaning as opposed to
revelational or experiential means and emphasized the authority of the individual
in religious matters rather than that of creeds, texts, officials, or institutions." All
three types are discernable in FWBO Buddhism, but the romantic and esoteric
types seem to play a stronger role at Sudarshanaloka than Mellor's representations
of the FWBO's public discourse in England would have led one to expect.

In nineteenth-century Europe, the romantic strand manifested as a desire
to recover a lost "genuine spirituality" through the study of Sanskrit texts (Baumann 2002a, 86). More recently, the counterculture (hippies, neo-pagans, and
some dimensions of environmentalism), in their critique of the industrial and
post-industrial age, often perpetuated this fantasy. Alongside this developed a related notion about a prior age in which people were part of nature rather than
alienated from it. In such a view, indigenous cultures retain this spiritual connection with nature, thereby holding the key to planetary salvation. The interest in
nature-centered spirituality is expressed through various forms of neo-paganism,
including among New Zealand feminist ritual makers expressing "the desire for
a spirituality which celebrates connection with the earth and the natural world"
(Rountree 2004, 106), but the ways that it emerges in contemporary Western Buddhism in interaction with the more "rationalist" strand have been largely over-
looked, and I return to this more "poetic" strand in the FWBO throughout this
book.

The other main feature of the FWBO and similar Western Buddhist movements that has attracted scholarly attention is the emphasis on personal development and how this is shaped by the ways the self is socially constructed in Western
society. Sandra Bell (1996) suggests that the FWBO's emphasis on personal growth
and self-awareness as leading to self-transcendence arises from the contemporary
pluralistic and atomized sociocultural scenario. Thus it is, in some ways, consistent
with "'high modernity' where most aspects of social life are open to 'chronic re-
vision in the light of new information or knowledge'" (88, quoting Giddens 1991).
In the FWBO, "transformation in the personal and public sphere is acknowledged
and actively encouraged to the point that it becomes integrated as an important
aspect of identity" (S. Bell 1996, 88), and "Buddhist identity can only be sought,
developed and cultivated" (89). Thus far I have discussed aspects of the FWBO
that Mellor, Baumann, Sandra Bell, and others have discussed at length. At this
point, however, I wish to turn to the ways in which Buddhism is attractive in contexts of cultural lacunae.

YEARNING FOR SPIRITUAL CONNECTION

I have already noted the FWBO's ecumenical approach. Is this movement just another example of the "spiritual marketplace" (Roof 1999)[19] appropriating desired Other practices within the context of imperialist power? Certainly, members of the FWBO enjoy the comforts and rights of other Westerners, privileges not accessible to the majority of people in the Buddhist societies from which they take many of their spiritual practices, and they do have far more scope in seeking out alternative religious possibilities.

But what drives such people to go searching for meaning beyond the borders of their own cultural heritage? The romantic construction of the exotic "East" certainly has some influence. The most significant outward flow of Buddhist teachings began to take place in the historical context of British colonization of South Asia. Edward Said writes about Orientalism as a form of knowledge, the essence of which is the "ineradicable distinction between Western superiority and Oriental inferiority" (1978, 42). This created a dualistic stereotype in which "[t]he Oriental is irrational, depraved (fallen), childlike, 'different'; thus the European is rational, virtuous, mature, 'normal'" (40). Said was particularly interested in criticizing Western understandings of Islamic peoples in the Middle East, but much of his argument contextualizes Western interest in Buddhism. When Westerners talk about a greater spirituality in India or some other archetypally Oriental place, such as Tibet, this is, arguably, "neo-orientalism" (Bartholomeusz 1998, 1), in which Westerners "mine" the "spiritual wealth" of Eastern religions for "personal edification"—perhaps as essentialist as the more overtly negative forms Said described and criticized.

A New Zealand woman who visits a Tibetan Buddhist institute in Auckland told me that she thinks that, in comparison to Westerners, Tibetans are a "more spiritual race" and "much closer to nature." Perhaps part of the appeal of an archetypal, exotic Other is this supposed closeness to the mythical Western ideal of nature and their appearance of belonging to a place and community—a pervasive theme in critiques of modernity. The appeal of the exotic does not fully explain this, however, for it does not tell us *why* the exotic is so appealing. Why not, for example, shop around within the range of Western alternative spiritual expressions?

In this context, it is significant that a number of FWBO members report negative experiences of Christianity during childhood and/or disagreement with Christian doctrine, which drove them to seek alternatives that they find "more helpful in explaining the world as they experience it" (Kurtz 1995, 14). One Order member accounts for what he calls the failure of "orthodox Christianity" by saying that it "brought about its own demise because it repressed and distorted the previous mythological systems, . . . it damaged those previous patterns of meaning, it didn't incorporate them, and in repressing and distorting them it sowed the seeds for its own destruction" (Aloka 1994, 3). I have heard several similar dismissals of Christianity among long-term FWBO members. Sangharakshita's "problem" with Christian, Jewish, and Islamic morality is that they present it as a "moral rule . . . laid up on man by God" (quoted in Subhuti 1994, 131). Despite the fact that many people no longer believe in God, Subhuti writes, this "prescriptive morality is still dominant in Western culture," causing "a lingering and oppressive sense of neurotic guilt." To become "fully a Buddhist," someone brought up in Christian conditioning must learn how to "stop being an unconscious Christian." In some cases, "blasphemy against God and other aspects of Christianity may be a therapeutic necessity" (131–132).

Beyond the issue of why people reject Christianity and seek religious knowledge outside their own tradition, Signe Howell suggests that in addressing the question, we must avoid two pitfalls. The first is "[o]verestimation of First World supremacy," the second "[u]nderestimation of general diffusion," because knowledge flows in many directions, not just from Western to non-Western parts of the globe (1995, 171–172). Many commentators, Howell says, perceive the globalization of culture as a unidirectional flow of knowledge from First to Third Worlds. But "they" have influenced "us" just as we have influenced them. Phrases such as "the Easternization of the West" (C. Campbell 1999) belie the complexities of these flows of knowledge, practices, and material culture. The flows are multidirectional; for instance, the Soka Gakkai (a lay movement with Japanese origins that is almost a worldwide movement) has established centers in Southeast Asia (Metraux 2001); Tibetan Buddhist teachers have not only found disciples in the West, but have also found enthusiastic audiences in places where other forms of Buddhism have long been established or are being revived, such as Malaysia, Taiwan, Hong Kong, and post-communist Mongolia.

Howell notes that "[m]uch Western interest in Third World knowledge and cultural products is a kind of spiritual quest—a search for deeper meaning to life or art which somehow got lost during the industrialization of western societies" (1995, 166), and this is combined with guilt and insecurity about the West's role in colonization and exploitation of those same regions. Many such seekers would argue that our society is spiritually impoverished, blaming the materialist-oriented consumerist ideology that bombards us through the media.

A focus on the penetration of a cultural Other's religion into a Western heartland disrupts the neat equations of Westerner/exploiter, Third World/exploited. I suggest that while we cannot entirely extricate Western interest in Buddhism from the political context of cultural imperialism, the expressed feeling of "something missing" is a crucial point to our understanding of this particular situation. Sherry Ortner observes that Orientalism is "not only a kind of racist 'othering,' but also at the same time a yearning for solidarity and even identity with the other that (perhaps) makes Orientalism different from classic racism" (1999, 140). She does not pursue the point, noting only that it is an important dimension of the relationship between Sherpas and foreign mountaineers in Nepal. But a similar yearning also appears to motivate many Westerners to become interested in Buddhism.

Introducing a concept that more or less describes how syncretism can operate, Howell suggests that this Western hunger for spiritual knowledge arises out of cultural absences, or "lacunae," in Western society that become apparent when we are exposed to other ways of being. She explores the diffusion of ideas resulting from the encounter with new and alien knowledge. Rather than there being a prior sense of a gap in local knowledge, a lacuna (in Howell's usage) is an opening or interval (180, n. 2) that enters one's field of awareness only when contact with a previously alien knowledge[20] alerts people to something until now absent. This works through provoking a feeling of resonance that "activates a cultural latency or lacuna" (165) through which insiders appropriate alien knowledge, using it according to their own perceptions. In the process they often excise the knowledge from its context. Buddhism's expansionist trajectory and its persuasive power have helped provide the conditions in which it has stimulated these cultural and, I would add, existential lacunae, meeting the "unfulfilled needs of the western 'homeless heart'" (175, paraphrasing Berger).

As well as offering a sense of meaning to the individual, Buddhism offers answers to the problems of the world, often in a vein that appeals to people of a politically liberal orientation. Since I share many of the aspirations and feelings that I have described as being important to FWBO members and this has important consequences for how I came to be involved in this research in the first place and how I conducted it, I now provide some personal background.

MULTIPLE IDENTITIES, SHIFTING POSITIONS

In a book review in the FWBO magazine *Dharma Life* Vishvapani expresses distaste for research that moves "away from focusing on what Buddhists believe, to considering what they do" (2001, 57). He suggests that the problem with this approach, which he considers an "anthropological" one, is that it represents Buddhists "as another strange tribe engrossed in their distinctive language games and arcane rituals. Buddhism appears as a simply cultural phenomenon rather than as a source of insight." Despite my disagreement with his characterization of anthropology, I think it is judicious to engage with FWBO concerns, some of which match anthropological ones and illustrate some of the differences between anthropological and Buddhist studies approaches. This also provides an opportunity to clarify the relationship between the FWBO and my research strategy and agenda; I am also aware that the FWBO has had a mixed response to social science researchers in the past (more on this below). Thus I think it appropriate to consider how I represent the FWBO and the differences between the aspirations of anthropology and Buddhist studies. Do I portray the FWBO as a "strange tribe" with "arcane rituals"?

As an anthropologist, I am indeed analyzing Buddhism in the FWBO more as a "cultural phenomenon" than "as a source of spiritual insight." Anthropologists try to understand the cultural and social place of religious practices, and in this case my task is to understand what is involved in the establishment of the FWBO in New Zealand. Despite Vishvapani's comments, however, the relationship between belief and practice is pertinent, since they shape one another. For me, Buddhist teachings are a source of insight into our existential conditions. However, the intellectual tools of my academic discipline can, I hope, also complement Buddhist insights.[21] Any person seeking spiritual insight is both enabled and constrained by cultural conditionings, so the development of a better understanding of such conditionings may in fact be helpful to Buddhists. Rather than being mutually exclusive, the two approaches can, I like to think, work together fruitfully.

The issue of outsiders researching the FWBO was raised over a decade ago, when Philip Mellor (1991) published an article about the FWBO in the academic journal *Religion*. Kulananda (a Western Buddhist Order member) wrote a brief response for the journal (1992), and Sangharakshita (1992b) wrote at length, pointing out Mellor's factual inaccuracies and using the opportunity to comment on other issues that he considered the article had raised.[22] My purpose in mentioning it here is to note that in it, Sangharakshita objects to Mellor's misleadingly impartial voice and calls for the parliamentary practice of "declaring an interest" (53) whereby one makes known any personal connections, "especially a prejudicial connection, with the matter under debate." He notes that Mellor is a convert to Roman Catholicism and should have taken an openly Catholic standpoint (54). He construes Mellor as claiming that the "FWBO is prejudiced . . . Mellor, himself, of course, is free from prejudice" (49).

Attempts to create inclusive portraits in social analysis can often entail violence to the mixed truths of lived experience. When Sangharakshita criticizes Mellor, for example, for representing the FWBO "as if it were a single, monolithic body" (1992b, 23), he is identifying one of the difficulties with which all anthropologists wrestle in attempting to represent and analyze human worlds. Even as I attempt to sketch out characteristics of the FWBO and fill this in with shades of local details, the image of the organization as an entity begins to disintegrate. In the very process of analytical writing, there are pieces that fit and other parts that unsettle the model. Nonetheless, the analysis of any "association of individuals" (a term that FWBO publicity favors over the word "group") involves discerning the commonalities, patterns of practice and discourse, as well as internal diversity. Further, if the FWBO does not operate, in some ways, as a single body, on what grounds does Sangharakshita defend "it" against misrepresentation?

Many, if not most, contemporary anthropologists would wholeheartedly agree with Sangharakshita that one should declare one's interest, and indeed I would recommend that anyone using ethnographic research techniques into such a complex field as that of religious beliefs and practices should consider doing just this. As an example, in *Guru Devotion and the American Buddhist Experience*, Daniel Capper (2002) delineates his research position, outlining his involvement and providing anecdotes involving himself as one of the actors. This gives the reader the impression of seeing the subjects through Capper's eyes, and he is frank about the extent to which he engaged with Tibetan Buddhist teachings on a personal level and as a researcher.

Despite some members' reservations about the limits of intellectual knowledge for the *practice* of Buddhism, Subhuti (1994, 40), referring to studies with a theological leaning, writes that modern academic studies of Buddhism are valuable and cannot be ignored; Sandra Bell (1996, 93) notes an occasion when Subhuti talked about the FWBO as being in a phase of what he referred to as "routinization of charisma," obviously referring to Weber. Indeed, many members of the FWBO and other similar international networks have a tertiary education, and there is an occasional intermixing of personal and academic engagement with Buddhism (e.g., Prebish 1999). There are several academics who are also Western Buddhist Order members; some of these work in Buddhist studies, philosophy, or religious studies, such as Robert Morrison, author of *Nietzsche and Buddhism* (1997). I, too, am an academic who (albeit with less depth of commitment) has participated in the FWBO; I therefore take up Sangharakshita's call to declare my interest, beginning with a brief outline of my personal background.

I am a fourth-generation New Zealander, self-identifying as a Pākehā, with Scots Protestant ancestry. I grew up in an urban, progressive, middle-class family, and curiosity led me to find out more than I was taught at school about the colonizing, settler culture into which I had been born. During my adult life I developed an interest in meditation, attending a ten-day retreat in 1988 run by followers of Goenka, a well-known teacher of a reformist *vipassanā* (insight meditation) movement with roots in Theravāda Buddhism. Eight years later I attended a meditation course with at the FWBO's Auckland Buddhist Centre. The trigger for this renewed interest, as well as my decision to embark on studies in anthropology, was my shock at the death of my then-partner Steve in a mountaineering accident in late 1994. While grieving, I felt hypersensitive to what I regarded as the failure of the society I lived in to acknowledge the reality of death and that as a result I had not developed a meaningful framework for understanding and living with the precariousness of life. Buddhist teachings seemed to offer me help with this.

Additionally, the discomfort I felt in learning about the displacement and dispossession of indigenous peoples in many countries, including my own, fueled my interest in the theme of white settler Buddhists seeking to build a spiritual relationship to the land. I also have a strong (and no doubt overly idealistic) interest in community-minded, socially and environmentally harmonious, and sustainable ways of living, and in that respect the FWBO's interpretation of Buddhism seems to have much to offer. As an anthropologist, though, my own involvement in the FWBO has been complicated by the discipline's insights about how human beliefs about the world, including my own, are socially constructed. Thus it came about that in the three years before I began the fieldwork for this study, I had participated in numerous FWBO activities, attending meditation classes, retreats, and study groups.

Two specific events that took place before I had conceived this research project ultimately became pivotal to this book: the dedication of the Sudarshanaloka stūpa in February 1997 (my first visit to the land) and the subsequent relocation of a statue of the Buddha from beneath a specific tree to the inside of the stūpa. As an undergraduate student at that stage engaging with Buddhism for reasons more personal than anthropological, my first visit to the valley left me filled with inspiration. The vision of the Buddhist trustees to create a sacred place, dedicated as a sanctuary for jaded people needing to heal themselves and, further, to healing the land, resonated with my own ideas and concerns. I have long been concerned about the ways humans have destroyed ecosystems and imprisoned the land under asphalt, dividing it up into blocks to buy and sell and fighting over it. Further, I am intensely aware of the unsustainable lifestyle of the world of which I am part, a world whose problems arise in part from hypermobility, wasteful consumerism, and gross maltreatment of the land, all powered by nonrenewable energy sources.

While this Buddhist retreat center is far from being independent of these systems, the project is inspired by the ideals of its founders: that if people deepen their wisdom and compassion through appropriate meditative and ethical practice, then this is ultimately a contribution to the healing of humanity's existential ills. At Sudarshanaloka, the ideal of appropriate practice has also come to entail learning to sense and respond to the spirit of the land, while also attempting at least partially to manage the inevitable *destruction* that accompanies the *construction* of the physical facilities they are establishing.

My personal enthusiasm for the FWBO has fluctuated: there is much about the movement, the institution, and the conduct of some individuals in it of which I am critical. However, I believe I have also learned much on a deeply personal level from my involvement with the movement, and in 2002 I formally took refuge as a Buddhist, becoming known as *mitra* in FWBO terms. For my doctoral research I attended numerous teachings in the Tibetan tradition, and at a personal level I continue with a daily meditation practice and attempt to apply Buddhist ethical principles in my daily life. Several factors, including my research entanglements, have led to reduced personal involvement in the FWBO. I now attend another, smaller group (the Long White Cloud Sangha) in Auckland, in the tradition of the Vietnamese Zen teacher Thich Nhat Hanh, and, like many others, I remain somewhat eclectic in my personal exploration of Buddhism, drawing inspiration from several teachers and their writings.

The implication of all of this for my research is that my personal ideals, meditation practice, and participation in FWBO activities enabled me to approach a sympathetic understanding of the interests and concerns of FWBO members. I have had some of the privileged access of a community member, without the kind of emotional investment that has the potential to suppress critical views of the institution. While such familiarity can in some ways hinder analysis, it was often advantageous because of my existing rapport and because I already had some understanding of the natives' points of view, to pluralize Bronislaw Malinowski's oft-quoted phrase (1953 [1922], 25). At the same time, I have had the opportunity to compare the FWBO with a range of other Buddhist organizations.

While my involvement with academic/intellectual knowledge might be regarded as distancing me from the deep, heartfelt participation of a more committed community member, taking a critical stance does not in itself make me an outsider, because there is frequent lively debate within the movement. My ongoing research interest in Buddhism has also had the contradictory effects of helping me to be tolerant of what I see as failings in convert Buddhist organizations while also creating something of a barrier to full participation.

Order members have tended to take a friendly, teacherly role with me, just as they do with newcomers and Friends. However, because I am not a member of the Western Buddhist Order, there are many aspects from which I am excluded, such as Order members' private "Chapter meetings." Likewise, the international Order members' monthly journal *Shabda* is a confidential document. Several of my FWBO interlocutors have told me they have found that our discussions stimulate them to see things in another perspective, and they have engaged with my research, reading and commenting on earlier drafts and expressing interest in reading the finished work. Thus this study is a tentative exploration of how anthropologists can work with the people they study (and who are likely to read at least some of my writing) in a way that I hope is mutually beneficial.

IMAGINING A NEW TRADITION

New religious movements with roots in established world religions face the challenge of being relevant in changing times while also demonstrating continuity with an established system of thought. In the case of the FWBO, its own literature depicts the movement as dynamic and innovative, while also taking care to assert continuity with the original teachings of the Buddha. For example, Vishvapani wrote of the FWBO's mission: "Western Buddhists are attempting to create a new tradition—a tradition of Western Buddhism within which individuals can develop beyond subjective experience, can grow through activity and engagement and finally come not just to follow the Truth, but to embody it" (1994).[23]

Likewise, in a conversation about the ways local groups were experimenting with bringing locally significant cultural forms into their ritual practice, one New Zealand Order member told me, "We're a new tradition." This odd expression suggests that the FWBO attempts to be sufficiently innovative to be relevant to its members, while also sustaining traditions that carry the core ideals held in common by a particular imagined community. As Prajñalila commented on a draft of this book, the FWBO seeks to hold to the "essential spirit while seeking relevant means to express them." In the next chapter, then, I introduce Sudarshanaloka and describe how FWBO retreat centers provide an opportunity for these new Buddhists to explore ways not only to manifest their dharmic aspirations on the land and deepen their personal spiritual practice, but also, more broadly, to realize their new tradition in a way that they consider relevant to the locale.

2 Unplugging from the Grid

Approaching the Coromandel Peninsula from the west, the green and jagged mountain range makes a dramatic backdrop to Thames (population approx. 7,500), the gateway town for the peninsula, after the flat farmland of the Hauraki Plains (fig. 2.1). Alongside the road at the town's northern end stand visible remains of Thames' historical role in gold mining, with old equipment and the entrances to mineshafts on display. Traveling northwards up the coast, the Firth of Thames is on the left. On the right, beyond one row of houses, are the same hills, clothed in regenerating native forest, commonly referred to as "bush" in New Zealand.

An easily missed side street serves a few houses and a camping ground before leading around a corner between two steep, overlapping spurs. Beyond a ford often barred by heavy rain, the narrow gravel road winds its way up the valley, passing the gated black hole of an old mineshaft in the clay of one roadside bluff and crossing the creek by way of several more crumbling concrete fords. After a kilometer or so, the valley widens out and vivid green, craggy peaks overlook the deep valley. Most of the land is steep, clothed in a mixture of native bush and invasive imported species such as gorse, broom, and wilding pines.[1] Although the impression, especially during the warmer months, is of lush and primal greenery, most of the bush is regrowth. The most distinctive plant is the native tree fern, which is often one of the first native plants to establish itself in regenerating bush. From the head of the valley, a walking track runs up to the ridge tops, through dripping forest, with gaps in the trees providing occasional glimpses of the valley and peaks. Other tracks take walkers to the occasional waterfall or clear, cool bathing pool.

Halfway up the valley, off to the right, a wooden sign, gateway, and fence demarcate the entrance to the Buddhist retreat center. A curved tree branch serves as a signboard that proclaims "SUDARSHANALOKA LAND OF BEAUTIFUL VISION." Entering the gate, the access road dips down to cross the creek via a ford. Sudarshanaloka is on a wedge-shaped piece of land, straddling a large, steep-sided spur. Tararu Creek and the Ohio Stream mark two of the property's boundaries; the upper boundary, adjoining Department of Conservation land, is less distinguishable, being situated at some point high in the bush. On hot summer days, people

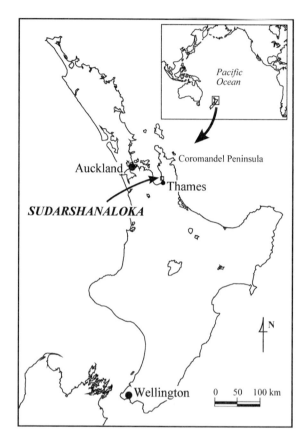

FIGURE 2.1.
The North Island of New Zealand showing Sudar-shanaloka, the Coromandel Peninsula, Auckland, Wellington, and Thames.

from the region come up the valley and swim in the waterholes, and their shouts and laughter can sometimes be heard from the hillside of Sudarshanaloka.

A flight of stone steps leads from the driveway up to the community house, past a rock garden and a painted horse skull attached to the trunk of a large *macrocarpa* tree.[2] This leads to the community house. Weathered but colorful flags printed with Buddhist symbols flutter on a nearby pole. Directly behind the house, steps cut into a clay bank lead up the hill to the community shrine room, a simple wooden structure built not long after the purchase of the land, with windows providing a view of two vertical slices of the neighboring forested hills and rocky peaks.

Beyond the shrine room is a small vegetable garden in a rough corrugated-iron enclosure and a large water tank to supply the house. Nearby is another large storage shed, which was used as a shrine room for two public ordinations. At the

FIGURE 2.2.
Kauri log. (Photographed by S. McAra in 2000.)

end of the flat section of the spur are three small huts (cabins) for community members and a path that rejoins the winding, unsealed road that we left to visit the community house. The road zigzags its way up the steep spur of land, at times pass-ing yellow and red-ocher banks of clay that stand out like scars on the land against the scrubby regrowth, and through the cool shade of one or two older stands of mature native trees.

From the last zigzag of the road the stūpa becomes fully visible, and when viewed from the final approach it sits against the backdrop of another bush-clad ridge, with the spire crossing the skyline. At this height there is an expansive view down the valley and across the Firth of Thames to the rolling hills south of Auck-land. Around a hundred meters from the stūpa, the first stage of the long-planned retreat facility is, in 2006, finally being completed. This site was in a mixture of re-generating bush and pasture when the trustees bought the land. Nearby lies an old *kauri* log (*Agathis australis*, fig. 2.2), and beyond that stands the *pūriri* tree (*Vitex lu-cens*, fig. 2.3) where, in the first dedication ceremony for the property, the trustees placed a Buddha statue at its base. These objects—the stūpa, *kauri* log, and *pūriri*—provide important landmarks at Sudarshanaloka (fig. 2.4).

FIGURE 2.3.
Pūriri tree. (Photographed by S. McAra in 2005.)

The FWBO has run meditation retreats in New Zealand since the 1970s, generally in hired out-of-town venues designed for school or church camps—buildings with a kitchen/dining area, ablutions blocks, bunkrooms, and a meeting space that they would convert into a temporary meditation/shrine room. However, it takes a considerable amount of work to organize and prepare hired venues, so members had hoped for some time to develop their own purpose-built retreat venue. Thus after a decade-long search, a group of Order members formed the Sarana Trust, which in August 1993 signed the deed of purchase for the Tararu Valley property now called Sudarshanaloka. The following year, four Order members (Satyananda, Taranatha, Dharmadhara, and Punyasri) formed a new trust named Friends of the Western Buddhist Order Tararu to legally manage it.[3]

In this chapter I provide an impression of the retreat center and tie this to the FWBO emphasis on retreats. Despite a sense that Sudarshanaloka is physically enclosed in a secret valley, the wider regional setting in which it is situated is important, so I also provide an orientation to the region and an outline of religion in New Zealand, with particular attention to Buddhism. I follow this by considering the aspirations behind the retreat center as a place of transformation, including the FWBO's utopianist notions of social transformation, while in chapter 3 I shift the

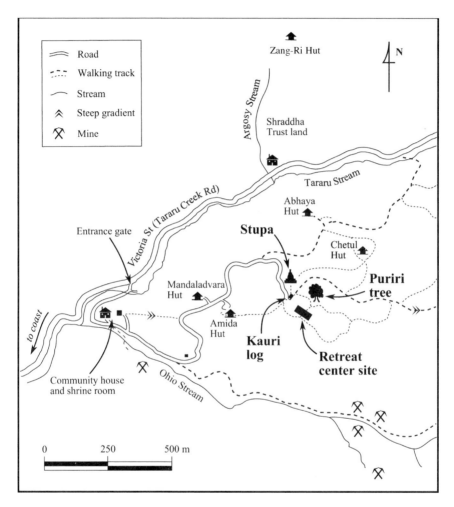

FIGURE 2.4.
Map of Sudarshanaloka showing relative locations of stūpa, *kauri* log, and *pūriri* tree.

focus to consider FWBO/NZ relationships with broader themes, including the nation's history of settler colonialism and notions of relationship with the land.

LOCAL CONTEXT

For many who go there, the Coromandel Peninsula,[4] or "the Coromandel" as it is often called, has the attributes of the quintessential place of idyllic "nature." The peninsula's main attractions include valleys cloaked in green forests with dramatic volcanic rock outcrops. It has a distinctive beauty and is accessible to urbanites (Thames being around an hour and a half's drive from Auckland) who may choose to engage in a range of recreational activities there. Expressions like "the bush," "hills," or "back country" evoke for many New Zealanders the idea of the wilderness. The bush is something of a cultural icon tied up with New Zealand identities (see, e.g., Grubb 2005), and thus my description of the bush in the Tararu Valley evokes a rugged place where people might choose to go hunting or tramping, rather than simply to take a leisurely stroll.

The Coromandel also boasts an abundance of white-sand beaches on its eastern side. Summer holiday periods see a flood of visitors from the urban centers who come to stay in holiday homes or the camping grounds. Holidays at the beach have been a long-standing Kiwi tradition. In the past, even many working-class families could afford to build their own "bach" (a simple holiday house) on small coastal sections in regions like the Coromandel or at least rent space in a beachside camping ground to pitch large family tents. However, land values have soared, and there are now a number of resort areas with luxury homes in the region. Property developers have also bought out many of the camping grounds, sparking fears that soon seaside holidays will be affordable only for a wealthy few.

During the 1960s and 1970s various people experimenting with alternative and communal lifestyles bought land on the peninsula, and even today some communitarian projects continue, albeit with adaptations to the idealism of their founders.[5] Intentional communities, organic cooperatives, and religious and secular retreat centers have been established in the region. On the western side of the peninsula there are, in addition to Sudarshanaloka, two other Buddhist retreat centers: the Mahamudra Centre for Universal Unity, not far from the town of Colville, and Dharma Gaia Centre for Mindful Living, which is connected with Thich Nhat Hanh's Order of Interbeing and based in a former Rudolf Steiner school on land belonging to the secular/New Age Mana Retreat Centre. On the eastern ranges near the town of Tairua is another venue named Te Moata Retreat Centre.[6]

Perhaps the diversity the region already boasts accounts for the apparent acceptance of Sudarshanaloka by the Thames community. Satyananda tells me that some locals without any interest in Buddhism are nonetheless pleased to bring friends to show them the stūpa, their local attraction. The retreat center's application for resource (planning) consent in 1999 was initially opposed by the local *iwi* (Ngati Maru) on the grounds that the applicants had failed to consult them directly, the result of an oversight in the process. This situation was resolved with meetings between the two parties, and Satyananda said that he felt there was now "a sufficient understanding of each other to form a basis for what will hopefully be an important and supportive relationship for both our people and theirs" (1999a, 11).[7]

Sudarshanaloka is known among community groups as being able to provide a place for people to have time out, and indeed at least one local Christian minister's wife sometimes stays in one of the retreat huts for quiet time. It is worth noting that Buddhist organizations with predominantly white membership such as the FWBO possess sociocultural advantages that enable them to win acceptance in the wider community. Further, many people, including locals and travelers passing along the nearby coastal road, remain unaware of the existence of Sudarshanaloka and its stūpa because of the fact that the valley is not visible from the coast road. In contrast, the elaborately decorated stūpa at the Mahamudra Centre has become a well-known landmark, since it stands right beside the main road to Colville, near the northern end of the peninsula.

NEW ZEALAND RELIGION BY NUMBERS

New Zealand officially maintains separation between church and state, and in general little attention is paid to religion in the public media. Buddhism enjoys a popular public image, being regarded by most as harmless. Some of the objections raised against temple plans by immigrant Buddhists in other parts of the country suggest a fear of unfamiliar religious practices, along with a more understandable concern about increased traffic flows (e.g., McLean 2001, NZ Herald 2001, R. Taylor 2002), but extreme hostility is rare. I know of one case of overt intolerance: Brian Tamaki, a controversial pastor who founded the Destiny Church in Auckland, describes the construction of the large Foguangshan Taiwanese Buddhist temple in south Auckland as "opening a door from Hell" (Brown 2005, quoting Tamaki). Linking Buddhism and Islam with "immigrants . . . who won't change their demon religions," Tamaki says these people "are 'pouring in' . . . as a result of a 'demon' looking around the world for openings where God has been pushed out."[8] When in 1997 the Foguangshan applied for planning consent for their Chinese-style temple, seventy residents and groups opposed the organization's resource consent application.[9] By 2006 the temple was complete, and they sought consent to build a 26.4-meter (86.6 feet) high pagoda as an addition to the temple complex; this sparked further objections, in part because locals were upset by the idea of a tower holding cremation ashes.

According to the last census, taken in 2001, New Zealand has a population of over four million people, of which around two million indicated an affiliation with a Christian religion. Beyond the uneven bicultural relationship between Māori and the British settlers that I discuss in the next chapter, New Zealand is a culturally diverse nation, with around 75 percent New Zealand European (Pākehā), 5 percent "other European," 14.7 percent Māori, 6.6 percent Asian (various nationalities including Chinese, Korean, Indian), 6.5 percent Pacific Islander, 0.8 percent "other".[10] The three largest Christian denominations in New Zealand are Anglican (17 percent of the population), Catholic (14 percent), and Presbyterian (11 percent) (Statistics New Zealand 2005). The largest non-Christian religions professed are still relatively low in proportion to the total population: Buddhism is the largest (1.21 percent), followed by Hinduism (1.16 percent), Islam (0.69 percent), and Spiritualism (0.47 percent). Buddhism is among the fastest-growing religions,[11] a pattern that has also been noted in other non-Asian countries (e.g., Prebish and Baumann 2002).

BUDDHISM IN NEW ZEALAND

In the 1996 census 82 percent of people who said they were Buddhist were Asian-born (CRAANZ 2000, 52), and the majority of these were born in Taiwan. Of the remainder, 19 percent of those who ticked "Buddhist" were New Zealand-born. These figures do not account for non-Asian immigrants to New Zealand who are Buddhist, and I have observed that of several international Buddhist networks I have spent time with, each has a fair share of members from Europe and North America. Māori participation in Buddhism is low: only 2 percent of New Zealand-born Buddhists said they had any Māori ancestry. The increase in numbers of Buddhists in New Zealand is in large part due to the numbers of immigrants from Asian Buddhist countries, but the numbers of Europeans (including those who identify as Pākehā) professing Buddhism has shown a greater intercensal increase: between 1991 and 2001, the number of European Buddhists increased from 8 percent to 20 percent of Buddhists. In the 1991 census, 90 percent of people who professed Buddhist affiliation were grouped under the category of "Asian" ethnicity (10,542 people), while 8 percent had a "European" ethnicity (2,157 people). In 2001, however, 72 percent of Buddhists were grouped as having an Asian ethnicity (29,835 people), while 20 percent of Buddhists in New Zealand were designated a European ethnicity (10,869 people).

The designation of affiliation with Buddhism on a census form does not account for people who, despite being influenced by Buddhist ideas, do not identify as Buddhist. I would suggest that as the North American studies have shown (Tweed 1999, Wuthnow and Cadge 2004), the influence of Buddhism on New Zealand society, especially among certain strands such as middle-class, tertiary-educated professionals, is far greater than current census statistics reveal. For example, many people will attend meditation courses and teachings by Buddhist teachers and read Buddhist literature without actually identifying as Buddhist.

New Zealand, like other Western nations, has a vast proliferation of different Buddhist groups following various approaches, from almost secular approaches such as Insight meditation (*vipassanā*) that eschew words like "religion" or "Buddhism,"[12] claiming instead to teach a method of mindfulness practice, insight, or awakening, to those that maintain the notion of their own way as being the only truth. Each group tends to have more commonalities with others in its international network than with neighboring groups. For example, the practices found in the FWBO in Britain and New Zealand have more in common than the practices found at Sudarshanaloka and the Mahamudra Centre, since these two centers are affiliated to two very different international organizations.

An indicator of the diversity of Buddhism is the number of centers and groups. One of the active directories (BuddhaNet 2005) has a list of ninety-six entries, which includes associations and their affiliates, trusts, retreat centers, monasteries, small meditation groups, and a hospice service. The listing includes both immigrant- and convert-oriented groups, incorporating approximately twenty Theravādin groups, twenty Tibetan Buddhist centers or groups, and about the same number of Zen-derived groups and centers.[13] There are also other branches of Mahāyāna (Ch'an and Pure Land) and several ecumenical groups (including the FWBO and the Wangapeka Retreat Centre in the South Island).

As Michelle Spuler notes, published material on the history of Buddhism in New Zealand is scarce (2002, 139), receiving only brief mention in one chapter of a book surveying the religious landscape of that country (Viradhammo 1996). Chinese immigrants brought the first Buddhist influences during the gold rush from 1863. Theosophy played an important role in bringing attention to Buddhism in North America and Australia, and one would expect the same to have occurred in New Zealand where, towards the end of the nineteenth century, theosophical societies became active (Parr 2000). Indeed, Olcott visited New Zealand in 1897 and lectured on Buddhism in Christchurch on September 9th of that year, but Parr finds little evidence of lasting interest in Buddhism after this visit. Through the twentieth century, *The New Zealand Theosophical Magazine* made only passing references to the religion (12). In the twentieth century, some New Zealanders encountered Buddhist teachers while traveling overseas or through literature. The Buddhist Society of New Zealand was founded in 1956 (Spuler 2002, 140) and was possibly the earliest such organization to be established in the country. By the

1970s the Buddhist presence in this country had increased and radically diversified, with monks and nuns from various traditions visiting, often at the invitation of New Zealanders who had met them while on overseas travels. Some of the groups founded at this time have led to the establishment of Dharma centers still in existence today. At the same time, immigrants and refugees brought their own specific Buddhist traditions. Linguistic and cultural barriers mean that, broadly speaking, Asian and Anglophone Buddhists seldom mix, although I am aware of instances where people of quite distinct cultural backgrounds do share the same teachers and practices. A fuller investigation of the history of Buddhism in New Zealand is beyond the scope of this book.

ESTABLISHING THE FWBO IN NEW ZEALAND

In 1970 a WBO member named Akshobhya returned from Britain and began holding meetings in his suburban Auckland home, which he named the Kalyana Mitra Buddhist Centre, marking the beginning of FWBO presence in New Zealand. This was only three years after the founding of the movement in Britain. Their meetings often centered on audiotaped lectures by Sangharakshita, and Sangharakshita himself visited the New Zealand FWBO groups in 1974–1975 and 1979 to teach and conduct ordinations. In 1974, members shifted to a city location and rented premises in a series of venues until they bought a building in the central Auckland suburb of Grey Lynn in 1990, now called the Auckland Buddhist Centre (ABC). From 1972 to 1979 there was an FWBO center in Christchurch, on the South Island, which closed when two of its organizers moved to Britain. During the time period on which this book is focused, the three formally established FWBO centers were in Auckland, Sudarshanaloka, and Wellington. Another center was established in Thames in 2002.

The FWBO in New Zealand has never been as isolated from Britain as its distance suggests, since so many New Zealanders involved in the movement travel there—for instance, to follow opportunities to work in the movement's Team-Based Right Livelihood enterprises as Diane did prior to her ordination as Prajñā-lila. It is because of this ongoing involvement with the movement internationally that much of my description of the FWBO in the previous chapter applies, on a smaller scale, to the New Zealand situation. In addition to the flow of New Zealand FWBO people to Britain, there are other flows between other FWBO centers around the world, with particularly close links to the Melbourne and Sydney Buddhist centers and the Vijayaloka Retreat Centre near Sydney in Australia. At any one time, several Order members from overseas are involved with the three FWBO/NZ centers. Some come from as far away as Britain to use the solitary retreat huts at Sudarshanaloka, often for quite a mundane reason, in that the exchange rate makes it cheaper for them to do long retreats here. Several Order members have come from overseas to help with building projects, and New Zealand Order members involved in the movement's Northern Hemisphere activities occasionally visit.

As a spatially dispersed, transnational network of people connected through shared understandings and through their communications and internal media, FWBO members "imagine" themselves as part of an international Buddhist community (cf. Anderson 1991). To maintain this community, FWBO members make extensive use of electronic communications, newsletters, news videos, and global travel. People involved in the FWBO are often very historically self-conscious, as reflected in the many published books, magazines, and videos the movement has produced about its short history. For example, the FWBO in Britain has produced a range of periodicals. A magazine called *Dharma Life*, formerly *Golden Drum*, which ran until 2005, presented itself as a magazine for Buddhists. Women in the movement had their own magazine, *Lotus Realm* (formerly *Dakini*) for some years. The *Western Buddhist Review* is their more scholarly journal, of which four issues have appeared since 1994. There are also several confidential newsletters—one each for men and women who have asked for ordination and another, *Shabda*, for Order members—and some specialized e-mail discussion groups. The FWBO has its own publishing house, Windhorse, primarily for Dharma books by Western Buddhist Order teachers. Windhorse has also released several volumes of memoirs by Sangharakshita, and various Order members are writing about their own lives (e.g., Taranatha 2006).

FWBO ACTIVITIES

Like most Dharma centers in urban settings, the FWBO in Auckland attracts new members by offering courses of meditation classes consisting of eight weekly sessions culminating in a weekend retreat. Numbers vary, but fifteen to twenty students per class would be about average. Order members run the courses with the assistance of *mitras*. The main reason for coming to the classes is that people wish to learn meditation, often because they have heard it is beneficial for reducing stress. Some students from these courses go on to become involved in the movement.

The ABC's regular community event, the weekly "Sangha night," involves a group meditation followed by a tea break and, often, a Dharma talk. There are also several annual festivals, including Buddha Day, Dharma Day, and Sangha Day, each of which is usually celebrated on a Saturday or Sunday and involves group activities such as meditation, *pūjās*, shared meals, socializing, and formal talks.

They combine some celebrations with the Sudarshanaloka/Thames sangha. For example, every February, the FWBO sangha marks the anniversary of the stūpa dedication, which coincides with the movement's observance of Parinirvana Day. The ABC offers regular weekend retreats. Often they hire a venue such as the Awhitu Environmental Camp, on the Awhitu Peninsula (a remote area on the western coast of the isthmus of Auckland), which is designed to host school camps. Like Sudarshanaloka, it is around two hours' drive from Auckland, but its amenities are more developed.

Like many nonprofit organizations, FWBO centers in New Zealand must raise funds whenever the generalized income is insufficient. The ABC relies on a variety of income sources, including donations, fees for retreats and classes (on meditation and Buddhism), bookshop sales, and the hiring of the center by other groups. While meditation courses and retreats have a two-tiered fee (waged and unwaged), this is negotiable for those unable to pay the full price—an adaptation of the Buddhist concept of *dāna* (generosity).

The funds for the initial purchase of the Tararu Valley property came primarily from loans and donations from FWBO members. During my fieldwork in 2000, a sign pinned to the wall behind a deep wooden bowl on a bookshelf in the living room reminded visitors that this is a "dana economy" and that it took about NZ$10 a night to keep a person fed and sheltered there. Five years later the suggested donation was NZ$30 per night. In the absence of the yet-to-be completed retreat center, Sudarshanaloka had no significant income-generating activities until 2002, when they opened a book and gift shop they called "Lotus Realm" in Thames. Soon after, they established the Thames Buddhist Centre (to teach meditation and Buddhism to locals), using some of the rooms behind the street-front shop. By 2005, Lotus Realm was providing enough money to fund the rent for the Thames Buddhist Centre rooms and financial support for several other positions, including a groundsman and an administrator for Sudarshanaloka. The shop has also become the town face of Sudarshanaloka and has links to other community groups.[14]

FWBO PEOPLE IN NEW ZEALAND

The majority of FWBO/NZ members, including those who attend meditation classes, could be classified as New Zealand European (or Pākehā, if they choose to adopt that label). Some immigrants also attend, mainly of European and North American backgrounds, and several from the Asia-Pacific region. Many are middle-class, middle-aged or retired, and tertiary educated. There are some younger members, both single and with young families, but other than one or two special retreats each year, few events in New Zealand are family oriented, and because other activities are not appealing to or designed for children and teenagers, parents of younger children rarely attend. This appears to be the case for many Dharma centers in New Zealand, although I have seen a greater proportion of younger people at an Auckland center with a Tibetan Buddhist affiliation.

The FWBO/NZ has a small core of dedicated members. Indeed, the number of Order members resident in New Zealand ranks the country third after Britain and India. Despite the FWBO's growth rate internationally, it is not yet clear whether the FWBO will grow significantly in New Zealand, since the membership is aging and few young people attend the events in the urban centers. As Robert Bluck has noted in a discussion of numbers of Buddhists in Britain (2004), record keeping at Dharma centers staffed by volunteers is seldom comprehensive. Another complicating factor is that there is also a much larger and more transient periphery consisting of people who have only a brief association with the center and the courses and events offered. Further, with the FWBO there is no formal membership. While the WBO keeps records on numbers of Order members, even this cannot be 100 percent accurate, since being an Order member does not always equate with active, long-term involvement, despite the intention for it to be so. Thus the "snapshots" of numbers in 2000 and 2006 I provide in chapter 1 must be taken as approximate.

The number of Order members in New Zealand is increasing, as people who have had a long-term involvement with the FWBO undergo ordination. According to Purna, a New Zealand Order member who compiled a list of New Zealanders who have been ordained in the Western Buddhist Order or who have resided in New Zealand, in 2006 the number of New Zealand-based Order members reached 49, with a further 17 Order members with New Zealand connections living overseas. The total of 66 consists of approximately equal numbers of men and women (34 and 32 respectively). There are two FWBO residential communities in Auckland: Amritadhatu women's community and Saranadipa men's community.

Establishing Sudarshanaloka

Although some people refer to Sudarshanaloka as a "community," this may mislead people into thinking that it is organized like the intentional communities where people exploring alternative lifestyles established their homes in the region. In actual fact, the residential community is very small, and residents are often short-term only. Sudarshanaloka operates more, then, as a "sanctuary" for urban and local members who periodically visit. Most people travel to and from the center for occasions such as meetings or retreats, while living and working elsewhere. During much of the year, there may be only three or four people living at Sudarshanaloka's community facilities.

An old farmhouse and several makeshift cabins accommodate the residential community. During my visits in 2000 there were three men (two of them ordained) in residence; in 2005 there were three men and one woman, Satyananda being the only almost-continuous resident over that time period. Until recently a few old caravans around the property provided extra accommodation, with cabins replacing these over time. The valley is not connected to the national grid, so the limited electricity supply comes from a generator and (more recently) a solar battery, so residents have to be more mindful of their energy consumption than they would be in the city. For several years candles and lamps provided lighting at night. A woodstove heats the water, and gas tanks provide the fuel for cooking.

The house is not suited for large numbers because of the limitations of the small bathroom and septic tank; there is space for a retreat of around ten to fifteen people. During the construction of the stūpa (1996–1997), however, up to thirty people stayed in the house and caravans. From then until this writing in 2006 there has been a small team of Order members and others who have been working on various construction projects at Sudarshanaloka. The house has something of the feel of a backpacker's hostel, with its combination of short-stay casual visitors, retreatants, and longer-term residents. The main house has five bedrooms, one of which doubles as a library. Another doubled as Satyananda's office until additional rooms were added upstairs.

The back of the house has a shelter, open at the sides, used as a dining area when there is a large influx of people for events such as the annual stūpa anniversary. In 2004, an upper story was added to give two resident Order members more privacy and to make the running of small retreats easier, since the facilities up the hill are still not ready for use. Buddhadasa, a male Order member living there since 2002, told me that now that a woman has moved into the community, the residents of this farmhouse may constitute the first "mixed" community in the movement, something of a departure from their norm of single-sex residential communities.

Beyond the shrine room, tool sheds, and residents' huts, further up the hill in various isolated locations are three self-contained huts (named Chetul, Amida, and Abhaya; see fig. 2.4) for the purpose of solitary retreats. Another house was constructed for Aniketa, an elderly Order member who wished to live in retreat-like conditions. Since her death in 2002, the house has been used for various purposes, such as a place for community members to stay when their houses are being used for small retreats. High on the hillside across the valley stands another, more remote cabin, Zang-ri, which people can book for longer solitary retreats; one woman completed a three-year retreat there.

Sudarshanaloka serves a variety of purposes. Order members sometimes hold their regular Order meetings there, and others, too, meet to meditate together, conduct *pūjās*, and study. They also help with various tasks: clearing tracks, chopping firewood, and carrying out general maintenance work around the property. At other times, using government employment schemes, locals without Buddhist affiliation have been employed for manual labor and as office administrative assistants. Sudarshanaloka sometimes takes Buddhist and non-Buddhist international travelers who work in exchange for food and accommodation. The whole summer is a busy period, with both casual visitors and intensive retreats. People (mainly from the wider FWBO Sangha but also some non-Buddhists) come to visit or stay from as far away as Britain or from around New Zealand. On alternate years, intensive "GFR" (Going for Refuge) retreats for Australians and New Zealanders training for ordination are held at Sudarshanaloka and Vijayaloka. Sudarshanaloka is the FWBO retreat center in New Zealand, and, as Satyananda noted, it will be the FWBO's first "purpose-built retreat center," being built from scratch rather than remodeling older buildings that had previous lives as farmhouses or country hotels, as has been done for FWBO retreat centers in the United Kingdom and elsewhere.

THE ROLE OF RETREATS IN CREATING THE "NEW SOCIETY"

In the Western cultural imagination today, admiration for Buddhism extends well beyond the numbers of actual converts (Wuthnow and Cadge 2004), evinced by the high sales figures for books bearing the face and name of the Dalai Lama and other famous Buddhist teachers. Buddhism is popularly imagined as a philosophy of peace, something that one can choose to follow as a method of individual, inner spiritual transformation. Internationally, there are many examples of so-called "engaged" Buddhism in which Buddhists try to address contemporary social problems and thus transform society. Many Buddhists would argue that all Buddhist practice is engaged, being concerned with the welfare of all living beings, but the term is used as a response to a popular representation of Buddhism as self-indulgent navel gazing (see, e.g., Queen, Prebish, and Keown 2003). In response to such criticisms, FWBO Buddhists often say that self-transformation is a necessary basis for the transformation of society, and this inner work facilitates the task of effecting social change.

The theme of disenchantment, of yearning for meaning, appears in FWBO literature and among FWBO members' personal stories of their encounter with the movement, primarily in discussions about people's reasons for being attracted to Buddhist teachings. It is not surprising, therefore, that many of the people who became involved with the FWBO in its founding days were participants in the countercultural movement, through which young people attempted to resist what they regarded as the "system." FWBO Buddhism had a utopianist tendency, appearing to propose an ethical and, at the same time, liberal way of being in the world. Sangharakshita tries to explain why people convert to Buddhism, suggesting that perhaps the commonest reason is that people are

> dissatisfied with themselves, or with life, or even that, in Karl Jaspers' phrase, they "feel ill and suffer from their psychic state." . . . They experience a sensation of lack, of there being something missing, and . . . out of this sensation they go searching, with varying degrees of determination and clarity, for that missing something, or at least are on the lookout for it from time to time (1992b, 42–43).

Sangharakshita describes alienation as a "metaphor for the human condition" (1993, 95), adding that "we are alienated from our own higher selves, our own better natures, our own highest potentialities. We are alienated from Truth, from Reality." Feeling such alienation and dissatisfaction, the newcomer comes "into contact with Buddhism" and feels that "the missing something has been found and that the sensation of lack is no longer there" (1992b, 45). In a booklet based on a talk at a training retreat for ordination, Aloka explains that people need spiritual meaning to counter anomie.

> In the West we have lost our overall patterns of meaning, we have lost our myths. . . . [Christianity] replaced magic with dogma . . . which cannot address a human being in his [sic] entirety. . . . The creative spirit . . . can only be repressed for so long before it rebels and destroys whatever is repressing it. . . . [A] contextless human being, in the sense that I am using it of mythic context, is prey to the demons of anxiety, fear, insecurity, lack of confidence. All these things are symptoms of a lack of real significance and meaning in our lives—these are very common, very modern, problems that people have—and without this context it is well-nigh impossible for a human being to experience himself in his fullness (1994, 3).

Doctrinal differences aside, the individual account of a sense of something missing that is then filled by Buddhism is not unlike the discourses of conversion to Christianity that Peter Stromberg (1993) documents.

The late modern trend toward so-called personal and spiritual development in which Western Buddhists participate has been portrayed as rebellion by a younger generation against their parents, but I concur with Howell that it is also an attempt to transform a society whose ills are perceived as stemming from the failure of materialism, rationality, and economic development "to produce individual and social 'happiness'" (1995, 175). The FWBO, then, is very much a product of late modernity, albeit one that attempts to improve upon its ills. It is clearly situated in a utopianist current, and I now turn to its founders' ideals of transforming not only the self, but also society and the role of retreat centers in this project.

FWBO members tend to regard Buddhist teachings as a way to transform both self and society. Team-Based Right Livelihood enterprises are one very deliberate attempt to change socioeconomic structures of Western society, although the accompanying discourses have changed from "revolutionary" to "accommodation and transformation of existing structures" (Baumann 2000, 372–373). In Britain, there are many such enterprises, including, among other things, a publishing house and gift stores, while in New Zealand the Sudarshanaloka-affiliated shop Lotus Realm follows a similar principle. In these businesses, the guideline for people dealing with donations and profits is "Give what you can, take what you need," a slogan much quoted in the FWBO that echoes Marxist ideals. This could be read as a refusal to accept the norms of mainstream Western society, including (ideally, at least) a refusal to be complicit in the destructive and exploitative practices of capitalism,[15] but in practice the businesses, like other sources of livelihood, operate in a capitalist society. It is clear, then, that these are not the socially withdrawn Buddhists described by Weber, a stereotype that has dominated sociological studies of Buddhism (Baumann 2000, 375).

Sangharakshita (1992a, 19–20) dismisses the idea of compromising Buddhist teachings in trying to integrate them into Western society. "[W]hat we really have to do is integrate Western society into Buddhism. There is much in Western society that needs changing. Buddhism can help us change it." In a series of talks originally given in 1976, he outlined a seemingly utopian ideal when he spoke of four things that the FWBO has to offer people: "a method of personal development to be practiced, a vision of human existence to provide inspiration, the nucleus of a new society to be enjoyed, and a blueprint for a new world to be worked for" (Sangharakshita 1996a, 54). His "new world" is one

> in which we relate to one another as individuals, a world in which we are free to develop to the utmost of our potential, and in which the social, economic, and political structures will help us to do that. The new world will be, in short, a spiritual community. . . . Our aim, therefore, must be to transform the present world into a spiritual community (1996a, 47–48).

He contrasts two views of how this radical change could be achieved: the first is that we must change the system; the second is that it is "up to the individual, *the basic unit of society*, to change" (48, my emphasis). He claims that the FWBO uses both approaches together, trying to provide, by example, an alternative world. The FWBO's utopia is, through its alterity, a silent but cogent critique of the ills of the West.

The FWBO propounds a utopianist "New Society" as a model for a Western Buddhist community based on Buddhist ethical principles (Subhuti 1994, 221ff). For example, living in an FWBO community and working in an FWBO Team-Based Right Livelihood cooperative are regarded as opportunities to effect positive change in oneself and society (Baumann 2000). Attending retreats, in which outside distractions are minimized, allows the FWBO member to develop inner spiritual practices and thus deepen the level of personal transformation. By way of illustrating how this is seen to effect social transformation, Sangharakshita notes that the prospect of a return to less helpful conditions can make people reluctant to leave a retreat, and the change they have experienced "does not always last." Nevertheless, he points out, "there is one lasting benefit: we have seen that it is possible to change, that—given the right conditions—we can develop." He summarizes his views about why retreats are beneficial, while demonstrating the FWBO interest in transforming society: "[I]t is not altogether true . . . that to offer a blueprint for a new world is to dream of something that does not exist. On retreat we experience, at least to a small extent and for a short time, what the new world could be like. We can even say that on a small scale a retreat is a new world (Sangharakshita 1996a, 49)." This suggests that retreats are a place to experiment with the utopianist ideal, and Sudarshanaloka is one of the few FWBO retreat centers outside of Britain for this ideal to be put into practice.

THE RETREAT AS A PLACE OF TRANSFORMATION

FWBO meditation retreats are presented as opportunities to intensify meditative practice, and the ideal is to provide the conditions in which retreatants can "develop" (Sangharakshita 1996a, 49), meditating together, taking part in *pūjās*, listening to talks on the Dharma, and participating in discussion groups. They involve living in conditions, at least temporarily, that are deemed

> more conducive to personal development. And in these improved conditions, people change. . . . They might arrive on retreat feeling worried, harried, anxious, tired, and irritable—but gradually they become more relaxed, they cheer up, they begin to smile and laugh. . . . They become

more aware of themselves, of one another, of their surroundings, of nature, more aware that they are living and breathing on this earth. They also become more free and spontaneous, more themselves. Although I have seen this happen many times, each time the change occurs it seems almost magical (49).

Indeed, I have often experienced this feeling of a temporary change in consciousness as a result of being on a retreat, a refreshing and vital sense of peaceful awareness. This may simply be a result of taking time out from the frenetic pace of city life and spending some quiet time in a place where there is open space, trees, fresh air, and a sense of perspective about my concerns; nonetheless, I am sure many would argue that the resulting sense of inner stillness helps spiritual transformation, including awakening to compassionate feelings for others, to take place.

In one conversation with Prajñalila about retreats, I explained the anthropological concept of "liminality" (V. W. Turner 1967), a situation in which people undertaking a rite of passage are separated from the day-to-day world to effect some kind of transformation or change of social status (such as the transition from boyhood to manhood) before reintegrating with society. She agreed that the term could be used to describe the sense of separation, transformation, and reintegration of retreats and added,

> Even to go away for a weekend, not even in our own retreat center, [you have to] unplug, prepare yourself, to leave things all in order. You step into this place, there is a dedication [ceremony] so you're orienting yourself for the practice that weekend. And as you leave, usually somebody will say, be careful, protect these states that you've been able to sort of cultivate in this weekend, because you know you will [go] back, and sometimes the interface with the world is awkward again, because there has been a transformation (Prajñalila 2000a).

Unless the retreat is for the purpose of ordination, the transformation is not an overt change in social status, but there is an inner transformation, in part because of the inner stillness gained by allowing one's daily preoccupations to drop, but also because one feels changed on arriving in a peaceful place. Ideally one brings something of this experience back to one's mundane life when returning from a retreat, and one is able to interact with the world in more beneficial and skillful ways. The notion that this transformation can then be of benefit to wider society helps to persuade people to support the proposed retreat center at Sudarshanaloka:

the brochure promoting the proposed facilities says that "it is essential in these troubled times that there be sacred places . . . dedicated to training the heart and cultivating insight" (Sudarshanaloka n.d.).

Guhyaloka is the principal retreat center for men's ordinations into the Western Buddhist Order and is located in a mountainous region of Alicante, Spain. A Web page promoting the center uses language that evokes the "mythic" emphasis in the FWBO, oddly juxtaposed with promotional language echoing vacation advertising.

> Far from the hustle and bustle of the modern world Guhyaloka is a place to relax, unwind, and live a simpler life alone or in the company of other people. As soon as you arrive at the remote Spanish valley where we are based you will understand why it is called Guhyaloka, which means the "secret realm." It is a magical place that provides a beautiful natural setting in which to deepen one's experience of meditation and further one's understanding of the Buddha's teaching (Guhyaloka n.d.).

While I have not conducted fieldwork in Britain, I know that British FWBO members are also concerned with what place means, because when Satyananda gave a talk at the North London Buddhist Centre and showed photographs and a video about Sudarshanaloka, people asked questions like "How can we make a sacred place, too?" Satyananda reflected that people want to have a "mythical element" in their lives and need places like Sudarshanaloka as a refuge or sanctuary.

To arrive in the enclosed Tararu Valley is to be noticeably parted from the outside world. After passing through the gateway to Sudarshanaloka and following the gravel road, one often sees stones from the creek piled up in the shape of small stūpas, often referred to as "stone stūpas" or "mini-stūpas," by the gate in the creek bed (fig. 2.5). Similar mini-stūpas are dotted along the private road and some of the walking tracks that crisscross the land, from the creek all the way up the spur. Flags, banners, the stūpa, and the stone stūpas all contribute to an aura of Otherness, something a little different from the typical New Zealand landscape. For some, these elements provide an aesthetically pleasing effect in the bush and stream setting and enhance the peaceful atmosphere of the valley. For those with an awareness of the symbolism of stūpas, such objects "point to the Transcendental," which in FWBO parlance means they evoke something beyond our everyday concerns and help remind us of aspirations toward spiritual liberation. Retreatants physically create a sacred place with objects of symbolic importance to evoke the

FIGURE 2.5.
Stone mini-stūpa
by Tararu Creek.
(Photo © Sudar-
shanaloka Trust.)

right feelings, and they perform rituals (formal and informal) for the same reason. There is a sense of entering another realm, which I certainly experienced on my first visit, when there were numerous colored banners standing out against the dark green of the bush-clad valley.

In the FWBO practice of going on retreat, rites of separation from the mundane world begin with the journey from the city to the retreat center. An article in the *Tararu Transformer* suggested that the point where the road crosses the creek could serve as "a ritual area where you can wash your hands and ring a bell before entering the property" (1999, 5), an attempt to consciously enact a rite of separation and purification. Typically the first evening of a retreat includes a simple ritual that dedicates the place and people to the purpose of the retreat, then people remain in the shrine room to meditate or retire in preparation for rising early the next morning. During the retreat, the timetable is usually quite structured, with periods of Dharma study, quiet "free" time for reflection, and group seated and walking meditation practices. On longer retreats people often designate extensive time periods for what they call "noble silence," breaking it only for specified purposes such as when one is participating in study group or shared chores that require discussion. This silence in the presence of other people increases the sense of being in an *other* space and time. At the end of the retreat, reintegration begins to take place with cleaning up the retreat buildings, dismantling the shrine (if using a hired venue), and sitting in a circle to "report out" and "dedicate the merit" gained by participation in the retreat to the welfare of all beings (this is regarded as reminding the retreatants that they do their practice to benefit all beings, not just themselves). The necessary journey to and from the retreat center is an extension of this ritualistic separation/reintegration.

Retreat center as maṇḍala

The FWBO members most involved with Sudarshanaloka intentionally reconceptualized the land itself as a maṇḍala (a model of the universe derived from Indic cosmology) with several gateways that lead deeper into the "mythic dimension" of Sudarshanaloka, and the valley itself and its particular features add to this sense.

> A maṇḍala is a sacred circle, a sacred space . . . [with] several gateways, and protective circles to cross, as you enter it. . . . The transcendental does not need protecting from the mundane world, because it is *other* than, but if you want to enter it, you need to be susceptible to transcendental influences. One needs to purify to go through these gateways. . . . So there seem to be some natural gateways up to the valley. There is the narrow valley itself, you enter it and you feel like you're actually going through a—you're feeling like . . . the town, and the big world behind is dropping away. Because the phone line is erratic, and power is generated from the sun, or a generator, you're also sort of unplugging from the grid, and you do become more reliant upon the elements (Prajñalila 2000a).

Sudarshanaloka, Prajñalila says, has tiers. Around halfway up the hill, an area they call Mandaladvara (Gateway to the maṇḍala) marks the shift from what they call public land (the lower part of Sudarshanaloka, around the community house) to retreat center land. Inscribing a maṇḍala on the land itself, it is "a symbolic gateway, to the private, to the more intensive practice, to the retreat center itself"— that is, to the innermost part of the maṇḍala, the center of the universe. To the left of the road, a pathway leads down to the small house built for Aniketa in 2000, and to the right there is also an unsealed parking lot, where future retreatants will leave their vehicles when going to stay in the retreat center so that they "leave behind another layer of the world." Within the inner maṇḍala is the stūpa, *pūriri* tree, and proposed retreat center site. The architectural plans for the retreat center shrine room incorporate what Prajñalila called "the inner sanctum," which is the heart of both the retreat center and the maṇḍala, being the focal point of retreats.

Prajñalila hoped the retreat center, when established, would "make a lot more things possible here. Just the kinds of retreats that we can run. The people that we can make it available to, so they can have a taste of something that they've never experienced in their lives. You know, some other possibility that they had never imagined really. So nourishing" (2000a).

The first brochure (Sudarshanaloka n.d.) promoting the planned retreat center, produced soon after the completion of the stūpa, is noteworthy for the words and imagery it uses that exemplify the kind of approach that has been developed: "At the core of the Sudarshanaloka vision is the desire to create a place of refuge and sanctuary, a place that will support people's efforts to become more aware and ethical, more emotionally positive and creative—in other words, to develop their fullest human potential" (n.d.). The text not only discusses the plans for the retreat center, but also discusses the land and their relationship to it. The imagery in this brochure features several photographs of the *pūriri* tree, some of native bush, one of a stone stūpa, and another of a lotus flower. The stūpa is a recurring image, with four photographs, one in close-up silhouette, two in the landscape with prayer flags around it, and a close-up of the spire with flags. The brochure also shows the architectural impression of the retreat center, some photographs of people, a shrine, and a solitary hut.

THE THREEFOLD BUDDHIST SOCIETY AT SUDARSHANALOKA

In many Buddhist societies and modern Buddhist organizations, the laity (the lower tier) seek to accrue merit[16] through giving alms to the monks, and the monks (the upper tier) seek to attain enlightenment. Many Western Buddhists are critical of this approach, since they understand Buddhist practice through their own notions of self-transformation and personal development. While I must observe that at times this elevation of convert Buddhists above those who are born into

Buddhist ways of life is problematic, the politics of this are beyond the scope of this book.

Western Buddhist Order members are not monks or nuns, and only a small number elect to take vows of celibacy. Further, while the traditional monastic code ranks women monastics below men (the seniormost Buddhist nun is ranked lower than the juniormost monk), the FWBO provides an equal ordination for men and women.

FWBO teachers place a strong emphasis on the importance of "spiritual friendship" (kalyāṇa mitratā) and the sangha as essential dimensions of the spiritual life. The ideal of spiritual friendship entails cultivating long-lasting and supportive friendship with others in the sangha, including those of similar levels of involvement and those who might be regarded as more experienced (Subhuti 1994, 154).[17] FWBO members repeatedly emphasize that such relationships are central to the spiritual life, citing a story in the Pāli canon where Ananda, a close friend and attendant of the Buddha, suggested to him that "half the spiritual life" consisted of spiritual friendship. The Buddha replied, "Say not so Ananda. Say not so. It is the whole, not the half of the spiritual life" (FWBO n.d.-d).[18] Spiritual friendship is described as having both "vertical" (one's mentors) and "horizontal" (one's peers) components (Subhuti 1994, 151ff).

In line with these ideals of spiritual community, FWBO members in various cities have affiliated residential "communities," almost always single-sex, where members of varying degrees of involvement live together. They have also developed "Right Livelihood" businesses, as discussed in chapter 1.[19] Several dedicated retreat centers have been established around Britain, including single-sex centers: Padmaloka (Norfolk) for men and Taraloka (Shropshire) for women; there are other centers where mixed retreats are held. In Spain the FWBO has established two centers: Guhyaloka (in Alicante) for men's ordination retreats and Akashavana (purchased in 2004 in Aragon and still undergoing renovation) for women's ordination retreats. The movement is not large in Spain, but land is cheaper there than in England, and thus such centers are suitable for FWBO members from around the world to travel to for their ordination retreats. Ordination retreats are also run on occasion in other venues around the world, including Sudarshanaloka.

In their experimental communities, FWBO members have found validation in Reginald Ray's (1994) discussion of the threefold model. Ray, who is a Buddhist scholar based at Naropa Institute (a Buddhist university founded by the late Chogyam Trungpa in Colorado in the United States), proposes that the "forest renunciant" (a Buddhist who renounces the institution of the monastery and practices alone) adds another dimension to the two-tiered model, with each of the three types of actors supporting one another. Ray argues that monastics and lay-people are involved in a "complex web of interdependence," but less obviously the forest renunciants, too, are part of this web (437). For example, like the monastics, they depend on laity for material sustenance (436), and they may become spiritual teachers. The laypeople support the other two groups materially and receive merit and spiritual guidance in return. The forest renunciants are likely to be the most dedicated spiritual practitioners and thus gain high esteem, providing inspiration to both monastics and laity. The monastery preserves the texts and traditions so that the essential teachings are maintained. The threefold model leads to a "more interactional picture of Buddhism."

> [T]he tradition will then be seen to consist of a series of relationships of different individuals and communities, . . . rather than as a unilinear tradition defined by a fixed and monolithic norm. Instead of a two-tiered model, a threefold model of Buddhism would provide a useful tool to illuminate not only the Buddhist past but also its present (435).

Such notions, with some reinterpretation consistent with earlier FWBO discussion on sangha, now appear in FWBO discourse.[20] Subhuti notes, for example, that the meditator/renunicant provides

> an important critique of devolutionary tendencies within the institutions. These sort of degenerations and devolutions are almost inevitable . . . [because] when people get together in institutions, group forces can easily take over. It's probably going to be those who are following more solitary pursuits who are going to ask what has happened to the ideals for which the institutions of the movement were originally set up. They can do this because of the uncompromising idealism of their own way of life and be-cause they are not caught up with those institutions: they should see their value and significance, even for themselves, but without identifying with them in an egoistic way (1996b, 19).

Subhuti observes that these three kinds of roles can be seen today in "three trends or tendencies both within the sangha as a whole and within the life of each indi-vidual" (Subhuti 1996a, 21). There is a trend relating to the forest renunciant in the "kinds of spiritual practice that require solitude," including spiritually moti-vated artistic pursuits. Instead of monastics there are people living and working in Buddhist institutions (for the FWBO, this includes Dharma centers, Team-Based

Right Livelihood businesses, and residential communities). The lay trend is found in those whose main activities are conducted outside Buddhist institutions (Subhuti 1996a, 21). Order members, *mitras*, and Friends can all participate in a short-term, quasi-monastic lifestyle by going on group retreats, or they can practice as quasi-forest-renunciants by going on solitary retreats (lasting from perhaps a weekend to three years). Thus people participate in all three trends to different degrees, "devoting varying amounts of time to one or other trend at different stages of our lives" (Subhuti 1996a, 21). Extrapolating from Ray's model, then, contemporary Buddhist retreat centers such as the established FWBO centers in Britain and the one envisaged at Sudarshanaloka provide an institution that is in some ways parallel to monastic centers.

In conformity with egalitarian notions that commonly influence contemporary reformations of Buddhism, Subhuti (1996a, 22) emphasizes that none of these lifestyle options should be deemed superior to others. Rather, all three are necessary, and individuals will place more or less emphasis on one or another way at different times in life. He draws out a distinction between a "hierarchy of conditions" and a "hierarchy of attainment." In the former category, some conditions are ranked as more supportive of spiritual effort than others. In the latter, one who consistently makes a "sustained individual effort . . . within the least favorable conditions can attain much more than one who makes little effort in the most favorable conditions."

The ideal FWBO community is, then, a supportive network for Buddhists trying to live according to the ideal that humans have the potential to become enlightened (Subhuti 1994, 122). In seeking a precedent for their approach at Sudarshanaloka, FWBO members engaged with Ray's model and Subhuti's interpretation of it (e.g., Aniketa 1999, 4) and used it to envisage their project of creating a "total Buddhist society," a venue for retreats for people to "deepen" their spiritual practice not just by undertaking inwardly focused retreats, but also by participating in a spiritual community. This was to become, they envisaged, a "complete context for practice." It has given them another way to think about their purpose, and the concept can act as a guide (rather than a model), providing for all three trends at Sudarshanaloka. Group and solitary retreats are one way in which people living in what they call the "mundane" (i.e., quotidian) world can at least temporarily experience the other two trends, that of the monastic and forest renunciant.

The FWBO members involved with Sudarshanaloka are attempting to create a Buddhist society accommodating these three trends. Table 2.1 shows how these

TABLE 2.1
Relationship between Ray's Threefold Model of Buddhist
Society and Its Application at Sudarshanaloka

A. THREEFOLD MODEL OF SANGHA	B. THREE "TRENDS"[1]	C. THREE AREAS OF PROPERTY AT SUDARSHANALOKA
forest renunciate/hermit	solitary retreatants	solitary retreat cabins
monks/nuns	Buddhists who live and work full time for Buddhist ideals	proposed retreat center
laity	those who still have competing interests	community house, Shraddha Trust

[1] The three trends are fluid since people move between them.

trends (B) correspond to Ray's model (A) at Sudarshanaloka. Sue Thompson, a *mitra* who took ordination in 2004 as Akasamati, told me that she and Prajña-lila arranged their video *On the Dharma Road* around these three themes (C) in showing footage of three aspects of life there.

CONNECTING WITH THE LAND

The people who go to Sudarshanaloka talk about the place in diverse ways. Many say they love going to Sudarshanaloka. For some this is because of a "connection" with the stūpa; some enjoy the rough conditions because they enjoy the outdoors; others find the place too harsh. There is also a prevalent theme about the land having a soothing effect, inducing peaceful states of mind and a sense of connectedness with all life. After a pleasant summery weekend at Sudarshanaloka, a *mitra* named Karenza enthused about the place.

> There you don't have to use the car, you can just walk. . . . [I]t's great not having to drive places. . . . I love being there, it warms the heart. I love being physical, using the body. . . . You just feel connected to the planet, . . . to life, to the world . . . the sound of water, birds, wind. You feel at peace with the planet. Being at a retreat center—I can empty my mind of city things, because of the sound of the water, because of the land. In the city there is too much input, pressure, and visual noise, which is such an onslaught on the senses after time on a retreat. On the land I can feel life all around me. It's such a relief (2000).

This kind of response is characteristic of those who hold that the land has a pro-
foundly positive influence on our well-being and for whom being in "nature" is
a source of spiritual nourishment. Karenza's contrast between the effects on her
mind of city and bush shows the concerns of meditators seeking to reduce unneces-
sary "input" to gain stillness and clarity. In this way of thinking, retreat centers
like Sudarshanaloka provide a place where the outer conditions can, at least for a
short time, facilitate the meditator's access to spiritual clarity. Ideally, the imprint
of this experience then nourishes the meditator when he or she is once again in
the urban environment.

British FWBO members have retreat centers in rural settings and most likely
express similar enthusiasm for being in nature. However, some FWBO/NZ members who have lived in Britain have suggested to me that their British counterparts
do not have such strong rhetorical emphasis on connecting with the land. There
are exceptions, primarily the growing phenomenon of FWBO events at British
festivals such as Glastonbury (Buddhafield 2005; see also chap. 3) and the "Ecopractice" group, a small network of FWBO members trying to encourage the movement to adopt a "five point eco-action agenda"[21] (FWBO n.d.-a).

Sudarshanaloka is different, and I expect that this is because of particular
emphases and concerns in the New Zealand (and, more specifically, Pākehā settler)
context. In the next chapter I therefore continue by providing an overview of the
themes of settler and indigenous relations in a (post)colonial society and of the
role land plays in Pākehā identity construction.

3   A Spiritual Home

> We wanted to create a spiritual home, a piece of land if you like, that was
> ours, in terms of our spiritual center. I think this is tied up much more for
> us with our own [Pākehā] culture. The indigenous culture in New Zealand,
> the Māori have quite a high profile, I think, in our conditioning.
> —Satyananda, speech given at the FWBO's North London Buddhist Centre, 1999

Some FWBO members are attracted to the idea of sacred place and, related to
this, indigenous notions of connectedness with the land. This is evinced in their
British-based arts magazine *Urthona*, which has at least twice featured the theme,
first in "Spirit of Place" (issue 16) and later in "Visions of the sacred earth and
mythic landscapes" (issue 20). The latter issue included an article by a well-known
New Zealand ecologist describing the "placental connection" that Māori claim to
have with the land (Park 2004; see the explanation of *whenua* below). As Satyananda suggests, Māori notions of spiritual connection to the land have influenced
the ways he and other Pākehā think about land, and this has played an important role at Sudarshanaloka. The desire for specifically Buddhist connections with
the land is not unique to FWBO Buddhists: Ani Kunzang, a New Zealand-born
Buddhist nun in a Tibetan tradition, also expresses such a yearning.

> In the early days when Buddhist teachers first came to this country, we had
> our meetings and retreats in church halls or university lecture rooms . . .
> nowhere of our own, nowhere Buddhist. I used to dream of a Buddhist
> place here, within the culture. Then the Centres began to flourish, Maha-
> mudra, Wangapeka: at Wangapeka I saw my first stūpa on native soil, so
> severe, such a beautiful form and so inspiring for people to see (Kunzang
> n.d.).

In this chapter, then, I investigate how key people involved with Sudarshanaloka
represent themselves and their project in relation to the wider FWBO through
their own and wider FWBO media in ways that highlight both their connections
with and difference from the British FWBO, and issues of belonging and identity

of concern to New Zealanders generally. I follow this with a brief outline of the role that the complex relationship between Pākehā and Māori plays in constructing New Zealand identities and the implications of this for any attempt by non-Māori seeking a sense of place-based belonging. This "place discourse" is comparable to that emerging among non-indigenous Australians in response to Aboriginal claims (Ellemor 2003, 238). In investigating this I touch on a wider, more public debate over whether or not Pākehā, through developing affective ties to the land, can ever be "indigenous" to New Zealand.

Related to this, I also introduce a theme that has an unlikely intersection in New Zealand's mainstream self-presentation as a "clean green" tourist destination and in alternative spiritualities that seek a deeper "reconnection" with nature, often in tandem with a romanticization of indigenous peoples. My main purpose in this chapter is to introduce these themes because of the ways they articulate with the stories I discuss in chapter 4 and to provide local context for the urge by converts to Buddhism, such as Kunzang and Satyananda, to establish identifiably Buddhist places in a new land.

FWBO MEDIA AND IMAGINED COMMUNITY

The FWBO makes use of a range of media to provide the sense of a community that expands beyond local Dharma centers (cf. Anderson 1991). Most of these media are produced in Britain. The long-standing *Newsreels* are compiled in and distributed from Britain using video footage and news from FWBO-affiliated centers worldwide. In more recent years the FWBO has made increasingly comprehensive Web sites, expanding the resources accessible through the official FWBO homepage at www.fwbo.org and, more recently, a range of less formal Web logs such as www.fwbo-news.org, containing information about the movement and a wide range of articles. During the time when the stūpa was being planned and built, several FWBO/NZ members, especially Prajñalila, produced a wealth of vivid stories and images through the media of video, photography, and newsletters. During and after the construction and dedication of the stūpa, Prajñalila wrote, compiled, and designed the *Tararu Transformer* newsletters, with contributions from other key participants. These were distributed around the New Zealand movement and beyond, providing rich narratives about the place that encouraged people to visit from as far afield as Dublin. I draw on the stories in these newsletters throughout this book.

The *Newsreel* items about Sudarshanaloka have also inspired British members to take an interest in their antipodean counterparts, and this in turn shapes how the FWBO/NZ members conceptualize themselves as offering something with a different flavor to the British FWBO. As Prajñalila says, "The nature of the land here is so significantly different from anything that you're likely to experience [in Britain]" (1999).

Another videotape, *On the Dharma Road* (Quin and Thompson 1999), was intended to present Sudarshanaloka to the international movement, and Satyananda took it with him on a visit to the British and North American FWBO centers in 1999. It opens to the haunting strains of a Māori flute over nature shots of Sudarshanaloka. As with other representations of Sudarshanaloka aimed at the wider FWBO, the video aims to convey the unique flavor of the place, showing that what was happening there was not just a copy of what was happening in Britain. The use of images depicting both the natural beauty and the "ruggedness" of the land has this function, providing a place-specific sense of identity. This intersects with a prevalent nature theme in the broader self-presentation of New Zealand to the wider world, especially when targeting potential tourist markets, a topic to which I return below.

Of the collection of photograph albums, the most carefully compiled is a set of three large spiral-bound albums spanning the years 1996–1998. These provide a record of the stūpa-building process, including research, construction, and dedication, also depicting a few events that followed in later years. Photocopied pages from various reference books are pasted into the first of these albums, and I return to these in chapter 5. Prajñalila told me that in compiling these albums she wanted to build a "connection with the land. . . . It's about people who come, how they responded" (1999). These albums present an important record of what has happened, the story so far, and images from them have been shown at other FWBO centers around the world. The last of the spiral-bound stūpa albums has a few blank pages at the end, and on the top of the first of these Prajñalila wrote, "Pages for Stories, Anecdotes, the making of the myth." The pages have remained blank, and except for records in private writing, newsletters, video, and now also in this book, the stories have continued to be primarily oral.

The stūpa albums reflect an increasingly conscious effort to provide visual documentation of Sudarshanaloka. The earliest of the albums appear to be assembled less deliberately from photographs gathered together over several years, with photographs printed in various formats. Many of the early photographs emphasize the wildness and beauty, including several pages depicting the bush and streams running through the valley, similar to many New Zealanders' snapshots of tramping trips in the bush. They convey a sense of discovery, exploration, and exuberance. But one photograph proclaims their presence in the valley by showing the multicolored Buddhist flag[1] flying over the community house, with a caption announcing "Buddhists in residence." This evokes a similar sense to Satyananda's expression of a wish to have a place in which the Buddhists could put down roots. What are the implications of this? By way of answering this, I first provide some background about the New Zealand cultural and historical setting.

PEOPLE OF THE LAND

Polynesian navigators first settled the southern Pacific archipelago now called Aotearoa, or New Zealand, around one thousand years ago, and over time they developed the distinctive Māori culture and language. From a European perspective, Capt. James Cook (1728–1779) is credited with "discovering" New Zealand in 1769. Following this, European whalers and sealers visited the islands from the end of the 1700s, trading such items as nails, axes, blankets, and muskets with Māori tribes to obtain goods such as New Zealand flax (*Phormium tenax*) for ship rigging.

In February 1840 the British Crown and Māori chiefs representing specific tribal groups reached an agreement known as the Treaty of Waitangi, which is now represented as an important founding document in the nation's history. However, its interpretations are contested, not least because the Māori-language version of the treaty safeguarded *tino rangatiratanga* (sovereignty or self-determination) among Māori tribal landowners, while the English-language version has Māori ceding sovereignty to the Crown. After British settlers began arriving in large numbers from the 1850s, the treaty did not prevent widespread alienation of land, and colonization and dispossession has caused enduring harm to Māori.[2] In 1975, an act of Parliament established the Waitangi Tribunal to inquire into and make recommendations on specific grievances. Its role also includes examining proposed legislation and making recommendations relating to uses of state-owned land (Waitangi Tribunal n.d.). Inquiries into claims and subsequent settlement processes continue.

In their arguments for restitution, Māori often draw on discourses of spiritual connectedness with the land. The Māori term for inhabitants of a locale is *tangata whenua*, a term that emphasizes ancestral links with a particular piece of land: *tangata* means "people," and *whenua* has the double meaning of "land" and "placenta." Māori have a tradition of burying the placenta in the tribal homeland, and it is through this connection that *tangata whenua* claim spiritual affinity with the land, which helps provide a form of moral legitimization of their political task of reclaiming resources and land lost since British colonization (Levine 1990, 6).

Significantly, the common English translation of *tangata whenua* is "people of the land," but the Māori usage also has the more politicized sense of the "primary custodians of a given geo-political territory" (Kawharu 2000, 349). As custodians, they consider their role to be one of *kaitiakitanga* (environmental stewardship).[3] While there are no treaty claims on the land I discuss in this book, the fraught history of Māori-Pākehā relations creates a major undercurrent affecting the way many FWBO members conceptualize their relationship to the land.

"WHITE NATIVES"? THE PROBLEM OF WHITE SETTLER IDENTITY

Many New Zealanders of European ancestry who have the means to travel to Europe say they sense deep layers of history there that they do not experience in their own country. Such an approach suggests that they feel New Zealand has no such depth; however, some Pākehā, including FWBO members, are now beginning to claim a sense of connection with the land itself. At the same time, they begin to identify more strongly as belonging to New Zealand rather than Europe. But in doing so, they have unexpectedly raised a sensitive issue stemming from the history of colonization.

In my use of "Pākehā" as an identity label, I follow Augie Fleras and Paul Spoonley (1999, 83) in referring to the settler culture, that is, "New Zealanders of a European background, whose cultural values and behavior have been primarily formed from the experiences of being a member of the dominant group of New Zealand." This usage excludes immigrants and New Zealand-born minorities such as Chinese, Tongan, and Indian, and the reference to the "dominant" status is worth noting: Avril Bell (2004a, 122) observes that the term "positions Pākehā in terms of contemporary [unequal] power relations," still shaped by the colonial relationship with Māori of the past. Those who consciously adopt the Pākehā label signal a degree of "commitment to the bicultural and/or bi-national politics of contemporary Aotearoa [New Zealand]" (Fleras and Spoonley 1999, 81). I find the term appropriate in this book because my discussion includes the theme of how these descendants of a settler society attempt to establish a sense of belonging and "assert a distinctive national culture" (A. Bell 2004a, 131) through their engagement with a specific place and its history. I should note, however, that many people reject the label, believing it to be insulting or because they consider the notion of biculturalism that it evokes to be "politically correct."[4] One survey notes that around 35 percent of European New Zealanders use the term to describe their ethnicity, the rest preferring to mark their national identity as "Kiwis" or "New Zealanders" (Liu 2005); in contrast, 60 percent of Māori use the term to refer to European New Zealanders. The word "Kiwi" explicitly signifies a nationality, but in practice often implies the "unmarked" white category. Most official documents use the more neutral term "European New Zealander" in place of the word "Pākehā."

Taken with the progressive weakening of ties to a British home after two hundred years of settlement at the other end of the earth, Pākehā have been prompted to identify with the landscapes of New Zealand as home. Their geographic, cultural, and temporal distance from their Anglo-European cultural roots means they do not regard Britain as "home" the way the earlier generations of white settlers did. But their status is ambiguous: on the one hand, they belong through having been born in New Zealand; on the other, Māori stories of their own deep spiritual roots in the land and numerous political claims for redress of past land-related wrongs highlight the fact that Pākehā claims lack temporal depth. Thus many Pākehā feel somewhat unsettled by anything that reminds them that Māori have a special status as the original inhabitants (Fleras and Spoonley 1999, xii). Of a similar colonial legacy of unjust displacement in Australia, David Day writes that the Aborigines

> survived on the margins of white society. As such, they remained as a permanent and living reminder of that original act of invasion and dispossession. Their brooding presence blocked the way to white Australians developing . . . [a] secure identity linked to their recently purloined soil. . . . It was difficult to develop distinctive national myths celebrating possession through peaceful settlement, if the original possessors of the soil remained to contest it, even silently (1998, ix).

With this unsettling undercurrent, many settler societies derived from the European colonial expansion have nonetheless engaged in attempts to create their own national cultural identities. Indeed, some non-Māori New Zealanders in search of a distinctive cultural identity have begun to speak and write about their feelings for the land. The most well-known exemplar of this is the influential public historian Michael King (1945–2004), whose book exploring Pākehā identities bears his credo on the cover: "Pākehā New Zealanders who are committed to this land and its people are no less 'indigenous' than Māori" (1999). Pākehā culture, he says, arose "in response to a relationship with the land and its flora and fauna. . . . And a major and influential part of that transforming interaction was with Māori" (235). King's books have been popular, and the claim to Pākehā indigeneity has been taken up by others who express a similar desire to belong here: for instance, in 2004 the coordinating minister for race relations for New Zealand's Labour Party, Trevor Mallard, said, "Māori and Pākehā are both indigenous people to New Zealand now. . . . We've left behind a British identity" (Young 2004, A6). The concept of "being Pākehā" (King 1985), then, has become part of this quest for a distinctive identity expressing something separate from European cultural influences.

Some Pākehā have used this claim of an affective connection with the land in Waitangi Tribunal hearings. Michèle Dominy (1990) has conducted ethnographic research among sheep-farming families of European descent in the South Island's High Country. She sparked a heated debate about cultural politics in New Zealand when she wrote of her decision to provide evidence for the High Country Committee of the Federated Farmers of New Zealand as part of their submission to the Waitangi Tribunal.[5] Dominy notes that while Māori claims to spiritual connection with the land receive recognition today, Pākehā are still broadly represented as having utilitarian relationships to the land. In her evidence, she argues that High Country farmers told her that they "recognized in hearing Ngai Tahu testimony an expression of feeling for the land which resembled the farmers' own feeling for the land" (11). In response to Dominy's article, the New Zealand Association of Social Anthropologists (NZASA) suggests that she conflates "two very different sets of values, historical experiences and ways of thinking" when she uses the "rhetoric of 'spiritual affinity' for both Māori and Pākehā linkages" with the land (NZASA 1990, 3). Further, High Country farmers' claims to an affective connection to the land do not justify retaining a position of privilege that abrogates the rights of others (1990, 3).

While I empathize with the feeling of love for the land, as an anthropologist concerned about the effects of colonization, I also agree with King's critics who assert that this discursive focus on the robustness of Pākehā relationship with the land whitewashes the unequal power relations. King says people become indigenous when they develop a commitment to this place rather than the ancestral homeland, but Avril Bell (2004a, 132) points out that this new commitment occurred at the same time as the alienation of Māori land and related practices of the colonial era. She argues that Pākehā appropriation of the term "indigenous" through claims to having "an emotional bond to this land" neatly separates contemporary Pākehā from the actions of their colonizing ancestors, thus falsely absolving them of any responsibility for the ongoing impact of colonization (133) and undermining the "political value" of the term "indigenous" for Māori and other colonized peoples (cf. Kenrick and Lewis 2004).[6] Where King does acknowledge the harm done by colonization, Bell suggests he neutralizes it by positioning it in the past and attempts to equalize it by noting that that his Irish ancestors, too, were subjugated and that Māori, too, have "skeletons . . . in their historical closets" (A. Bell 2004a, 133, quoting King 1999, 237).

Avril Bell suggests that Pākehā appropriate some aspects of Māori cultural symbolism as "identifiably specific national signifiers" to differentiate themselves, since otherwise, she thinks, they're "just another colonial Anglo-Celtic offshoot" (2004a, 131). In so doing, Pākehā want some of the things Māori appear to have, that is, "a secure claim to this place, a clear sense of cultural distinction" even though, ironically, colonization has "undermined these for Māori also" (2004a, 131). Ani Mikaere (2004) maintains that according to *tikanga Māori* (protocols and other culturally specific customary knowledge), people who are here by right of the Treaty of Waitangi are *manuhiri* (guests or visitors to a tribal place) who thus should not claim *tangata whenua* status; stating a similar idea, Nandor Tanczos MP, the Green Party's treaty spokesperson (2004), says that *tangata tiriti* (people of the treaty) can feel secure in their legal right to live in New Zealand, but they should also observe the obligations that come with this right.

Thus when Buddhists in New Zealand seek to establish something of a spiritual home in this land, they are (unwittingly) overlooking this power imbalance. My concern here is to understand what FWBO members say about their own feelings in relation to this often only partly apprehended situation. This emerges in stories about feeling connected to the land, or wanting to be more connected, and often accompanies critiques of Western alienation from land. There are several aspects to this, but here my focus is on the role of both Māori and land in Pākehā constructions of national identity and belonging. Michael Attwood (a Pākehā from the ABC) had been on retreat several times at Sudarshanaloka but was in the middle of several years working in the FWBO's Windhorse Trading in England when I was writing this book. In an e-mail he suggested to me that there were qualities or energies of the land itself specific to New Zealand that influenced people, which he missed. In England, he said,

> myth is buried a lot deeper I think. And the land is tamed and, in East Anglia at least, pretty featureless. So there aren't the roots to tap into. Here things are more intellectual, more head driven. Which isn't to say that myth has no place, but just that as Kiwis we do seem to be very much a part of the land (2004a).

He did not believe this special relationship with the land derived from Māori influence.

> I have pondered this [and] I think it is the land itself which has this effect on us, rather than, say, some influence of Māori culture. I could be wrong

but I think the land has a similar effect on us Euro's [sic] as it did on the Māori. But Euro descended I may be, I am definitely a foreigner here [in England].

Michael, then, associates the mythic feeling with direct contact with the natural (as opposed to built) environment or the history of its human inhabitants. In contrast, Satyananda describes how the indigenous relationship with the land (as he understood it) influenced his own involvement with Sudarshanaloka by showing him what he did not have. He said in a talk at the FWBO's London Buddhist Centre during a visit in 1999,

> The indigenous culture in New Zealand, the Māori, have quite a high profile, I think, in our conditioning. [. . . Part of] my conditioning was that I lacked a certain amount of identity of who I was, as I grew up. . . . Through our exposure [to] the Māori . . . and their whole identity with land, their tribal identity, there was a part of me that felt I was missing out on something (1999b).

Satyananda is emphatic that a spiritual home is important for identity.

> It gets talked about quite a lot about the sort of Celtic background that we're not in touch with, who are we, and all that sort of thing. But for me in New Zealand it was more to do with, I felt like I didn't have a home, you know, so it was part of I think the cultural conditioning in New Zealand, is that we feel we're missing out, 'cause we can't go home to our spiritual home. Somewhere where the "Tribe" in inverted commas, belongs. . . . So part of what we wanted to create there was a spiritual home. Somewhere where it didn't matter where we were in the world, we actually had this identity with land.

Satyananda represents New Zealanders in the FWBO as having different issues around identity than the British members; for him, connection with land and having a sense of connection with a particular place *in New Zealand* was more important than any "pagan" or "Celtic" background that some FWBO people of British ancestry attempt to rekindle, a topic I return to later. He seems to be expressing a feeling of lack, which, as in Howell's description of cultural lacunae (1995), was highlighted by the proximity to another people who *do* appear to have a sense of belonging and "spiritual home."

When Jayaghosa, another Order member, talked about his understanding of why the FWBO built the stūpa at Sudarshanaloka he talked about *tūrangawaewae*, which he interpreted as meaning "standing in your own power" (2000b).[7] He said that the stūpa was "something symbolic and concrete" that reminded them to do this. This blending of a Māori concept with his background in counseling warrants more exploration than I can give in this book, but as I read it, the specific understanding expressed here assumes the concept emphasizes psychological empowerment with regard to the FWBO's establishment of a place to which they can belong, rather than political empowerment of one disadvantaged group relative to another more dominant group (which is the sense in which some Māori use it today).

"CLEAN GREEN" AND NATURAL

In the last chapter I mentioned how people find retreats in natural settings to be restorative; this interlinks with the ways that New Zealanders seek to differentiate themselves from the rest of the world through presenting their land as a place of unspoiled natural beauty. I regard FWBO/NZ understandings about nature as being interlinked with wider contexts of issues that concern liberal Pākehā. Although most New Zealanders now live in cities, discourses about the land remain salient, especially celebrating New Zealand's so-called "natural beauty." I was struck by the importance of the landscape in how we represent ourselves to people abroad when I helped a friend to select books about New Zealand to send as gifts to overseas friends. She sought books depicting beaches, mountains, lakes, and forests because the scenic beauty was what she felt was distinctive about New Zealand. As John Taylor (1998, 9) observes, "nature is . . . unrivalled in its status as New Zealand's most lucrative tourist commodity," and indeed brochures, postcards, and tourism Web sites focus almost exclusively on scenic images. Nature rhetoric is widespread, and despite environmentalists' protestations that it is deceptive (given some major failings in New Zealand's environmental record), it is much exploited in tourism and marketing language, where New Zealand landscapes and produce are "clean" and "green."

Prolific nature photographer, publisher, and environmentalist Craig Potton produces books, calendars, and postcards that celebrate the beauty of "wild" places to both external tourists and the New Zealand market. His photography and writing provide a glimpse of how this notion of nature has deep emotional resonance for some Pākehā. Potton, who studied Eastern religions at university, writes of being in the wilderness as a source of spiritual connection and nourishment, even while commodifying his images. One quote that he places in his book of photographs about Tongariro National Park demonstrates the guilt-tinged concern about destruction of the environment felt by many liberal Pākehā: "The time has come, not to forget, but to forgive ourselves the past, to begin again in humility to relate to our land" (Hooper 1981, quoted in Potton 1995, 153).[8] Such approaches demonstrate an awareness of past damage done to the land, a desire to redress the situation, and attempts to incorporate *tangata whenua* views in ways that could be read as trying to make space for Pākehā. Potton writes,

> [I]f there is too much planning and order something inside us gets suffocated. There are occasions when we need a huge place where time and space is measured out by natural rhythms, and where we see, hear, taste and smell only what we can never create. In other words, times when we need wilderness and its solitude (1995, 178).

I quote this statement as an example of the feeling of a need articulated by many New Zealanders (including myself) to experience places of natural beauty. Potton goes on to reflect that "there is a sense in which [wilderness] parks are a giant meditation arena. . . . [A]nyone who encounters the wilderness will return to their daily lives at least a little changed" (178, 183), a phrase redolent of the sentiments FWBO members such as Karenza, quoted in chapter 2, express about going on retreat and evoking a long tradition, in many societies past and present, of spiritual seekers withdrawing into monasteries in wilderness surroundings in search of solitude.

The "green" and unspoiled image that New Zealand has overseas is reiterated in an article titled "Pioneers in a new country" in an FWBO women's magazine from the U.K. Two women described New Zealand as geologically young, with a "varied and for the most part unspoiled environment" (Chasteau and Furdas 1990, 9). Incidentally, the invocation of the ideal of "pioneering" resonates with the way FWBO members take particular pride in their exploration of re-expressing Buddhism in a Western context as well as the history of Pākehā settlement in New Zealand.

The rhetoric about the land as a source of spiritual nourishment for Pākehā as per Potton and King demonstrates a contemporary attempt by Pākehā to legitimize their presence in this land. While I do not reject this yearning for spiritual nourishment, I must agree with Stephen Levine's caution that this "apparent convergence of affinities" has the potential to drive the two contending parties further

apart, due to the "broader implications of cultural and territorial displacement arising from one people's appropriation of another people's language and self-imagery"
(1990, 5-6).

NATURE-CENTERED RELIGIONS

The search for a spiritual connection or "belonging" to the land is part of a more
widespread search among members of late modern society who are critical of sense-
less consumerism and the generally unsustainable exploitation of natural resources.
Among the alternate religious movements that tap into such critiques, nature-
centered spiritualities are finding expression in forms such as neo-paganism, where
members of predominantly urbanized, post-industrial societies try to recreate a
connection with the natural, as opposed to the built, environment. These discourses of connection to the land provide a multitude of avenues for people to
attempt to distance themselves from harmful human activities of past and present.

As alternate religious movements, Western Buddhism, New Age, and neo-
paganism, as well as the earlier Theosophy movement[9] have developed in post-
industrial societies from various waves of countercultural explorations of utopianist alternatives to mainstream society. For example, it is common to find among
such movements critiques of the way that lifestyles in post-industrial society have
distanced us from the natural (nonbuilt) environment. Various forms of neo-
paganism (Pike 2001, xxii) and "Eco-Buddhism" (Harris 1995) demonstrate concern for the welfare of planet Earth and its inhabitants. This concern that we need
to develop a land- or nature-centered spirituality if we are to save the Earth from
environmental destruction has prompted a range of writings including that of Zen-
influenced Gary Snyder in the United States (e.g., Snyder 1990, 1995; Snyder,
Woods, and Shoonmaker 1985; Strain 1999) and Jungian psychoanalyst David
Tacey in Australia (Tacey 1995). In New Zealand, *Celebrating the Southern Seasons*
(Batten 2005), a book now in its second edition, provides a particularly interesting insight into the idea of connecting spiritually with the land in order to save
the world. Juliet Batten advocates the creation of a calendar of rituals based on
the seasons of New Zealand, rather than observing those derived from the Northern Hemisphere, where Halloween is an autumn festival, Christmas is celebrated
near the midwinter solstice, and Easter is a rite of spring. Batten presents a lively
combination of suggestions for rituals for the southern seasons, using New Zealand plants and imagery. Advocating a bicultural approach that appeals to liberal
Pākehā, she also interweaves Māori and Celtic mythology. Another Pākehā author, an academic addressing discrimination against Māori, notes in passing that
renewed interest in spirituality helps us relate "to a wounded land that we should

heal, ... to understand that the ancestral land is like a living body" (Ritchie 1992, 78). There is also a strand of liberal Christianity that similarly explores a relationship with the land (e.g., Bergin and Smith 2004).

Sangharakshita recommends that Western Buddhists befriend and channel their own unconscious energies, in part through the exploration of neo-paganism, which refers to an imagined pre-Christian spirituality connected with "nature," a term that, in this discourse, appears to be imagined as opposite to culture and romanticized as pure and original (cf. MacCormack and Strathern 1980). Sangharakshita encourages this "re-connecting with nature" approach because the individual's spiritual progress is "dependent on a healthy and integrated self-awareness, not one cut off from the most basic forces of life." The concept of paganism, as he uses it, has a positive valence: to be pagan, he says, is to "sense nature as peopled with living forces, animating every stream or tree or mountain," thus "engender[ing] a realistic but positive relationship with the forces of nature" (Subhuti 1994, 285–286).

Many FWBO members explore aspects of this mythical engagement with nature and, more specifically, land. For instance, in the issue of *Urthona* titled "Spirit of Place," Satyagandhi writes, "[R]eceptivity and connection with the natural world can take us beyond the boundaries of place, self and other to the common spiritual ground of humanity" (2001). The same issue includes an article reflecting on the role of the Green Man in understanding the "traditional British 'spirit of place'" (Chintamani 2001). The author of this article also built a stūpa for an Order conference that included the Green Man motif in its base, with the explicit intention of evoking a "pre-Christian image for the forces of the land and nature as a supporting protector for the higher life ... [to remind Buddhists] of the sort of ... foundation that we need to live the higher [spiritual] life," which the stūpa represents (1999, 53, quoted in Harris 2002, 379).[10] A number of people have taken this idea to heart, tapping into environmentalist, neo-pagan, and land-based spirituality movements in Britain. These eco-Buddhist advocates claim such an approach allows a reconnecting to the "forces of the land and nature as a supporting protector for the higher life" (Chintamani 1999, quoted in Harris 2002, 379). For instance, some FWBO members have used the Green Man to explore "links with indigenous features of the British religious landscape, an adaptation strategy linked with the movement's desire to break free from an 'orientalist' approach to the practice of Buddhism" (Harris 2002, 379).

The clearest example of this is the FWBO collective called Buddhafield, which runs events at alternative festivals like Glastonbury in England, its own five-day festival, and open-air retreats (Kamalashila 2001). It is the most marked instance of this exploration of the marriage of Buddhism with pagan or nature-centered spirituality. The Web site advertising the 2005 program in Britain bears slogans like "Buddhism and Ecology: connecting with our land" and includes themed retreats oriented to newcomers (Buddhafield 2005). Some of these entail a fascinating bricolage: for example, one meditation retreat is promoted as a mobile pilgrimage on foot "through the ancient sacred landscape of Britain" to Stonehenge for the summer solstice celebrations there. At Sudarshanaloka in 2005 and 2006, Buddhafield-style retreats were held, a logical extension of the interest in the lively synthesis of Buddhist and neo-pagan or nature-centered practices that certain FWBO members are exploring.

A BUDDHIST PLACE

In this chapter I have attempted to show that Sudarshanaloka is a focal point in which FWBO/NZ members attempt to work out what it means to be Buddhist and Pākehā. Most FWBO/NZ members are Pākehā, and many come from progressive, tertiary-educated backgrounds. As such, it is almost impossible for them to ignore the fact that Pākehā settlement in this country was based on the displacement and dispossession of the *tangata whenua*. Simultaneously, some FWBO members express a desire to find or create a place to which they may belong—partly due to the Pākehā yearning to belong, but also because they want somewhere that enables them to explore a Buddhist identity. Māori resistance and resurgence has contested an earlier, more secure sense of Pākehā right to be in New Zealand. The attention to land that FWBO/NZ members show reminds me of Anthony Moran's (2002) account of Anglo-Australian settler society's uneasy attempts, given the legacy of dispossession, to make their own affective associations with the land while also accounting for Aboriginals' claims to it. Moran argues that discourses of "indigenizing settler nationalism" constitute a concerted attempt to respond to such challenges.

This concern with identity and land colors narratives about Sudarshanaloka. A nationalistic dimension is present in the association of New Zealand-ness with a certain idealized construct of nature and land, but national identity is not of explicit concern to these Buddhists. Nonetheless, I perceive an "indigenizing settler" discourse at Sudarshanaloka and regard the project as having an aspect of nationalism insofar as it is an attempt to channel some of the emphasis away from the FWBO in Britain to create a New Zealand node in the movement. In the narratives about Sudarshanaloka I also hear an anxious wish to belong to this land. In this context, through their creative interactions with the place, the human actors reinvent themselves with discourses of "indigenizing Pākehā Buddhism." This co-evolves with another discourse of "universalizing Global FWBO Buddhism" claiming to transcend national identities and link people around the world. I have used this and the previous two chapters in introducing important influences that have shaped the FWBO and its plan to build a retreat center at Sudarshanaloka.

In the following chapters I discuss events that happened as they engaged in redefining the property as a Buddhist retreat. In chapter 4 I explore the critical conjuncture in which two key events occurred, and the damaged state of the land, which could no longer be ignored. The resulting increased awareness of the importance of developing an appropriate relationship with the land led to a transformation in how the trustees thought and talked about their project and led to a shift in plans.

4 Unsettling Place

Despite New Zealand's "clean green" reputation internationally, around the country the land and its ecosystems have suffered severe damage from human activities, and this has had a marked impact at Sudarshanaloka. The stories that I explore in this chapter demonstrate a growing awareness of this impact and the intention not only to create a place conducive to healing people spiritually, but also to heal the land itself. The increasing awareness of this larger purpose takes place as a result of two key incidents that draw on issues of how people in the FWBO in New Zealand have incorporated the desire both to be connected to the land emotionally and spiritually and to achieve harmonious relations with unseen presences. These pivotal events, linked to specific sites *on* the land, shape an emerging narrative about the development of a friendship *with* the land.

A CONJUNCTURE

Lush, regenerating bush dominates the Tararu Valley, but ample evidence remains of the destructive past. In parts of the Coromandel region, including this valley, gold mining (which peaked between 1868 and 1871) has left lasting scars on the land, and today hidden disused mineshafts present a real hazard for walkers in the regenerating bush. European settlers also deforested most of the peninsula during the late nineteenth and early twentieth centuries, harvesting the tall, straight *kauri* for their fine-grained timber, and today only inaccessible pockets of the older trees remain. Pastoral farming followed, encouraging erosion of the steep, deforested slopes, while introduced possums, pigs, and goats devastated the struggling ecosystem.[1] In spite of all this, the forest is regenerating.

After purchasing the land with a vision of creating a retreat center, FWBO members began to encounter problems and, over time, came to realize that they needed to transform the way they related to the land itself because of the past damage that had been wrought upon it. Taranatha, Satyananda, and Prajñalila all provided similar outlines of the history that underlies this book, but Taranatha's tale adds a particularly relevant slant in linking the quest to heal the land with his own journey of transformation from a Wesleyan farming background that he

described as destructive (see also Taranatha 2006). This narrative begins with dis-
connectedness from and domination of the land, which through the medium of
the Dharma transforms into friendship, healing, and aspiration towards spiritual
liberation.

> My beginnings . . . were in pioneer farming. And it was a very domineering
> destructive sort of life. I mean, in back country farming, you destroy plants,
> and you kill animals, and it's the work you live for. . . . And I did a lot of
> killing in my youth which, I've discovered since, required a great suppres-
> sion of awareness. . . . Of course, the karma of that has come out during
> my meditation years. . . . And when I saw . . . how the land was defiantly
> restoring itself, I realized that that's what I'd been doing for the last . . .
> 30 or 40 years. Restoring myself after the destructive early phase. And it
> became an increasingly conscious myth of mine, to move into partnership
> with that process (Taranatha 1999a).

Meanwhile, he says, in the Tararu Valley

> the timber had been removed, the forest had been clear-felled, it'd been
> burnt. There was an attempt to sow it in grass, and while all this was going
> on it was being burrowed and mined and dug about for gold, and it was just
> a wasteland. And all that terrible destruction wasn't the action of people
> who were evil or sinful, it was people who were very sincere, and doing the
> right thing, but they were just misguided, they just had "Wrong View."[2]

There are many relics left from the mining and logging days that so changed the
face of the Coromandel Peninsula. A farm harrow and bones from farm animals
(see figs. 6.5 and 6.6 in chap. 6), and the *kauri* log (fig. 2.2) all became reminders
of the valley's destructive episodes.

Alongside the evidence of past destruction, other aspects of the land have
an impact on those who visit it. The choice of a steep, rugged piece of land in an
enclosed valley with a rough road was not unanimously supported. Some FWBO
members dislike the drive up the valley to Sudarshanaloka in the winter, because
they say it is dangerous to drive on the narrow and muddy road, with its many blind
corners. Some have difficulties walking around the steep and uneven terrain, while
the damp in the house is a further disincentive. One Order member planning to do
a solitary retreat in early winter told me she intended to drive to a beach when she
wanted walks, rather than go for walks in the bush, which, she said, felt closed in,

dank, and dark. A *mitra* said he preferred the FWBO retreats held at Awhitu Environmental Camp because it has a sense of spaciousness, with its wide-open vistas, and a beach within walking distance, while Sudarshanaloka is enclosed and dark. He said he preferred to be close to the sea when on retreat, finding the quietness of the valley "unnerving," especially at night. Another *mitra*, an English immigrant accustomed to tamer landscapes, said that he found the land too harsh, with gorse (a noxious weed in New Zealand) "almost on the back doorstep," and expressed a preference for a tamer and what he regarded as a more aesthetically pleasing environment, like a Zen garden. Some report feeling sad about the destruction wrought by milling, mining, introduced pests, and farming on the land. Others commented on the silence, which for some evoked a sense of peace, while for others it was eerie.

Many people, including some who liked Sudarshanaloka and some who disliked it, talk about how the land feels "raw," a metaphor that evokes a dual, contradictory sense of the land being raw like a wound because of human interference, and raw like untamed nature, unspoiled by human interference. A European *mitra* who disliked going there said she found the land "raw and inaccessible." Prajñalila, who clearly had a heartfelt connection with the place, remembered initially feeling that the land was "really *raw*, it had really been *ravaged*. It potentially could offer a place for retreat, but initially it was just an overwhelmingly huge piece of land that had been so devastated by these successive waves of mining, forestry and farming" (1999). She told me that she had felt "from the beginning a streaming of energy down the main ridge. It only really stopped when the stūpa was complete. By which time much had changed in our sensitivity to the land and the way we became partners with it" (2000b). The energy felt grieved, she said, and reiterated the Friends of Tararu team's realization that they had to become friends of the land itself at Sudarshanaloka: "there was no question, really, that to make this a place of retreat, to bring out its beauty again, we needed to *be* there. Re-clothe it, [and] pacify it. Say that we're not going to try and sort of *take* any more out of it. We were going to put into it. Put our energy back into it so that it can be at peace with itself" (2000a).

The reconceptualization of this property in terms of Buddhist sacred geography is also the creation of a liminal space for transformation, from a raw and damaged (or, alternately, untamed) space into a place of healing of both land and those who go there. Some who visited the land in the early days after the purchase recalled that it felt even more raw in the first sense before they effected the transformation in the relationship with the land.

Several of the people most involved in the Sudarshanaloka project told and retold stories of their search for meaningful ways to relate with their environment, a way compatible with the Buddhist teachings that they aspire to live by. Satyananda's wish to create a spiritual home highlights how FWBO members engage both with their position as members of a settler society on a quest to put down roots and as FWBO members in relation to what their British brethren regard as a remote outpost of the movement. On two occasions he talked about the obstacles and the "dark" energy they had encountered in the first years of their ownership of the property.

> We arrived, there was a lot of difficulty. A very tough piece of land. . . . It was very dark, in some ways, when we first bought it. There'd been a lot of killing, . . . pig hunting . . . it was real New Zealand back country land. And then there'd been gold mining on it as well, forests cut down, for gold mining and stuff like that. And there was a bit of a strange energy, initially. So, we moved on, we started trying to build . . . and things went wrong. . . . (1999b)
> We found ourselves in one battle after another—local authorities, natural obstacles like slips or road washouts, accidents, and eventually the death of one of the community members [Denis] in a local road accident (1997, 2).

Before this untimely death, Denis's response to the place had begun to have a particularly marked influence on the way they related to the land. Prajñalila told me that Denis undertook the task of clearing the energy of the land, and as part of this project he began building stūpas of river stones, one stone balanced atop another, around the riverbed and ford and the gateway to the land (fig. 2.5).

> Denis . . . found the land very overwhelming, and he thought, "Well, I'll start at the gate." He began to clear the pathway onto the land, through the gate. And around the river and the ford, he began to make little piles of stones, little stone stūpas. It was about that time that Satyananda thought "A-ha! Perhaps the first thing we actually need to do is build a stūpa" (Prajñalila 1999).

These mini-stūpas resemble other kinds of stone stacks and cairns, including the track markers familiar to trampers (hikers) in New Zealand mountains. One can also see similarities with Tibetan mountain cairns (*laptse*), which are the abodes of local gods (Samuel 1993, 159), and Japanese stone stūpas. In Tibet the presence of sacred objects such as cairns, stūpas, and prayer walls "grounds" Buddhism and sacralizes the landscape. For Buddhists, then, encountering holy objects such as these while walking around the land can stimulate "mental transcendence of the here-and-now concerns of personal sustenance and social obligations" (Barnes 1999, 102–103). The practice of making such cairns also appeals in more secular contexts: one young woman told me that at "The Gathering," an outdoor rave that incorporates New Age elements, there were various themed zones for different concerts and other festival activities. In one such zone, the atmosphere was set in part by small stone cairns much like the mini-stūpas. At Sudarshanaloka, the presence of these small stone piles similarly sets a kind of atmosphere. They also make focal points around the land, reminding people who encounter them of their own spiritual aspirations.

Denis, then, came to have a significant impact on how people talked about their relationship with the land, and his death caused something of a crisis. However, there was something else he had done that marked the land, in a way that came to have significance in marked contrast with the small rock stūpas.

THE *KAURI* LOG

Around the rugged property lie the remains of several *kauri* trees, reminders of the era of logging. Denis had retrieved one log (already depicted in fig. 2.2) from the bush higher up the hill and shifted it to a spot not far from where the stūpa was later built. They intended to make use of the high quality wood, but the log lay at that spot for nearly a decade, providing a meeting point for people planning to perform rituals at the nearby *pūriri* tree, stūpa, or retreat site. Derived from an enormous crown section of a *kauri*, it bore the scars of the burning and cutting of the logging days. From one truncated limb hung two bells made from old gas cylinders. This log was one of many "relics of the magnificent bush that originally clothed the land" (*Tararu Transformer* 1995, 1).

Denis had just decided to move from Wellington to Tararu so he could live on the land full time when, in April 1995, he and his partner were involved in a car crash. She died immediately, and Denis remained in a coma until his death some months later. Satyananda speculated that there was a connection between Denis moving the log and his subsequent death.

> In the Māori tradition that's *tapu* [taboo] . . . to move things like wood in the way that he did. . . . Although there was not necessarily a definite relationship between him doing that and him getting killed a couple of days later, a *myth* sort of built up around it. . . . We started to create a mythical sort of relationship with what was happening, and we decided

that it was time to stop what we were doing and try and just arrive on the land. And make our peace with the local entities, the local spirits on the land (1999b).

Taranatha also saw Denis's main influence as being the way he had turned people's minds more to the overall Buddhist vision of creating a sacred place and away from dominating the land. Some visitors and residents continue building these mini-stūpas, especially alongside the road and foot tracks around the land and beside the two creeks that flow down two borders of the triangular property. The mini-stūpas are fairly transient; those near the road and river have been knocked over or washed away from time to time, but as Taranatha said, "they're still breeding, popping up all over like mushrooms after an autumn rain" (2000a).

It was with hindsight that they were able to see Denis's influence on the place, and, reflecting on how he felt the death of Denis had changed people's re-lationship with the land, Taranatha said,

> For some reason I never quite caught up with, we suddenly found we weren't all into dominating this land anymore. We wanted to feel its spirit and move into partnership with it. And so . . . that attitude has been devel-oping and deepening ever since. Just before Denis's accident, we'd modified the road, and I had tramped through the scrub with a machete, cutting a track for the bulldozer to follow, didn't so much as think about the trees we were destroying. It was only scrub, but, even so. Well, we don't do that anymore. If we need to destroy a tree, we hold a pūjā and have a cere-mony, and become completely aware of what we're doing. [Pause.] I don't know whether we would have developed such an empathy with the land if weren't for the shock of Denis's death (1999a).

Incidentally, Prajñalila, in response to reading this quote in an earlier draft, told me that she found Taranatha's initial response of wanting to dominate the land unsettling and said that from the beginning she had been aware of the effects of the damage already done and did not wish to add to it.

As a result of Denis's death and what had gone before it, Satyananda real-ized that if they were to create "a real spiritual refuge, a place of harmony and of deep quietude" (1997, 2) this "meant more than just moving to an isolated plot of land and putting some buildings up." What they needed was a "spiritual focus." The mini-stūpas that Denis had built contributed the seed of an idea, ultimately contributing to the impetus to build the stūpa itself. Such tangible, visible signs

helped to bring out the symbolic aspects of the project of establishing a retreat center, reminding people of the vision of a Buddhist "spiritual home" that had inspired
them to buy the land in the first place.

A PEACEFUL GROVE?

There was another event that also changed how the trustees conceptualized and
articulated their relationship with the land, connected with the *pūriri* tree that
stands on the hillside a short walk from the *kauri* log and adjoining the site of the
planned retreat center. The *pūriri*'s large canopy creates a peaceful grove. Prajñalila told me that the tree "has been quite significant, and nearly everyone who visits
it feels that it has quite a special quality of energy" (1999). The grove is quiet and
still inside, giving a sense of enclosure. In an article written for an international
Buddhist audience, Taranatha provides an eloquent description.

> Near to the prospective retreat center buildings was a noble pūriri tree
> whose dense, evergreen foliage cast so deep a shade that little grew in the
> filtered, green light beneath it. Under its protection was a natural clearing
> some 25 meters [82 feet] across, carpeted with dead leaves and surrounded
> by a wall of tree ferns and hanging vines. A place of peace and rever-
> ence, whose silence was disturbed only by the song of the many birds that
> gathered to feast on the tree's abundant berries. This was more than just a
> forest tree. Here was a presence that evoked from all who encountered it
> responses of respect, reverence and even a sense of the sacred (2002, 40).

Taranatha continues, "Here we built a shrine to Shakyamuni Buddha. Here we recited a Buddhist pūjā, placing, so some of us thought, our Buddhist stamp on the
land." Indeed, when the Buddhists performed a dedication ritual for the property
not long after signing the deed of purchase, they placed a terra-cotta statue of a
meditating Buddha at the base of the tree (fig. 4.1), facing the uphill slope where
people sit during the *pūjās* that are sometimes performed there. This was a reference to the Buddha's association with trees: his birth, enlightenment, and death
all took place in the shade of trees, and he often taught beneath one. I have often
heard FWBO members liken this particular grove to the sacred groves in which
the Buddha taught his followers.

  While this grove indeed has a peaceful feeling, if one considers the history
of the valley, it is deathly quiet. While it is true it does attract birds, due to the
past deforestation and ongoing possum damage, the chimes of *tūī* and bellbirds or

FIGURE 4.1.
Buddha statue under *pūriri* in 1994. (Photo © Sudarshanaloka Trust.)

the rustlings of the heavy wood pigeons are not as common as they once were, and other species have altogether vanished.[3]

Vessantara, a senior Order member from the FWBO in Britain who visits FWBO centers in other countries from time to time and is respected as a strong meditator and good teacher, had an unusual experience in the *pūriri* grove in 1996. I heard the story of his experience, which circulated among people at the ABC, even before my first visit to Sudarshanaloka in 1997, so during the course of my research in 2000 I wrote to him asking about his encounter, and he replied thus.

I first visited Sudarshanaloka in '94. At that time I felt that the grove around the pūriri tree had a very special atmosphere; very tranquil. On my second visit in '96, I visited that part of the valley again with Satyananda, who was showing me the proposed site for the retreat center. As we were looking round, someone came to see him on business. I wandered off, and decided to go into the grove around the pūriri tree. As I approached the opening to the circle of trees encircling the pūriri, I became aware that the grove appeared to be glowing with a brilliant emerald light. I went forward a pace or two, but ran into what felt like a physical barrier, or force field, which prevented me from entering. I tried a couple of times with the same result. It felt intuitively as if something was happening in the grove and it was "closed to the public." As this was likely to be my only chance to enter the grove on that visit to NZ, I decided to ignore this feeling and to push through the invisible barrier. I managed to do so, though as I began to enter the grove I had the continuing feeling that I was not welcome (2000).

Vessantara said he did not know about the history of dispossession of indigenous people with connections to the valley, having only ever made brief visits to New Zealand. Nonetheless, his sense that the spirits were hostile to him and his persistence in entering the grove somehow echo the attitudes of earlier colonists and their ways of relating to the land. Thus

I chanted various Buddhist mantras associated with love and compassion silently to myself as I began to circle the pūriri tree. My experience of using these mantras is that they virtually always help to change the atmosphere of a place for the better. However, on this occasion, I sensed that they were not appreciated. I felt as if I was in communication with some kind of spirits of the land. I gathered that the land had been ravaged in various ways, including gold mining and inappropriate timber felling. Now there were yet more people coming onto the land—these Buddhists— and the local spirits were wary and suspicious of people with another ideology taking the place over for their own ends. There was a small shrine with a Buddhist image on it, which had been set up on the far side of the tree from the entrance. I sensed that this was a most unwelcome intrusion for the spirits of the land. I carried on slowly circumambulating the pūriri tree. I dropped all thought of Buddhist mantras, and began generating a feeling of loving-kindness which was universal, and had no Buddhist connotations. I repeated inwardly "May all beings in this place, whatever they may be, be well and happy." In this way I completed a circuit of the grove, and then left. I still had a sense that I had been unwelcome, a gatecrasher, and that it was only through generating thoughts of loving-kindness that I had managed to complete the circuit, and then very much on sufferance. I came out of the grove feeling very strange, almost as if I had been dealt a blow.

He says that he "dropped all thought of Buddhist mantras" and began "generating a feeling of universal loving-kindness" with no "Buddhist connotations," at which point he repeated the phrase "May all beings in this place, whatever they may be, be well and happy," which itself echoes phrases taught as part of Buddhist meditations on loving-kindness. This seems to involve a contradiction, but Buddhists offer the explanation that the Dharma is universal, and so too is a non-Buddhist loving-kindness.

Soon afterwards, an FWBO member arrived to drive him back to Auckland.

> As we drove out of the valley I was in an agitated and unhappy state. Once we had driven off the land I asked her to stop the car, and went and poured water over myself at the stream. . . . It felt as if I was carrying something with me from my experience in the pūriri grove which was bothering me, and I needed to purify it.

He reflected on his experience.

> I am quite intuitive by nature but also, I like to think, fairly hard-headed. I would not want to speculate much about what I experienced. I have described what happened in the terms which do most justice to what I subjectively experienced. I leave it up to the reader to draw their own conclusions. At the time I knew a little of the history of the valley. I did not know what I was subsequently told—that the pūriri tree was probably sacred to the local Māori.

By "history," Vessantara was probably referring to the stories of the destructive activities of milling and gold mining by the Pākehā settlers. In using the term "sacred" with reference to the tree, he was unlikely to be aware of the nuances of *tapu*, which is only partly equivalent to "sacred" (itself a rather slippery word): *tapu* refers to a ceremonial restriction with a sometimes dangerous power, and when associated with the dead it can be contaminating; the violation of a *tapu* results in calamity (Wakareo ā-ipurangi n.d.-a). It is interesting to note that Māori use water to remove *tapu* after contact with ancestral treasures or the dead and that Vessantara poured water over himself at the stream after his experience in the *pūriri* grove. I do not know if someone explained the *tapu*-lifting practice to him or if it was something that he did "intuitively."

Several of the Pākehā Buddhists who had a basic awareness of *tikanga Māori* wondered if the tree had had an old *tapu* on it. Here the stories that were told and retold about Vessantara's experience implied that he had the sensitivity to detect something that most Pākehā would not be aware of but that Māori knew well. Perhaps for FWBO/NZ members this affirmed one of their key teachers' spiritual powers. Considering the possibility that he possessed a strong intuitive capacity, I wondered, from my own many-layered subjective position, had he "tuned into" the undercurrents of colonization and desecration that so affected the land, but out of habit or curiosity acted in a way reminiscent of a colonial-era missionary? He demonstrated this second aspect by entering the grove despite the evident hostility of its inhabitants.

Vessantara singularly departed from such missionizing or imperialistic patterns, however, in his acknowledgment that the local spirits, too, had their place and that the onus was on the newcomers to reach some accommodation with them, rather than suppress them. Having pushed into the grove despite sensing a barrier, he intuited the reason for the hostility, and this ultimately became crucial in convincing people of the need to reassess their relationship with the land, indicating the need to prove to these indigenous deities that their intentions on the land were friendly. It was Vessantara's account that led to the trustees deciding that it was "not always appropriate to use Buddhist rituals, it is a different space" (Prajñalila 1999).

Despite the ways this story of hostile spirits sits in the narrative of transformation of their relationship with the land, there appears to be an irreconcilable paradox within a paradox. First, while thinking Buddhism was universal, they recognized that at Sudarshanaloka they needed to cooperate with local forces. Second, within this paradox another exists: while talking about friendship with the land, they continued to bring in heavy machinery to develop the road in order to allow increased vehicular traffic that the retreat center will bring, thus doing further damage.

Creating what Appadurai calls a neighborhood (a context within which meaningful social interaction can take place) is "inherently an exercise of power over some sort of hostile or recalcitrant environment" (1995, 209) that involves "implicit violence." Such acts can be regarded as "inherently colonizing" because they involve "the assertion of socially (often ritually) organized power over places and settings which are viewed as potentially chaotic or rebellious." Altering the land in attempts to construct a building can be regarded in this way. My interlocutors, however, do not consider their own activities to be colonizing: Nagabodhi (a senior Order member based in Britain who visits New Zealand every two years because of his role as honorary "president" of the New Zealand centers) equated colonization with missionaries coercing people to take on a new religion, while he thought Buddhism offered "a kind of universally applicable key, that can be used anywhere, under any conditions, and even sometimes in active cooperation with pre-existing forces" (2000).

As a result of Vessantara's experience, the trustees began reconsidering the appropriateness of imposing specifically Buddhist symbols on the *pūriri* grove, and it became a focus for the acknowledgment of localized spirit presences.

> [Because we're] Buddhists, we wanted to bring our own cosmology. . . . But, there clearly were spirits in the land. And it seemed very arrogant to think that we could automatically bring in our energy, without considering [the spirits]. . . . It took a while to know how to best do that. . . . We found it inappropriate often to use Buddhist things, and more appropriate to [offer our support to] the guardians of the land, as we call them, and say: "We are here as caretakers as well, can we work in partnership?" And we found appropriate verses, that were sort of like transition pieces. They also came from a Buddhist source, but they were more generalized in nature. In a sense [we tried] to not frighten the land (Prajñalila 1999).

This narrative, like others from Prajñalila, Satyananda, and Taranatha, reflects the trustees' increasing articulation of the idea of *inviting* the local energies to join with them, rather than forcing Buddhism upon them, keeping the *pūriri* grove clear of specifically Buddhist symbols.

Nonetheless, in their rituals addressing the spirits of the land, they can refer to various canonical Buddhist sources. This is something that is done elsewhere in the FWBO, too. Gunapala, a visiting New Zealand Order member who has lived at Guhyaloka, told me that before they embark on a project they read a specific Buddhist text excerpted from the *Ratana Sutta* (1999).[4] This scripture details an occasion when the city of Vesali was besieged by spirits that caused a plague and famine. The Buddha arrived and addressed the local spirits, instructing them in the Dharma and exhorting them to look after the city's inhabitants. Taranatha told me he has read the *Sutta* at "various earth-blessing ceremonies" at Sudarshanaloka, including the stūpa site dedication,

> at the installation of the present pagan shrine under the pūriri, and at the dedication of the [Shraddha] Trust land[5] across the road. Maybe other times too—certainly in my private rituals at the pūriri. . . . It is aimed at

tuning in with the spirits of the land—the energy that was there before we came along to add our bit. To co-operate with rather than try to dominate the existing forces (2000b).

Another Buddhist text, the *Karaniya Mettā Sutta* (1999), relates to disturbances caused by local deities for monks attempting to live and meditate in the forest. The Buddha's advice to the monks was to send the spirits loving-kindness (*mettā*). The power of this *mettā* so affected the spirits that they then allowed the monks to meditate in peace. The concept of communicating *mettā* to the local spirits is one that Taranatha, like Vessantara, has taken seriously. He told me that every time he visits the *pūriri* grove, which for him embodies the spirit of the land, he chants a refrain whose words wish happiness for all beings: "*Sabbe sattā sukhī hontu*" (Pāli for "May all beings be happy"). He told me it is important to go on declaring friendship, expressing a wish that humans "work together" with spirits to "overcome our limitations."

LOCAL SPIRITS, DHARMA PROTECTORS

I have shown how some FWBO members speculatively linked certain mishaps to their own failure to acknowledge and accommodate local spirits or energies. People began to weave the stories about Denis's death (tentatively linked to his shifting the *kauri* log) and the stories about spirits (linked with the *pūriri* grove and Vessantara's story) into a narrative or myth about transformation and healing. This was not necessarily intentional, but rather happened through retelling the stories, perhaps just because they felt significant. When I first heard these stories prior to embarking on my research, although I could not have explained why, they certainly felt meaningful.

For FWBO/NZ members, the project of creating a Buddhist sacred place came to mean accommodating the local nature spirits. "Spirit religion" has generally been associated with "traditional" Buddhist societies in places like Sri Lanka (e.g., Gombrich and Obeyesekere 1988), in contrast with "Protestant Buddhism," which tends to be associated with modernist elites. Debates have raged about whether such practices are "Buddhist" or syncretic cultural baggage (e.g., Gombrich 1971, Spiro 1967), but from an anthropological perspective I consider the notion of a pure, authentic Buddhism to be untenable. Suffice it to say that in many societies where Buddhism is well established, people embarking on a new building project make offerings to the local spirits they are disturbing in order to compensate them for the human imposition, and although this is often associated with more traditionalist Buddhists, it is not exclusively so. Accommodation of local spirits is variously spoken of as a matter of winning their favor, pacifying or converting them through making offerings, and befriending them to turn them into "Dharma protectors" or allies of Buddhism. Notions of local deities and spirits are inextricably intertwined with Buddhist traditions, and the influence of Indian spirit-religions permeates early Buddhist iconography (DeCaroli 2004). In some instances, practices combining Buddhism and animism serve as a useful environmentalist strategy, such as in northern Thailand (see, e.g., Darlington 2003). A wide range of scriptures acknowledge many kinds of local spirits and deities, including ones that inhabit caves, bodies of water, and trees.[6] In legends telling of the establishment of Buddhism in Tibet, the appeasement of local spirit forces was essential (e.g., Mills 2003, 13–17). Likewise, in accounts of his mythological visit to the island of Sri Lanka, the Buddha expelled violent *yakkha* spirits using his supranormal powers to facilitate the establishment of his teachings (Trainor 1997, 108). *Nāgas* (serpent-like beings associated with rain and fertility, as well as being guardians of treasure) are powerful beings that can become devoted followers of the Buddha when subdued (126). However, these beings can help (or hinder) humans only in mundane matters such as the weather, success of crops, and fertility; they are not able to help people attain enlightenment (Lewis 1997, 343).

Modernist or reformist Buddhists, including many Western Buddhist authors, tend to be dismissive about stories of magical or supernatural beings, which they regard as mere superstition. This is consistent with materialist world views in which numinous entities are either not regarded as existing or, where they are acknowledged, it is usually only on certain ritualized occasions, and then only by the ritual specialists, such as when preparing the ground for a new building (e.g., Kolig 1997, Van Dyke 1997). Further, where supernatural powers are mentioned at all it is with regard to the development of *siddhis*, which are portrayed as mere side effects of deep meditative practice. To become concerned with these powers would be to digress from the ultimate aim of enlightenment.

It may therefore seem somewhat surprising for the FWBO to adopt practices relating to spirit presences—even more so given that at the level of public discourse the FWBO urges Western Buddhists to differentiate true Dharma from "cultural baggage" or "ethnic Buddhism" (cultural practices not conducive to spiritual enlightenment). However, the FWBO's "mythic dimension" and interest in paganism provides a framework in which Buddhism needs to integrate the psychic energies of people and place. There are indeed precedents in Tibetan Buddhism, about which Sangharakshita has written (1996b). In the case of Sudarshanaloka, the accounts that lead to the eventual ritual acknowledgment of local spirits give the impression that it was not a choice but a necessity to learn to work with such unseen chthonic forces. Satyananda (1997, 2) said that people "had been [so] caught up in the mundane tasks of building" that they lost sight of their purpose, which was not only to establish a retreat center, but also to work for the enlightenment of all beings. This, among other things, meant learning to be sensitive to the spirits, as reinforced by Vessantara's experience. Satyananda said of this time period,

> So it was a bit like Śāntarakṣita, when he went to Tibet. He [worked] all day and then woke up in the morning and everything he'd done, during the night was pulled down by the local [demons]. [It was] like a war zone. I remember Nigel, who lives in Norwich, was with us for three months, and he wrote when he left that he felt like he'd been living in a war zone. Just one thing after another, cyclones.[7] . . . But anyway, we stopped. And we decided to build a stūpa (1999b).

Satyananda's reference to Śāntarakṣita (not to be confused with Sangharakshita) is fleeting, but it is important in that it indicates a shared understanding among at least some of the audience that Buddhism, as a missionizing religion, has had to find strategies to introduce the religion in new cultural situations. Śāntarakṣita was an eighth-century Buddhist scholar whom a Tibetan king invited to introduce Buddhism to Tibet. He gave lectures on the Dharma in several places in Tibet and tried to establish a monastery, but he was "not very successful," eventually giving up when, because of resistance by local deities, epidemics broke out all over the country (Sangharakshita 1996b, 21).[8] He then recommended that the king invite Padmasambhava, who was not only an accomplished scholar, but also possessed shamanic powers and was "a formidable yogi, a great meditator and a mystic." It was Padmasambhava who subdued the local demons, "converting them into guardian deities of the Buddhist faith" (1996b, 21). Thus Padmasambhava is often regarded as something akin to a patron saint for the establishment of Buddhism with Tibetan connections in new lands.[9] This story suggests that the successful establishment of Buddhism in Tibet required not only the conversion of local spirits, but also the adaptation of Buddhism itself, adopting the local spirits as guardians, thus channeling otherwise irrepressible energy.

In the story of the transformation of Tararu into Sudarshanaloka, we see a parallel to the Padmasambhava story. When Satyananda mentioned Śāntarakṣita's failure to establish Buddhism in Tibet, he was correlating this account with the struggles of the FWBO in New Zealand to bring Buddhism to a piece of land in the Coromandel. This link is made material in the form of a shrine among ferns in a kind of grotto caused by subsidence of the ground (see fig. 6.6 in chap. 6). This shrine, which included a reproduction of a Tibetan painting of Padmasambhava, was assembled by a Buddhist who was doing manual labor. around the property using the bones he found around the land. As well as the fact that bones are used in Buddhism to index the transience of life, I read this as an attempt to transform the destructiveness of farming by putting it into the mythic context, using the shamanic powers attributed to Padmasambhava.

Nagabodhi reflected on the significance of the talk about strange energies or spirits.

> There are people that say that they feel a very, very powerful force [in the *pūriri* grove], and there are even little myths beginning to develop in the FWBO about the power of the place. You know, when Vessantara went there, and felt some really strange thing and got ill afterwards, or well afterwards, one or the other. And I know when I came and heard people talking about it a couple of years later, they were talking about it with, you know—disbelief seemed pretty suspended. And I'm agnostic on the subject. But it's interesting to see how . . . gradually the grove is beginning to develop a kind of mythic dimension, which people feel. How that will fit in with Buddhist practice I don't know (2000).

I have noted that Vessantara's story helped to convince many who heard it that there was some kind of spirit presence in the land. To what extent are stories of spirit presences influenced by *non-Buddhist* concepts of local spirits? Various stories about visions and hearing voices in the trees or creek have become woven into people's accounts of Sudarshanaloka, including one about the man who sold the land to the FWBO, a farmer and hunter. According to the *Tararu Transformer*, he had told Satyananda that he had "heard Māori women singing in the trees, and felt his hair stand on end at Fisher's Flat" (1997a, 2). Pākehā understandings of Māori spiritual forces in the land, including the notion of sites placed under the influence of *tapu* and the possibility that the tree had once been a "placenta tree" added another level to the concept of a forest world inhabited by unseen and sometimes hostile spirits.

In chapter 1 I noted that in contemporary Buddhism reformist-minded teachers such as Sangharakshita attempt to extract the "essence," that is, the pure, universalistic teachings from so-called "cultural baggage" so that practices that may have been appropriate in one context are not imposed on another, where they become meaningless. The idea that the "ethnic" and canonical elements are incompatible is itself part of the modernist approach, which holds that "pure" and universal Buddhist teachings are found in canonical texts and that spirit cults, shamanism, and spirit possession are localized practices. Similarly, as mentioned above, many scholars identify the "spirit cult" and "Buddhist" strands in Buddhist societies. At Sudarshanaloka, however, people draw on Buddhist cosmologies inhabited by many kinds of unseen entities, intermixing these freely with neo-pagan concepts, derived from various indigenous cosmologies, of spirits animating places. Such beings are real for some participants, while others in the FWBO see them as useful or not so useful ways of relating to the unknown.

JUNGIAN ARCHETYPES OR INDIGENOUS INHABITANTS?

The extent to which FWBO members now talk about local spirits might be regarded as intriguing, given that in line with the reformist approach to Buddhism they reject beliefs and practices that they regard as cultural baggage. However, I have already noted the sympathy that many members have towards rediscovering their imagined pagan roots. The FWBO are not alone among Western Buddhists in considering nature spirits part of the world. There is much overlap among those with interests in nature-centered religions and deep ecology. Buddhist-influenced Californian poet and ecologist Gary Snyder argues for a re-engagement with place (he calls this a "bioregionalist ethic"), paraphrasing an unnamed Crow elder as saying,

> I'm not really worried about what white people are going to do on this continent. If anybody lives here long enough, the spirits will begin to speak to them. It's the power of the spirits coming up from the land. . . . That's what it taught us, and it would teach everybody, if they'd just stay here. The old spirits and the old powers aren't lost; people just need to be around long enough to begin to [let them] influence them (Snyder et al. 1985).[10]

What I think Snyder is attempting to convey here is the way that the spirit of a place can influence us; we can then choose to personify this spirit as "local spirits."

The "healing the land" discourse resonates with attempts to return to a nature-centered spirituality and provides an alternative to the dominant ideologies that separate "man" from "nature," which many environmentalists blame on the Judeo-Christian tradition. There are parallels to neo-pagan ideals, which emphasize the need to "focus on healing ourselves, our communities, and the planet" (Pike 2001, xiv). According to neo-pagans, this healing can take place only through relationships, that is, "an intimate connection with the natural world, with a goddess or god, and with one's community."

The FWBO "spirit discourse" might be understood in terms of FWBO discourses about the mythic dimension and its role in spiritual development. FWBO members seem to imagine spirits less in the sense of a literal belief in real spirit beings and more as a way of personifying unseen forces. In line with this, Sangharakshita (1996b, 21) provides a Jungian interpretation of the Padmasambhava legend, referring to the local deities as "archetypes of the Tibetan collective unconscious." He suggests that the Tibetan psyche "put up resistance" to initial attempts to introduce "the higher and more spiritual ideals of Buddhism" because initial attempts did not take into account how the Indian and Tibetan collective minds differed, and the Tibetan collective unconscious generated an enormous force that blocked the teachers' work, released only when it was accommodated as an ally rather than something to be repressed.

Noting the influence of Jung on Sangharakshita, I asked Taranatha what he thought about the view that spirits were aspects of the psyche projected onto the land, and he agreed, adding that the way to cope with anything beyond comprehension is to make an image of it and then interact with that image. He explained that an Order member's visualization practice of a tantric deity or bodhisattva is a personification of an abstract ideal, and this helps the meditator to connect imaginatively with what would otherwise remain an inaccessible concept.

Having imagined these unseen forces as spirit beings, then, the trustees are able to interact with them. The personification of deep, barely conscious processes into spirits, is something that can be done in a very deliberate way. In an edited volume on spirit beliefs in the Pacific, Alan Howard and Jeanette Mageo argue that

> cultural borrowing and subsequent cultural reinventions are often highly
> self-conscious and reflective. All cultures reimagine their identities and
> histories. . . . [W]here spirits survive, they are an important medium for this
> reimagining process. The process is, moreover, a means by which people
> effect historical readjustments of cultural values (1996, 4).

Spirits can be regarded as a "necessary complement" to the concept of gods or, I might add, to the agnostic rationalism of Western Buddhist modernism, providing ways to cope "with darker, unorganized thoughts, feelings and sensations" (10). Likewise, I suggest that FWBO contact with spirits is part of the re-imagining process of a more holistic interrelationship between oneself, the social group, and the environment. The Friends of Tararu have been exploring ways to help themselves and others to connect with these ideas at Sudarshanaloka. The ways they talk about the *pūriri* grove and its resident spirits may be seen as an attempted readjustment of their cultural presumptions to create ways of being in the world that are compatible with both their Buddhist ideals and the land they are attempting to inhabit.

TRANSFORMING TARARU

Sudarshanaloka is an explicit attempt to create a spiritual sanctuary through ritual, as an early brochure says: "the land has a mythic dimension that informs our growing connection between its presence and our potential. Ritual is an integral element in all that we undertake as its caretakers, to develop its natural sanctuary" (Sudarshanaloka n.d.). This is not taking place in some pristine wilderness, however; rather, it is in a cultural landscape permeated with complex and often contested histories. I have noted that sangha members' discourses about their relationship with the land at Sudarshanaloka express concern with restoring and healing the environment, which fits the wider settler-indigenous discourses about place and environmentalist concerns in New Zealand society.

In this chapter I have described events that led people to talk about their relationship with the land in new ways and imbue it with new meanings, thereby transforming Tararu into Sudarshanaloka. However, as Prajñalila told me, they did not wish to interact with the place as "owners."

> Satyananda was quite clear from the start, that we were there as caretakers, that we had no ownership as it were. Good stewards. But we had to . . . [let the land] know that, because the land didn't seem to have had that experience. Certainly not in the last 100 years. And the energies around it seemed to suggest that it wanted to throw off any further "ownership," you know, sense of ownership or occupation, taking anything more from it (1999).

Despite the environmentalist spirit of acting as caretakers or stewards[11] (terms that evoke the Māori idea of *kaitiakitanga* mentioned in the previous chapter), the Buddhist precedent of Padmasambhava gives the impression that the local spirits should be pacified and converted into Dharma protectors. While I think the notion of pacifying the land is drawn from Buddhist rituals for preparing a new site for a temple or stūpa rather than being intended to imply this sense of domination, as I noted in the previous chapter, the relationship between people of Pākehā settler and indigenous Māori origins has shaped the ways people think about place, and there is a slightly uneasy echo of this in their talk about the energies of the land.

At Sudarshanaloka they came to consider that placing a Buddha statue in the grove might be seen as an imposition, repeating the mistakes of earlier colonial ideologies. The *pūriri* in its grove inhabited by spirits is not just a reminder of the need for friendship with the energies of the land; it also provides a place for the reciprocal enactment of that friendship—that is, it is actively involved in it. Further, whether intentional or not, the link that Satyananda and others made between the story of Sudarshanaloka's incorporation of local energies to Padmasambhava's introduction of Buddhism in Tibet has the effect of providing a form of legitimization of their project both to themselves and to the wider Buddhist world.

Related to this, the attempt by Pākehā to find or claim a spiritual connection with the land could be read as a way of securing their place in New Zealand, echoed in Satyananda's wish to create a spiritual home. Something about the stories of spirits and rawness at Sudarshanaloka highlights an underlying atmosphere of insecurity, an affliction of what might be called the "post-colonial anxiety" of a settler society.

In connection with wider, transnational FWBO interests in personal transformation, the land is both consciously and unknowingly implicated in the transformation of the individual and society. For many members of the FWBO/NZ, their relationship with the land they call Sudarshanaloka has become an important index of personal and group belonging, as well as a way of re-imagining and adjusting to the difficulties the people have encountered due to the wider sociohistorical processes into which they have been born. Although from the beginning they had undertaken various Buddhist rituals, such as the dedication ceremony used at the beginning of retreats, Denis's death and Vessantara's account of his encounter in the *pūriri* grove stirred people to rethink the ways they related to the land.

Discourses about universalism, including those suggesting that anyone at all can claim a spiritual affinity with the places they feel attached to, can be employed to claim a right of access to what are portrayed as more "spiritual" traditions. Meanwhile, it is easy to overlook how we came to be in a position to have this privileged access (cf. Bartholomeusz 1998). FWBO/NZ members express sadness about the past and present environmental destruction and dispossession of the indigenous people in New Zealand, albeit with far more emphasis on the former than the latter, with regard to Sudarshanaloka. The "healing the land" narrative could be regarded as an attempt to make amends, but more directly it is a self-conscious attempt to engage with marrying Buddhist traditions about spirit presences in the land to locally specific concerns. Perhaps there is also an unarticulated attempt to legitimize their presence on the land by pursuing the kind of spiritual relationship ascribed to the original Māori owners. Members' stories about developing a "friendship" or healing relationship with "local spirits" or "the land" may reflect a desire to resolve their own discomfort about the complex past that shapes the land they are now trying to transform. While some FWBO members personify unseen energies of the land as nature spirits and openly reflect on this act, they intend the stūpa to be a representation of the refinement of those energies, and it is the construction of this distinctly Buddhist edifice that I discuss next.

5   The Stūpa Is Dhardo

> We thought . . . the best thing to do is to actually try and arrive, put our-
> selves on the land, and get some sort of spiritual center [on the land at
> Sudarshanaloka]. So, that's what we did. And initially we thought we'd
> build a little stūpa, . . . [which ended up being] seven meters high! . . . So
> the whole process for us, from the moment we decided to build a stūpa,
> became more of a mythic journey, one that involved a lot of ritual, and a
> lot of symbol. And in a way, we've been working like that ever since.
> —Satyananda, speech given at the FWBO's North London Buddhist Centre, 1999

Although a popular notion of Buddhism paints the religion as seeking to transcend
the "material" world, in another sense of the word, material culture is the necessary medium through which people interrelate with the ideologies they hold. For
the expression of beliefs, the physical world is the "only medium available to us,
our physical surroundings organized by internal narrative" (Pearce 1997, 2), so we
communicate abstract religious concepts through the mediation of the material
world. Buddhist sacred sites, including stūpas, can provide a place for people to
interact with what might otherwise be abstract, intangible ideals. Indeed, many
Westerners initially became interested in the Dharma through visiting historical
Buddhist pilgrimage sites in Asia, or through an aesthetic response to Buddhist art.
In the ABC's newsletter *Sangha Scene*, a Western Buddhist Order member talks
about how, before he had become a Buddhist, he was "affected by the peaceful
atmosphere" at the Buddhist sites he visited in Asia, which he had "never experienced before. I thought 'How do they create this?'" (Guhyasiddhi 2005, 12).
Places, then, can have a powerful effect on people, and his experience of certain
sacred sites awoke his desire to learn about the Dharma.

    The stūpa at Sudarshanaloka paradoxically embodies a transcendental ideal
through the medium of a seventeen-ton concrete structure. Sue Thompson writes
that the stūpa "helps us to value spiritual qualities; in fact it reminds us of them"
(1996a, 3), and Prajñalila writes that the stūpa is "intended for devotional practice
alone" (*Tararu Transformer* 1996, 1). According to Adrian Snodgrass (1985, 353),
stūpas have three primary purposes: as reliquaries containing relics of the Buddha

(or saints), as memorials marking the location of an event in the Buddha's life, and as votive offerings. Paul Mus argues that they model the cosmos and refashion the Buddha in the image of a royal god (1998, 342ff).

Besides the intended religious effects, stūpas also have social efficacy. In marking their presence in a place, whether they inscribe the walls of a cave, fly a flag, or construct a monument, people not only give a site special significance, but also claim a connection, control, or even ownership of it. In this chapter, then, I investigate how the Sudarshanaloka stūpa was designed, built, and consecrated and the effects, both intended and unintended, that this had. I also ask how the construction of the stūpa came to be represented as an act that healed the land and channeled its energies. I explore meanings and interpretations of the stūpa, address the ways in which its particularities encapsulate and constitute aspects of the FWBO/NZ, and investigate the ways in which members use conventional Buddhist symbolism and re-imagine themselves as a community undertaking a "mythic journey," as Satyananda calls it in the epigraph that opens this chapter.

The stūpa helps people to think about enlightenment, a paradox because the statement is made in the material world, while intending to point to something beyond it. Beyond its intended dharmic symbolism, the stūpa participates in the mundane, social realm. They are not just static symbols, but rather operate in human ways and have considerable social utility and local relevance in the current flourishing of Buddhism in the West. Anthropologist Alfred Gell contends that humans "form what are evidently social relations with 'things'" (1998, 18), resulting in these things having social agency. As Tim Dant notes, when appropriated into human culture, objects "re-present the social relations of culture, standing in for other human beings, carrying values, ideas and emotions," and some objects, like the stūpa, do this more obviously than others. As such, they provide "a means of sharing values, activities and styles of life in a more concrete and enduring way than language use or direct interaction" (1999, 1-2).

I suggest, following Gell's concept of art objects as agents, that they are also objects in reciprocal relationships with the people who believe in them. This concept of material agency is a potent one with regard to the stūpa in that it meshes with the ways Buddhists attribute metaphysical powers and enlightened essence to the stūpa. It also shows that objects such as the stūpa have consequences beyond those their builders intended.

BUDDHIST STŪPAS

In the Asian Buddhist heartlands, the stūpa can be a site for pilgrimage and worship, and in its variant forms it has become "a focal point and the singular landmark denoting the tradition's spiritual presence on the landscape" in all major schools of Buddhism (Lewis 1997, 329–330). The stūpa's role as a reliquary makes it into a substitute body for the Buddha or Buddhist saint. Clockwise circumambulation of an object such as a stūpa ritually enacts its centrality in the Buddhist life. Besides these religious functions, stūpas harness sacred power for the benefit of the community and the locale. For example, the people who build them often regard them as subduing chthonic energies or spirits that hinder both mundane projects such as the success of crops and sacred projects such as the establishment of the Dharma (e.g., Mills 2003, 13–17, 149–150, 330–331). Throughout much of history, Buddhist elites have commissioned stūpas that embodied the cosmological and political center of, for instance, a particular historical kingdom.

Today, international Buddhist networks are constructing stūpas as part of the work of establishing their centers of power and, as they explain it to themselves and non-Buddhist locals, to bring a peaceful atmosphere to a place.[1] An Anglo-Australian Buddhist named Yeshe Khadro writes of such effects at the Chenrezig Institute in Queensland, Australia, a community founded in 1974 in the context of the Foundation for the Preservation of the Mahāyāna Tradition (FPMT) and incorporating a nunnery, meditation temple, and housing for laypeople. Over time they built two stūpas, a massive prayer wheel, and various other holy objects "because of their power to increase the harmony and positive energy of the center and its members" (1995, 123).

THE SUDARSHANALOKA STŪPA

The *Tararu Transformer* records that in June 1996 the Friends of Tararu launched the stūpa project with a small procession from the river to the stūpa site. At the river, the participants selected a stone and made offerings of rice to the "non-human inhabitants" (Thompson 1996b, 1). The river was chosen as the starting point because it is the entrance to the property and the place where "Denis [had] played in the river building his mini stone stūpas" (1996b, 1). At the stūpa site they made offerings to "the local spirits and the five Jinas [*dhyāni* buddhas]" and circumambulated the site, then placed their stones at the center.

In attempting to convey to me the importance of stūpas, an Order member e-mailed me an excerpt from an explanation by the Tibetan teacher Tarthang Tulku, who is one of the longest-established teachers of Tibetan Buddhism in the United States. Tarthang Tulku attributes the contemporary problems to the imbalanced nature of the cosmic age in which we live.[2] He suggests that "forms which reflect patterns of stability and order," such as representations of Buddhas, maṇḍalas, and statues, help to offset this negative state. They do this by using shape, colors and proportional relationships as a basis of focusing psychic power. Mandalas have a positive energy which balances disruptive forces and heals rifts of time and space in the universe; their healing energies are reflected in our own world. These are not recent ideas or my own thoughts, but realities that Buddhists throughout Asia have known and acted upon for centuries.[3]

The language he uses here resembles New Age and neo-pagan discourses about psychic energies, powerful places, and healing the land, which themselves draw on such sources as Tibetan Buddhism.

When the FWBO/NZ sangha (primarily the Tararu trustees and Friends of Tararu team) initially decided to build a stūpa, they discussed the idea with Sangharakshita, who approved and, further, decided to bring some of his late teacher Dhardo Rimpoche's ashes to inter. The Tibetan refugee community in Kalimpong where Dhardo had lived had divided his ashes into five portions, of which four were given to the FWBO. Portions are enshrined in other FWBO stūpas at Taraloka, Tiratnaloka, Padmaloka, and Guhyaloka. According to Sue Thompson, having these ashes was an "important and auspicious gift" and required a special "repository" that would "signify the rootedness of [the FWBO] . . . through the efforts of Bhante [Sangharakshita] and his teachers—in the rich soil of Buddhist history, as well as being a marker for our present faith and aspiration and a signpost towards the future" (1996a, 3).

The Buddhist converts had little or no experience of building stūpas, and during 1996 Prajñalila produced three issues of the *Tararu Transformer* as a way of drawing people to become emotionally and spiritually inspired to participate in the project. As she commented on reading an earlier draft of this book, she wanted to encourage people to connect with the "land, project, dharma, each other and, hence to help create [the place]" (2000b).

DESIGNING THE STŪPA

The established Buddhist traditions leave much of the planning and ritual to specialized experts. For instance, when the Dhargyey Buddhist Centre built a stūpa near Dunedin in New Zealand's South Island, the rituals and consecration ceremony were overseen by Tibetan monks. In this case there was an interesting adaptation to the locale in that Māori elders (in their role as *tangata whenua*) participated in the consecration rites (Kolig 1997).[4] But what I wish to stress here is that in this case, most of the convert Pākehā Buddhists were peripheral supporters, their roles being worldly ones (e.g., supporting their Tibetan teachers and providing the land on which the stūpa was built). In the FWBO, in comparison, it was the convert Pākehā (and other Western) Buddhists who conducted all aspects of the planning and ritual.

The degree of creativity and bricolage that the Friends of Tararu put into planning, building, and dedicating the Sudarshanaloka stūpa is remarkable. They had no single design precedent from the FWBO when they began designing the stūpa, nor did they have a stūpa expert to advise them. Rather, they considered themselves able to select from the whole array of previous stūpa designs, from all Buddhist traditions, recombining components to compose their own form, much as Sangharakshita had selected "essential" aspects of Buddhism from various Buddhist traditions. They also planned the ritual details for the dedication procession themselves, drawing on a range of sources and calling on occasional advice from Sangharakshita. Their legitimation came through their connection with Sangharakshita.

The trustees' final design choice was a combination of many ideas. Initially they sought Sangharakshita's approval and advice, and he encouraged them to place their activities

> within an all-encompassing "greater mandala" of aesthetic appreciation and playful activity. . . . From the minutiae of making tea at team discussions to the grand task of alchemically transforming steel and cement into a transcendental symbol we practice an attitude of beauty, metta and playfulness—"that the whole project be like one great pūjā from beginning to end," as Satyananda has put it (Thompson 1996b, 1).

FWBO members involved with planning their own stūpa and retreat center visited Buddhist temples and retreat centers in New Zealand and looked at photographs from Buddhist countries. The first stūpa album is compiled in a scrapbook-style collection of photocopied readings (about stūpa worship and visualization) and images relating to stūpas. There are also photocopies of information collected as the trustees educated themselves as to what was significant about a stūpa in terms of form and symbolism.

Books that provided inspiration included relevant sections of *Buddhist Saints in India* (Ray 1994), the same book that had provided inspiration for the three-fold model for the FWBO community discussed in chapter 2. They also referred to *The Symbolism of the Stūpa* (Snodgrass 1985),[5] which includes stūpa designs from all over the Buddhist world. A book on Japanese tantric symbolism associates the stūpa's underlying geometric forms with the human body (Rambach 1979). Vessantara gives a detailed table showing the Five Buddhas and provides an extensive set of "correlations" with each one (1993, 54–55). Other important sources for the research by the Friends of Tararu were Sangharakshita's discussion of stūpas in his book *The Drama of Cosmic Enlightenment* (1993) and two books by a German Buddhist named Lama Govinda, his earlier work drawing on Tibetan "mysticism" and the later being another compendium on stūpa symbolism (1960, 1976).[6]

Prajñalila told me they drew inspiration from what they wanted it to "manifest by its form," such as "aspirational" qualities (2000b). Further inspiration came from prior overseas trips. One example is clear from the Sudarshanaloka photograph albums that Prajñalila compiled in the late 1990s: several photographs of prayer flags and banners in Bhutan, and then a few pages later banners at Sudarshanaloka, arranged around the path leading to the stūpa in similar fashion. The photographs from Bhutan provided the inspiration and indeed the model for the arrangement of banners and flags at Sudarshanaloka.

The Tararu Team members separately drew stūpa forms, and when they met to compare ideas, found that they basically had all come up with very similar styles, so they had little or no disagreement. For refinement they passed their ideas to architects John Hunt and Hugh Tennent.[7] Tennent's company also provided the designs for the new retreat center.

Sangharakshita provided another source of information about stūpa building. He said that stūpas are "appropriate" in the West. "They could be a pleasing feature of the landscape, not necessarily in a completely traditional form, but having some link with tradition, based on the traditional five element structure" (1993, 160–161; I return to the five-element structure below). However, he thought features such as the "Nepalese-style stūpas with eyes" would look rather bizarre in the British landscape and that a brightly colored one would be "gaudy and tasteless." He preferred Tibetan style and Sinhalese bell-shaped stūpas to the tower-like pagoda. He did not think all FWBO stūpas should be one design style, but preferred simpler designs, and "the bigger the better." It is possible that Sangharakshita recommended a larger size stūpa because it could be seen from farther away, having the effect of proclaiming Buddhism's presence on the landscape. Some of what Sangharakshita describes about stūpas comes from his background of wide reading of both canonical Buddhist texts and scholarly works on Buddhism.

The original plans for the stūpa at Sudarshanaloka envisaged a structure three meters (under ten feet) high, which Taranatha had thought was already "big work" (1999a). But to make it fit the site they had chosen, in keeping with Sangharakshita's recommendations, the spire had to project above the skyline when viewed from the approach, and it had to be seen from a distance. Because of the height of the ridge across the valley that forms its backdrop, it needed to be at least seven meters high to satisfy these requirements.

As it has eventuated, the stūpa at Sudarshanaloka is like Sinhalese and Thai "bell-shaped" stūpas in form, with what Prajñalila calls "Thai aspirational height," and is white against the green background of the native bush.

The bricolagic approach that the Friends of Tararu engaged in to design their stūpa is a notable contrast to lineages more strongly affiliated with one cultural tradition, where certain style and ritual specifications are represented as having been passed down over many generations, following much more clearly prescribed guidelines (giving exact proportions and detailed protocols) than those the FWBO members had available to them. I now discuss the ways that the five-element and five-buddha symbolism was incorporated into the planning and construction of the stūpa.

THE FIVE BUDDHAS

Stūpa symbolism and Indic maṇḍala symbolism are closely intertwined, so that the stūpa is in fact a three-dimensional maṇḍala. Both stūpas and maṇḍalas provide a diagram of the cosmos and reference Mount Kailash (a spectacular pilgrimage mountain in southern Tibet), which in Indo-Tibetan cosmology is the center of the universe. Stūpas are built in alignment with the five directions: this incorporates the four cardinal points and the center of the maṇḍala (the cosmic axis, the directions of upward and downward).[8] In Meeting the Buddhas (Vessantara 1993), an FWBO book that interprets the spiritual qualities of many of the buddhas and bodhisattvas of Indo-Tibetan Buddhism, the five dhyāni buddhas of this maṇḍala are Ratnasambhava, Akṣobhya, Amitābha, Amoghasiddhi, and Vairocana. The five buddhas correspond with many other sets of five, including the five elements, five geometric shapes, five colors, five directions, and so forth (fig. 5.1, tables 5.1 and 5.2).

However, following the model of many stūpa designs there are two additional components. First, near the top of its spire and just between the bowl and the flame-shaped jewel at the top, the designers of the Sudarshanaloka stūpa have placed three Perspex rings—one red, one yellow, one blue—representing the three jewels (fig. 5.2). According to Snodgrass (1985, 324–326), the three rings fitted at the top of some stūpa spires relate to the parasol symbol, which in South Asia is "an emblem of kingship." Prajñalila told me that they adopted this symbol to represent the Buddha's "mastery of the mind" (2000b). Second, the stūpa also has a harmikā, a box-like shape above the cupola that references the Vedic sacrificial altar and represents the fire of transmutation.

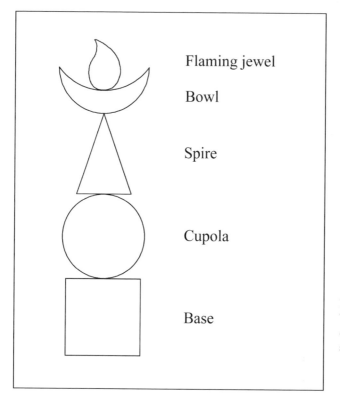

Flaming jewel

Bowl

Spire

Cupola

Base

FIGURE 5.1.
The five geometric
components in
stūpa symbolism.

In FWBO explanations these qualities signify the channeling, refinement, and integration of psychic energies (see below), and this symbolism led the Friends of Tararu to devise rituals based around these correspondences. At certain stages of the stūpa building, the trustees performed rituals and *pūjās* with different foci depending on the different phases of construction. For instance, inside the four "inner" stūpa shrines within the concrete base of the stūpa, they installed a colored plaster statue for each of the first four *dhyāni* buddhas and created corresponding "outer" shrines in the grounds around the stūpa. When they completed the stūpa base (earth element), they held a Ratnasambhava *pūjā*, during which they installed a yellow statue in the shrine to the south of the stūpa. They repeated this for each element of the stūpa, and when they installed the spire they placed a red Amitābha Buddha in the western shrine. They held the Amitābha *pūjā* at the summer solstice (in December in the Southern Hemisphere), which ironically, considering that Amitābha is connected with fire, was marked by torrential rain. The ritual for

TABLE 5.1
Stūpa Components with Corresponding Colors and Elements

STŪPA PART	ELEMENT	COLOR
flaming jewel	space	iridescent/rainbow
bowl	air	green
spire	fire	red
cupola	water	white
base	earth	yellow

TABLE 5.2
The Five Buddhas in Relation to Four Key Qualities
(as used in ritual at Sudarshanaloka)

BUDDHA	COLOR	ELEMENT	DIRECTION	TIME
Ratnasambhava	yellow	earth	south	noon
Akṣobhya	deep blue	water	east	dawn
Amitābha	red	fire	west	sunset
Amoghasiddhi	green	air	north	midnight
Vairocana	white	space	center	—

the installation of the fifth buddha, Vairocana, occurred later, during the following winter solstice of 1997, a ritual I discuss in the next chapter.

THE DEDICATION WEEKEND
The stūpa itself was built over a ten-week period during the summer of 1996–1997. The stūpa dedication was held on a warm summer weekend beginning on Friday, 14 February 1997, through to the evening of the 16th. It involved *pūjās* for the first four *dhyāni* buddhas and Vajrasattva (the buddha of purification, who is sometimes represented above the head of the fifth *dhyāni* buddha, Vairocana), a major procession, and a *pūjā* marking the Buddha's Parinirvana, which the FWBO commemorates in February. For the occasion, clusters of colored banners on bamboo poles relating to the five elements and *dhyāni* buddhas (yellow, blue, red, green, and white) were planted at various sites along the private road leading to the stūpa, creating a festive atmosphere.

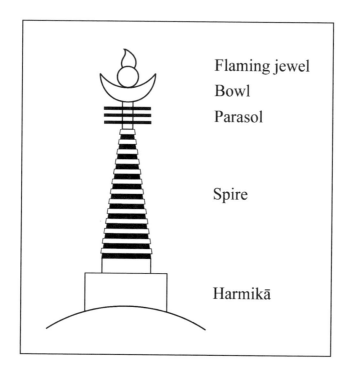

Flaming jewel
Bowl
Parasol

Spire

Harmikā

FIGURE 5.2.
Elaboration of five
elements with
additional compo-
nents (harmikā,
parasol) in stūpa
spire at Sudar-
shanaloka.

The procession that carried Dhardo's relics up the hill for interment in the stūpa was the climax of the weekend. Around one hundred people gathered by Tararu Creek near the gate to the property to receive a briefing on the day's ceremony. Participants were given instructions to chant the Buddhist refrain *"Namo tassa bhagavato arahato sammā sambuddhasa"* (Homage to him, the blessed one, the worthy one, the perfectly enlightened one!). Bearing the blue flags collected from beside the creek, the procession began moving up the hill, and the participants chanted the refrain in unison seven times over, with a single drumbeat between each repetition. At the end of the seventh repetition the musicians in the procession produced a "cacophony of whistles, drums, cymbals and bells" (Kennelly and Gill 1997, 1), followed by a moment of silence. This cacophony and the ensuing pause, the coordinator said, was intended to awaken the mind and sharpen focus, rather than fall into mindless repetition.

When they reached the community house, the procession halted, and Sangharakshita, bearing some of Dhardo Rimpoche's relics in a small ceramic container, came down the steps from the house with his entourage (all Order members: Paramartha, a New Zealander who was personal assistant to Sangharakshita, the

FIGURE 5.3.
Participants in procession photographing Sangharakshita. (Photographed by S. McAra.)

five Australian and New Zealand chairpersons, and Malini, who is the seniormost Order member in New Zealand). Since Sangharakshita was too elderly to walk with the procession up the steep hill, he was to be transported on a seat that had been fixed on the tray of a four-wheel-drive truck (sport utility vehicle). This borrowed vehicle was decorated with colored bunting and ribbons, a canopy improvised out of an Indian-style bedspread, and a Buddhist flag attached to the aerial. Participants' cameras clicked and whirred as they took photographs of Sangharakshita, this being for many newer FWBO members the first time they had seen him in person. As a participant, I had a momentary feeling of disjuncture at this break in the planned ritual, which prompted me to turn and photograph the photographers (fig. 5.3). I felt as if they were behaving more like tourists or fans or recorders of history than performers in a ritual, and this feeling of double consciousness perhaps stemmed from my dual background as a (then undergraduate) anthropology student and participant in a Buddhist ceremony.

The procession continued up the steep hill, resuming the Pāli refrain, with designated flag bearers collecting further colored banners at the selected points "until all five elements were flowing up the valley like a rainbow serpent toward

FIGURE 5.4.
Procession ascending hill to the stūpa. (Photo © Sudarshanaloka Trust.)

the stūpa" (Kennelly and Gill 1997, 1) (fig. 5.4). Prajñalila explained to me that the procession, with its flags, took the energy and elemental symbolism of the land and offered it to the stūpa "so that [it] would *hold* us, . . . anchor[ing] the energy of the land" (2000a). The procession seemed to evoke the Buddhist heartland for some: "The cacophonists took us into a timeless and almost spaceless realm. It could almost have been the hills of Kalimpong or Tibet, except there was no snow" (Malini 1997a, 2).

I went ahead of the procession to videotape its arrival at the stūpa for one of the English Order members. Satyananda's dog, Georgie, came up the hill ahead of the procession, and Malini later linked this to her memory of Dhardo, who, she said, "would probably have been delighted as his own dog was always by his side when I had seen him." Sangharakshita walked up the last stretch of the road before the stūpa, bearing the ashes. He circumambulated clockwise three times, in silence, before placing the relics on the shrine, and the flag bearers then followed suit, chanting the mantra of Śākyamuni Buddha (fig. 5.5)

Participants settled onto the grassy slope facing the stūpa and the view beyond, and, again, many took photographs, while Sangharakshita led a sevenfold

FIGURE 5.5.
During the 1997 dedication ceremony the flag bearers circumambulate the stūpa. (Photo © Sudarshanaloka Trust.)

pūjā and read a poem he had written about Dhardo Rimpoche on the first anniversary of his death. At the high point in the ceremony, Malini climbed a ladder that had been leaned against the stūpa and placed the urn containing Dhardo's relics inside the *harmikā* (fig. 5.6). As reported in two FWBO accounts summing up the intent of the ritual, "The cavity was then sealed and the stūpa thus dedicated, empowered by the enshrinement of Dhardo" (Kennelly and Gill 1997, 1) and "imbuing the valley of Sudarshanaloka with ever greater spiritual significance for all who go there" (Clear Vision 1997).

REFINING THE ENERGY OF LAND AND PEOPLE
Not only did the Friends of Tararu equate the stūpa with the Dhardo's body, but for them its structure represents the enlightened mind through representing the progressive refinement and "increasingly subtle energy" (Sangharakshita 1993, 150). In the form of the stūpa, the five elements are integrated in an enlightened being: "In the course of the evolution of the individual, yin and yang must be harmonized, synthesized" (152), an explanation that would no doubt sound intelligible to many

FIGURE 5.6.
Malini places the relics inside the stūpa; Sangharakshita stands to the left. (Photo © Sudarshanaloka Trust.)

New Age enthusiasts. As qualities of energy, the five elements represent a continuum from a gross to a subtle level. The stūpa helps one to refine and integrate energy; this applies to land as much as to people. The five-element symbolism incorporated in ritual at Sudarshanaloka helped members to reflect on the land itself. "During the stūpa project," Satyananda said, their awareness of the five elements

> brought out an interplay between us and the raw elemental nature of the Tararu environment. We shifted tons of earth, cement and gravel [earth], formed the curve of the cupola [water] or climbed the heights to work on the spire [fire and space] all in the context of Tararu's very strong weather, [including] cyclones, heavy rain, much wind and too few hot fiery days. This certainly gave us a direct experience of the different elemental levels symbolized by the stūpa: levels we had read about many times but now understood through direct experience (1997, 2).

Andrea, a *mitra* living in Thames, reflected on this too.

The five elements are already very much present. Here the rugged red *earth* contains hidden gold; the *water* is ever-present in mist, rain, rushing streams and the sea; there's cold *fire* in the stars and its heat in the hearth and friendship; the *air* is always active from a tickling breeze to a howling gale; and the flaming jewel drop of *space* and consciousness resides within and without everything here (Gill 1997, 2; emphases in original).

Here Andrea and Satyananda refer to the five-element meditation practice, a contemplation that involves applying one's imagination to the ways that the physicality of bodies are the same as the elements of the universe (e.g., the element water is found in our bodies in blood and urine, etc.; the element fire is found in our body heat; the element air sustains our life via our lungs). This practice is intended to give a sense of unity with the cosmos and a feel for the composite and transient nature of what we imagine to be the separate self. A variant of this contemplation, which I once learned on a retreat at Sudarshanaloka, involves visualizing a colored geometric shape for each of five idealized components of the stūpa (fig. 5.1) and equating these with the five elements and related qualities of energy. For the FWBO practitioners, the stūpa becomes the body, helping meditators to integrate and refine their energies in their spiritual practice.

Prajñalila told me "I have a sense of having a stūpa inside of myself since being part of [the stūpa project] over the years, and that really helps me keep my motivation focused" (2000a). When Taranatha was doing the stūpa visualization practice in Spain, Prajñalila told me, he had experienced "the parallel between the nature of limestone and the nature of bone" and felt less "separate." She reflected that if we all "carried that sensibility," we would "make *saner* decisions about the planet." This kind of comment, as well as the talk of integrating energies, evokes for me the way some New Agers, inspired by esoteric approaches to spirituality, talk about cosmic energy, but there is also an aspiration that this kind of practice is not aimed at narcissistic self-development. Here the bodhisattva ideal that the FWBO Buddhists say they attempt to manifest (see chap. 1) is intertwined with New Age and environmentalist discourses.

THE AGENCY OF STŪPAS

Buddhists portray stūpas as mediating spiritual agency because of the powers of the relics they contain. In representing the mind of an enlightened being, the stūpa is a symbol of transformation, pointing to the possibility of enlightenment for all beings. In Buddhist art, the stūpa and the Buddha's body are interchangeable. This is because its form is the "idealized structure of the Buddha's body" (Ray 1994, 326) containing the "spiritual charisma" of the relics within, and it is deemed to affect its environs. The Mahamudra Centre, also on the Coromandel Peninsula, issued an invitation announcing the consecration of their stūpa. The invitation explained the beneficial effects of the stūpa, claiming it "increases the power of prayers" and has a healing effect on both people and the region: "Many locals have commented that it has enhanced the energy in the local area already and therefore [is] beneficial to the wellbeing of the whole planet" (FPMT flyer n.d.). Although less direct in discussing its powers, FWBO members, too, claimed that the stūpa has had a transformative effect on the valley.

Engaging with the stūpa through "mythic truth," Buddhists treat the signifier, the stūpa, as if it were itself the *signified*, enlightenment. Core FWBO members repeatedly stressed to me that they regard or at least *try* to regard the stūpa as a physical embodiment of enlightenment. For example, upon reading an earlier draft of this work, where I was trying to discuss the stūpa's agency in the community, Prajñalila commented that it "symbolically represents the purpose of the move-ment, enlightenment" (2000b). Further, she said that "even if . . . viewed as 17 tons of concrete, [it] has an effect beyond its form." Satyananda (1997, 3) said a stūpa has an effect on people whether they are aware of its symbolic meanings or not and without their necessarily realizing it, and that even before the structure was completed, "its significance as a spiritual focus was having an effect. . . . [I]t reminds us of our priorities" (2).

Stūpas mediate the physical and spiritual levels of existence, providing physi-cal media for metaphysical principles (Kolig 1997, 207). Satyananda says that the stūpa is "myth in architectural form, just as ritual is in gesture or sutras in words" (1997, 3). Analytically, it is problematic to suggest that people who do not share the same meanings and understandings about something will respond to or be af-fected in particular ways by that thing, because it implies that it has an inherent meaning and efficacy, but this is exactly what these members were suggesting.

One Order member told me that there is something in stūpas that "draws me like a magnet," which she thought was universal (rather than because of any Buddhist associations it had for her). She thought it had something to do with the shape, which had a "transcending effect" as it reached up into the sky. Church spires and Islamic minarets could arguably have such meanings, too. In a creative re-interpretation, she speculated that the Auckland Sky Tower (a tourist destina-tion beside a large casino) could be re-imagined as a stūpa spire, even though I have heard other FWBO people refer to the same tower, because of its association with gambling, as a symbol of all that is wrong with society.

Jayaghosa told me that the stūpa is a lightning rod, both metaphorically and pragmatically, because it had to have something that would conduct energy to the earth and was also "something that touches the sky but is well rooted in the ground" (2000b). This was considered to have had a beneficial effect on the energy of the land, as Prajñalila told me.

> It was like putting an energy transmitter [makes a sign of a vertical rod with her hands]. Before that I had often felt the energy of the land running down the ridge and pushing people aside. But once the stūpa was there it seemed to *gather* the energy up and just sort of uplift everything. That was also quite palpable to those of us who'd been involved for a while, and we felt [we] were beginning to *pioneer* a whole new relation to the land. And at that point, many, many more people started coming. They just got really, really engaged and interested in what we were really doing there, even though we had [laughs] . . . only *one* solitary retreat hut, . . . at that point, and a community house still being made habitable for a community and small retreats (1999).

Anthropologically, the stūpa is an "ancestral" object because it contains the essence of one of the FWBO's spiritual ancestors and mediates his spiritual agency. Given that Sangharakshita, the FWBO's founder, dedicated the stūpa and that it contains the relics of one of his principal teachers, the stūpa provides an important link for the FWBO in New Zealand to the lineage of the FWBO. This gives the stūpa a sense of ancestral lineage much like that embodied in Māori meeting houses (see below). After Gell (1998, 256), I suggest that this sense of lineage is both tradition oriented or "retrospective" in that it refers to previous stūpas and deceased teachers, but also future oriented in that it is a model for the human potential to transform. The completed stūpa gave Satyananda a sense of the lineage of Buddhism.

> I sometimes look at the Stūpa and I can feel the strength and depth of practice going right back to the Buddha and stretching into the future. . . . I have gained a lot of confidence from seeing the Stūpa manifest at Tararu. Confidence in my own beliefs and confidence in others. It has given me a sense that the Buddhaland really is possible (1997, 3).

There is an interesting parallel with other built objects that have important roles in group identity construction. Coincidentally, there is a very apt New Zealand example in the Māori meeting house. Roger Neich (1994, 147, citing Jackson 1972) says that the Māori meeting house serves not only as a model of the cosmos, but also expresses group identity and symbolizes the idealized unity of the tribe that associates with it. After the 1870s many tribes used their meeting houses "to define their religious identity, their local and tribal identity, and their identity as Māori *vis à vis* the Pākehā" (148).[9] Such meeting houses were not so much symbols as "vehicles of a collectivity's power" (Thomas 1995, 103) and thus are well suited to the task of projecting collective agency (Gell 1998, 251–252). The meeting house does not simply memorialize the ancestor; it reinstates him or her in the form of the house (253).

The stūpa has a comparable role in Buddhism, modeling the cosmos as well as being a focal point for group religious identity vis à vis others; in the case of Sudarshanaloka this means non-Buddhist locals and other Buddhist groups such as the Mahamudra Centre up the coast. Like the meeting house, the stūpa is "collective" in that people are collected together by it (252). It thereby also acts as a vehicle to project the group's collective agency. Alfred Gell makes the point about meeting houses to argue that "artifacts like Māori meeting houses are not 'symbols' but indexes of agency. In this instance, the agency is collective, ancestral, and essentially political in tone" (252). Gell's argument can apply fairly closely to the stūpa, although my interlocutors will not be convinced by this interpretation, having told me that cultural identity creation is merely incidental to their spiritual intentions. On reading an early draft of this book, Prajñalila disagreed with my analogy between FWBO activities in relation to the stūpa and Māori meeting houses. She thought it problematic to draw parallels between "universal religion of Buddhism and ethnic culture of Māori," referring me to the distinction Sangharakshita makes between "universal" and "ethnic" religions (the latter, this argument says, are concerned only with the welfare of the tribe, while the former are concerned with universal welfare). However, I suggest that from an anthropological point of view a "universal" religion is purely an ideal type. Whatever their religious beliefs, adherents must still interact in the mundane world, and they use the medium of their culture to assist them. Similarly, Prajñalila differed with Gell's idea applied to the stūpa, writing that "[t]he stūpa is the vehicle of enlightenment, empowered by that and influences the collective who makes it accordingly. We gather there to expose ourselves to this. Enlightening"(2000b). She emphatically equated the stūpa with Dhardo and enlightenment. This equation of FWBO interpretations of Buddhist teachings with the universal truth and the ways they set this above so-called ethnic practices is similar to the equally problematic issue that I mention in chapter 1 around the ways many Western Buddhists create a distinction between their own understandings of the Dharma and the practices of Asian Buddhists.

DHARDO'S PRESENCE

After the ceremony dedicating the stūpa, Sangharakshita told Satyananda that the stūpa was now "Dhardo." A series of short pieces in the *Tararu Transformer* clarified for readers the significance of this enshrinement. An Order member named Purna explained that

> [t]he particular importance of the internment [*sic*] of Dhardo's ashes goes far beyond the dedication ceremony. Reginald Ray in his book Buddhist Saints in India [1994, 325] points out that, "The particular importance of the stūpa in the cult of the saints derives from the fact that, once ritually empowered, in an important sense the stūpa was the saint, although now the body was composed of mortar and stones, rather than flesh and blood" (Purna 1997, 3).

Buddhist tradition directly identifies the stūpa with the body of the dead person enshrined within it, but more importantly it also represents the enlightened mind of the Buddha and, by extension, any awakened being. Just as the human body incarnates the enlightened "essence" of a particularly wise and compassionate person, so the dedicated stūpa, as a built body, incarnates that same enlightened "essence" after the passing of the more ephemeral physical form.

Ray Taylor (later ordained as Kuladasa), a *mitra* who lived at Sudarshanaloka in 2000, became progressively more inspired by what the stūpa represented as he learned more about the idea that the stūpa is the body of a Buddha.

> If I was alive 2500 years ago, and the Buddha Gautama was on the hill, alive up there somewhere living up in a cave, how would my life be different to what it is now? And it's an unanswerable question really. For me. But it's very important, it's been an important question for me just to have. And to be aware of. . . . So for me now, the stūpa has come to represent my highest potential. At times I really enjoy going there, and at other times I don't at all [laughing]. And it very much depends on where I'm at in my mind (2000).

Members of the FWBO recount stories about meeting Dhardo Rimpoche when he lived in Kalimpong or talk about the powerful effect he has had on them without even having met him. They tell stories on various occasions connected to the stūpa (such as its subsequent anniversary celebrations), and several members wrote articles for the *Tararu Transformer*. One such account tells of the powerful effects of Dhardo's presence on the land.

> The highlight of my solitary [retreat], and perhaps its very foundation, was my daily pilgrimage to Dhardo's stūpa: climbing the hill . . . and to see this magnificent white form towering into the cold blue sky surrounded by puffy clouds, I immediately saw Dhardo's eyes, then figured I was imagining it and was just seeing the eyes of the Nepalese stūpas. Then I realized again, no, these eyes were slanted like Dhardo's, they were his eyes. I felt the care and compassion pouring out of them, as I had felt from his human form (Malini 1997b, 4).

She continues with a description of meeting him in 1982 and then adds,

> The sun of Dhardo's presence, his kindness, his compassion, his radiance and magnitude, thawed the coldness of my being and transported me into another realm. . . . I felt intense gratitude for having met Dhardo in this life and the fact that here he was with us in New Zealand. . . . I felt a lot of admiration for all the people who had put energy in one way or another to make this possible (4–5).

Thus it seems that the stūpa's connection with Dhardo is indeed compelling for those who share some sense of the kind of person he was or, more specifically, the kind of Dharma ancestor he embodies for the FWBO. The sense they have of him appears to have a more powerful effect than the more abstract concept that the stūpa is the enlightened mind.

Dhardo's relics provide a link between one of Sangharakshita's teachers and the land itself. A section of the *Tararu Transformer* pointed out that Sangharakshita had returned to Britain from India with the endorsement of Dhardo, who is said to have told him that as a Western monk he would be more effective in the West than any non-Western teacher (1997b, 5). This had the effect of sanctioning Sangharakshita's understandings of Buddhist teachings and subsequently provided validation for the activities at Sudarshanaloka. For FWBO members, their founder's authority to teach Buddhism was underwritten by Dhardo Rimpoche's endorsement.

In Erich Kolig's words, the stūpa is a vehicle for "recycling charisma" (1997), and in Alfred Gell's words it is a thing that spreads "personhood . . . around in time and space" beyond a person's biological lifespan (1998, 223). Satyananda explained his understandings of the stūpa as Dhardo in an interview with Anne Reich: "I do feel that . . . the Stūpa has in some sense been perfused with Dhardo Rimpoche's insight and has 'become' Dhardo Rimpoche. . . . I am just trying to learn how to live not only with a stūpa 'in my back yard,' so to speak, but also with Dhardo Rimpoche present" (1997, 2). Thus the stūpa is the *replacement body* of the deceased "ancestral" teacher. Being designed to stand for a thousand years, it is far more long lasting than the body of flesh and blood whose relics are enshrined within, thus prolonging the teacher's agency or effecting "a process of localization or spatial concretization of charisma" (Kolig 1997, 210).

The stūpa is made with everyday industrial materials, but through its symbolism, rituals, and narrative and through the connection that the holy relics inside it make, it becomes sacred, thus also sacralizing the surrounding land. It is an adopted (and adapted) alien object that, in the FWBO members' terms, is a deliberate anti-utilitarian statement. Sangharakshita liked the idea of a stūpa "being solid, a monument having no use. Not being able to use it—even as a temple—you can only worship it" (1993, 160). Indeed, this is a key point for FWBO members, for whom the stūpa marks a transformation from a more "utilitarian" approach typical of their Western cultural conditionings to one more in line with their spiritual ideals. It places the value of the transcendental at the center of the FWBO conception of existence.

Gell suggests that we treat works of art/images/icons (or any "thing" people imbue with ritual or religious significance) as "person-like; that is, sources of, and targets for, social agency. In this context, image-worship has a central place, since nowhere are images more obviously treated as human persons than in the context of worship and ceremonies" (1998, 96). Idolatry,[10] the worship of images, recognizes the "human, non-artifactual, 'other' as a copresent being, endowed with awareness, intentions, and passions akin to our own." FWBO members do not attribute biological life to the stūpa, but nonetheless, in thinking of the stūpa as Dhardo Rimpoche they acknowledge that through the stūpa's presence on the land he has influenced, and continues to influence, them. Although there are differences between Gell's analysis of idolatry and my approach to the stūpa, I concur with him in his emphasis that the idol permits *"real physical interactions . . . [to] take place between persons and divinities"* (135, emphases in original). The idol is an "emanation or manifestation of agency" (96) of the group that built it and the community that identifies with it, of Dhardo, even of the Buddha's life. Buddhists would argue that like the Buddha, the stūpa is not a god, but I suggest that it has

similar sociological effects, being a link to something outside of our ordinary limitations. It embodies, in concrete form, the highest state Buddhists aspire to attain,
enabling the ordinary, conditioned mind to relate to that ideal through a physical
presence.

A stūpa is somewhat like Gell's "ambassador," one who "is a spatio-temporally
detached fragment of his nation, who travels abroad and with whom foreigners can
speak, 'as if' they were speaking to his national government," and the embassy is a
"fictional mini-state" (1998, 98). In the same way, the idol represents the "god" as
a kind of ambassador, and the stūpa is an "ambassador" for enlightenment, visibly
re-presenting an abstract idea. It is the body of a spiritual being in artifact form,
not a depiction of that being.

PACIFYING EFFECTS

There is much literature attesting to the role stūpas play in controlling, pacifying,
or converting local spirits. In Tibetan Buddhist traditions, their power helps to
"suppress malevolent powers" (Mills 2003, 149). They were and are placed with
care in sites determined by ritual specialists such as geomancers and astrologers,
and not merely for the purposes of facilitating the establishment of Buddhism.
There was also the need to influence the spirits that controlled weather, for the
success of crops and so forth. The Tiseru monument, a great stūpa with 108 shrines
built near Leh in Ladakh, was built to subdue four demons that were causing "destructive winds that shriveled the local crops" (150). This apotropaic or "pragmatic orientation" (Samuel 2004, Spiro 1970) continues to motivate the construction of stūpas, with local groups constructing them to protect land (Stutchbury
1994).

Buddhist groups constructing stūpas in New Zealand have followed this practice. For example, Kolig notes that when preparing the ground for their stūpa, the
Tibetan community in Dunedin "pacified and bribed [the local spirits] to enlist
their help as protectors" (Kolig 1997, 212). Prajñalila was aware of the double sense
of either subduing or befriending the spirits by building a stūpa, because she wrote
on an earlier draft of this work that in referring to the need to "pacify" the land,
she did not mean "tame, or colonize, but be in harmony" (Prajñalila 2000b). She
told me that "the building of the stūpa was perhaps one of the most turbulent times
on the land," and with "tempestuous" weather: "In some ways, if you looked at it
in terms of the spirits of the land, it felt like that was the *final* resistance, you know,
to *embed* this object, you know, this strangely *foreign* object, on the land. But when
it came to the dedication, the day dawned clear and bright" (2000a).

When performing rituals, Tibetan Buddhists regard mild weather as a good omen, a sign that the local deity is pleased, while bad weather indicates its displeasure. Although FWBO members tend to take such ideas less literally, they do allude to them from time to time. I suggest that believing that they had appeased and befriended rather than subdued and conquered the spirits might also help to assuage any doubts they might have about the significant alterations they were making to the landscape. To prepare the hillside for the stūpa, a structure that is intended to spiritually benefit the people and environment, the trustees had nonetheless had to disturb that land.

STRANGENESS AND POWER

Recalling the value placed on holy objects in Buddhism, stūpas have been, and are now, important in the ways they embed Buddhism into the soil and channel or pacify local "energy." I suggest that stūpas *are* more than sacred symbols: they are a means of projecting the collective agency of a particular collectivity. As I noted earlier, various Buddhist communities in New Zealand have built stūpas in the last decade or so, and whether intended or not, each stūpa becomes a marker of identity for that community vis à vis other groups (whether Buddhist, Māori, or Pākehā). The Sudarshanaloka stūpa is a site at which members of the FWBO focus their idea of themselves in relation to other groups.

The stated intention in building a stūpa is to proclaim the potential that all human beings have to transform ourselves through "overcoming our limitations" rather than competing overtly with other groups, but there is talk of how this act empowers them in another, more psychospiritual way. Jayaghosa asked rhetorically, "Why spend $50,000 on a lump of concrete? Because it's meaningful to us, and puts down the mythological and spiritual roots" (2000b). As I noted in chapter 3, he invoked the notion of *tūrangawaewae*: "We realized we needed to be standing in our own power. . . . We needed to do something symbolic and concrete to remind us this." Thus the stūpa is a vehicle of the "power" of the *collectivity* that made, empowered, and uses it, mediating their agency, Dhardo's agency, and the FWBO's agency and, in turn, empowering its makers.

If many FWBO members have explored ways of integrating this agentive stūpa into their lives, others are uneasy with or unaware of such concepts. Not all FWBO members relate readily to a concept that remains "foreign" to their own cultural preconceptions. This is particularly noticeable among people who are not involved with Sudarshanaloka's projects. One Auckland *mitra*, for example, told me "the stūpa leaves me cold" and that it "doesn't resonate." He had not studied or had many discussions about it, so it had little meaning for him, and when he first saw it he was disappointed. He had expected something larger but also more integrated with its surroundings, perhaps using local materials such as mud brick, rather than what he called "industrial materials." I suggest that these sentiments are very similar to the views expressed by other liberal countercultural groups that wish to transform contemporary society, including neo-pagans. As Ray told me,

> I've had a reasonably neutral sort of response to the stūpa, when I first came here. But I came here with my ex-partner, we walked up the road, and when we turned around and saw this thing, the first thing he said was "*Why* would anyone build such a thing, in the middle of *this* [landscape]? So out of place! So incongruous! In the middle of the New Zealand bush! This isn't Asia!" [Laughs] . . . And it was an interesting question. And that's always colored my view of the stūpa really.

As a participant, while I often felt the "presence" of the *pūriri* tree, my own subjective feelings about the stūpa have remained mixed. On the one hand, my Western-conditioned self sees the stūpa as "just" a concrete monument, an incongruously "Asian" architectural form oddly juxtaposed with its New Zealand native bush setting. On the other hand, I believe I can appreciate its significance for FWBO members. On a five-day retreat at Sudarshanaloka in 2000 involving meditations on the five-element symbolism of the stūpa, I felt a tentative engagement with the idea expressed in FWBO circles that there was a mythical way to engage with the stūpa, a mythical realm in which a concrete structure had qualities beyond the everyday. This realm seemed to transcend the tensions involved between the encounter of an introduced Buddhism, Pākehā settler society, and myriad other factors needing to be addressed in the creation of a Buddhist sacred place. However, it remained a tentative feeling; I expect that FWBO members would suggest that it would take a longer and more solitary retreat and also that I would have to remove myself from my analytical, academic mode of thinking. The idea of creating an object designed to give inspiration rather than to advance political or commercial objectives does retain a distinct appeal. But at the same time, I still feel there is something out of place about seeing a stūpa on a New Zealand hillside. The original impetus for this book came in part from my desire to explore this strangeness.

A KIWI STŪPA?

Several FWBO members stressed to me that the stūpa is a "purely devotional structure." Yet they do recognize that in practicing Buddhism in New Zealand, there is a need to adapt to and identify with the locale. The feeling that stūpas are culturally incongruous in New Zealand landscapes is a common response among non-Buddhists. A *New Zealand Herald* article notes that when the FWBO Tararu Trust applied for a building permit, the Thames Local Authority had trouble fitting the stūpa into their categories and even (presumably in jest) suggested the term "transmitter." It was finally approved as an "'accessory building for community use'" (Guy 1997, A17). The stūpa was such an alien object, this report suggests, that the building regulations had no concept that could accommodate it. There was a less accommodating response when a Tibetan Buddhist group based in Dunedin applied for resource consent to build a stūpa. Local authorities required that because it was to be situated on a prominent hill, the group should plant native bush around it to obscure it from view, because it is alien to "mainstream aesthetics" and "[its] message is discordant with current (Pākehā) hegemony" (Kolig 1997, 216–217). While seeming to be an alien object for the non-Buddhist locals, the construction of the Sudarshanaloka stūpa drew on the skills of non-Buddhist locals such as tradespeople based in Thames; thus the profile of "the Buddhist center," as the locals refer to it, has become a more familiar part of the local community.

Sudarshanaloka has the effect of making the FWBO in New Zealand more noteworthy to its British counterparts. It has been featured on the FWBO's video *Newsreel* (e.g., Clear Vision 1997); on one of these items, an Order member at the Wellington Buddhist Centre says, on an FWBO *Newsreel* video, that the New Zealand FWBO centers were in an "isolated situation." The antipodean FWBO had functioned for many years as a "stepping stone" for people who eventually moved on to Britain, the "hub" of the movement, so they were always building up the ground but never able to do much more. The stūpa at Sudarshanaloka changed this. As Satyananda told an FWBO group in London,

> I believe what's happening in New Zealand and Australia is important for the movement. . . . It's a different culture, we aren't English, we do things differently, like a number of other parts of the movement. . . . All of these [varied cultural aspects] in the movement are very important, and I think the culture of Australia and New Zealand does have a part to play (1999b).

This speaks to wider concerns about New Zealand's emerging sense of nationhood. Prajñalila told me that the FWBO in New Zealand has "a different environment and social structure. . . . The land itself is helping to determine that for us. . . . We're not *English colonials* any more; we are New Zealanders, in a South Pacific Island, Pacific culture" (1999).

This is demonstrated in the ways that the Sudarshanaloka stūpa in its set-

FIGURE 5.7.
Padmaloka stūpa in highly built environment of Britain. (Photo © Sudarshanaloka Trust.)

ting differs from the stūpa at Padmaloka, the FWBO men's study retreat center in Norfolk, England (fig. 5.7). These two different stūpas are situated in two very different settings. The rugged environment at Sudarshanaloka, especially before the landscaping of the path and retaining walls around the stūpa,[11] contrasts strongly with the controlled brick and tile environment in which the English stūpa stands. Standing in its courtyard, this latter stūpa could lead a non-Buddhist Westerner to believe, at least at first glance, that it was a garden ornament such as a fountain, rather than a religious reliquary and key symbol for Buddhists.

The two stūpas embody the different sociohistorical and geographic contexts in which each is located, giving some indication of the consequent different flavors that one encounters in such varied locations. When compared, they demonstrate the distinct cultural flavors of the FWBO in two respective settings at opposite ends of the globe. The Sudarshanaloka stūpa is in a similar situation to the Dhargyey Buddhist Centre's stūpa among green hills of the Otago Peninsula near Dunedin. This latter edifice, Kolig notes, is well sited in an environment where its "cultural 'nature'" strongly contrasts with its "natural surrounds" (1997, 216). Thus it can broadcast its message "more openly and more keenly" than one in an environment "already filled with cultural edifices." The FWBO/NZ members are working

FIGURE 5.8.
Stūpa cake. (Photo © Sudarshanaloka Trust.)

in quite a different physical setting than their British counterparts, then, and this setting becomes a part of their identity and self-presentation.

The Sudarshanaloka brochure (n.d.) uses several photographs of the stūpa as an emblem of identity. In other ways, too, it has become a symbol of community, quite playfully so when on a festive occasion a stūpa-shaped cake was made and eaten. A photograph shows Sanghadevi, the women's preceptor who had just publicly ordained an Australian woman as Vimokshalehi, cutting into a cake that had the distinctive dome and spire shape of the Sudarshanaloka stūpa and was coated with white icing (fig. 5.8). In making a stūpa-shaped cake they lightheartedly evoked the stūpa as representative of what holds them together. In contrast, at a Tibetan Buddhist center in Australia where I have conducted research, several non-Tibetan members discussed the idea of baking a stūpa-shaped cake before a special occasion but quickly rejected the notion because it would be, they decided, "inauspicious" to cut up even an edible imitation of a stūpa.

Ray told me that he thought the stūpa represented friendship; "it's a mirror of . . . the thing that interconnects us all, really. It's the reason why we're all here. . . . [And also] the Buddha is the reason that we're all here" (2000). As Satyananda said,

[T]he stūpa brought a lot of energy together, I think it made the movement aware of what was going on [in New Zealand]. A lot of the people
who came over to do the stūpa job were from [Britain]. There was a time
there when there were [thirty?] in the community and I was the only New
Zealander. . . . Thirty people is not a lot of people here [in Britain], but over
there it's a huge number, especially when you've been living on your own
for three or four years! And it changed the whole nature of the project. It
made us more public, it made us more aware of the fact that we were involved with other people. 'Cause the stūpa of course now is a very public
thing, I mean people use it as a pilgrimage. Non-Buddhists, non-FWBO
people come too (1999b).

As well as creating a locally distinctive node for the FWBO in New Zealand,
the stūpa at Sudarshanaloka appears to contribute to a sense of international fellowship among the movement. FWBO members who visit New Zealand to maintain links with friends here are likely to visit Sudarshanaloka and see the stūpa.
Robyn, a New Zealand *mitra* who lived in England for several years, told me that
the sangha members there were captivated by the idea of an FWBO-built stūpa
in what to them seemed such a remote place. Drawing people to New Zealand is
not an explicit purpose of the stūpa, but a "by-product and incidental, except the
intention was to provide a means for people to connect to the land and project"
(Prajñalila 2000b).

As I have emphasized in earlier chapters, the ideal of a strong and supportive
sangha is a central one in the FWBO. Building the stūpa and performing devotional activities (including celebrating the stūpa anniversary) helps to recreate this
group by providing a place to strengthen friendships and re-establish a sense of
belonging. Sue Thompson wrote that this was to be "as much a Sangha-building
project as a stūpa-building project" (1996a, 3). Building and maintaining a sense
of connectedness and community is important in a movement that is geographi-
cally dispersed. To Jayaghosa, it was a "collaborative event" and is the "fruition of
spiritual community" (2000a). Satyananda reflected on its importance.

I certainly went through a lot of questions about priorities. Why not build
five solitary huts instead [of the stūpa]? It was quite obvious they were important. In having to take the vision of a stūpa to others and ask for some
of their precious time and money I had to contact my own faith first. It
has given me a much stronger confidence in the Dharma. Also seeing how
wholeheartedly the Sangha responded has given me a lot of joy and trust in

others. I feel that the practice of the Dharma is going deep in our Sangha. I have more confidence in the future of the Dharma in Australasia (1997, 3).

For FWBO members, one purpose of the stūpa is to have "a positive bridge for people of all types to use to meet the Dharma" (Satyananda 1997, 3). The FWBO/NZ had wanted to create a retreat center somewhere out of the city, but Sudarshanaloka has become a larger project, involving creating a Buddhist sacred place in New Zealand. As Satyananda reflects, the stūpa is

> a statement to others both Buddhist and non-Buddhist that the Dharma is here, and putting down roots in Australasia; that we believe that the Dharma has something to offer, through its traditional symbolism, in the west. . . . [With a] solid presence . . . one feels it will be there for a long time—so too, the Dharma (1997, 3).

The stūpa, then, effectively acts like Gupta and Ferguson's idea of a "territorial anchor" (1992, 11) in a world where people feel they have lost a sense of belonging to a place.

IMAGINING AN FWBO COMMUNITY

The iconic potential of the stūpa has led to its form and the stories associated with it being reproduced in various FWBO media. It was the subject of many articles in the *Tararu Transformer*, copies of which reached the British FWBO centers and even attracted visits from members there; other FWBO media such as the Sydney Buddhist Centre's newsletter and the FWBO *Newsreel* video also ran features about the Sudarshanaloka stūpa. An FWBO business that produced a series of greeting cards for sale in the movement's gift and bookstores made a card featuring the Sudarshanaloka stūpa at sunset. Thus stūpa-related activities could be read as media events, creating opportunities for the movement to represent its strengths to itself, thereby reinforcing participants' senses of an "imagined community" of Western Buddhists across the world (cf. Anderson 1991).

In creating Sudarshanaloka, both through narrative and through articulation of the physical world, FWBO/NZ members construct their past as an act of "self-identification" (cf. Friedman 1992, 856). Some key members reported, in hindsight, a change from being overly preoccupied with practical considerations such as the proposed retreat center to a wider vision that encompassed practical aspects but put everything within the context of the mythic dimension. In celebrating the stūpa anniversary weekend each year, they reiterate the centrality of that past in the present. What is distinct about the New Zealand movement is visible in some of the ways members interact with land and, more important, in the ways the environment itself shapes them: their cultural forms, material culture, and practices. But, as Prajñalila says, "the stūpa creates us." In other words, they built the stūpa and it, in turn, shaped (and continues to shape) them as a community.

FWBO members are collectively creating a distinctive worldview and identity in both global and local contexts. The stūpa is as far as it physically could be from the FWBO's "center" in Britain, while the Buddhist heartlands are in some senses culturally remote. Members' shared spiritual ideal of enlightenment gives them a sense of unity with the FWBO sangha in Britain and elsewhere. The stūpa embodies this shared ideal and so "states very clearly in a quite beautiful form that we are Buddhist" (Satyananda 1997, 3). In the FWBO in England, Sandra Bell writes, "[o]ld symbols are rejected or reworked, while new symbols are adopted and put to work to make 'new traditions'" (1996, quoting Giddens 1991). All along, members of the FWBO/NZ have had a "historical consciousness" that they were "pioneering" or inventing a new tradition in New Zealand. The physical work of creating a "sacred place" and specifically of building a stūpa had social consequences, strengthening the sangha that created it in an ongoing, fluid process. The stūpa acts as an anchor for the FWBO/NZ at Sudarshanaloka: while for them this is a spiritual anchor, to refer back to Gupta and Ferguson, it also acts as a territorial anchor.

For Taranatha, the stūpa "brings our energy to the land," but he also says this needs to be "reconciled with the energy that is already there." After the stūpa consecration, then, the trustees decided that there was a need to remove the small Buddha statue that sat beneath the *pūriri* tree, creating in its place a focal point for the spirits of the land. It is on this rite of redress that I focus in the next chapter, which along with the stūpa dedication was one of the key definitive actions in this enactment of a new relationship with the land.

6 Interanimation

Whatever beings are assembled here,
Whether of the Earth or Air,
May you all be happy.
Please listen now to what I say:
Please send your Metta, day and night,
Toward the human race,
On whose behalf we make this offering.
Please give us your protection—We are your friends—
And all you fleshly beings and spirits,
Gather round.
Let us together salute the [Three Jewels]
The Tathagata [Buddha] is honored by gods and men.
May there be peace!
—*Ratana Sutta*, trans. supplied by Taranatha, 2000

Until the stūpa was built, the *pūriri* grove was treated as the spiritual heart of the land and a focal point for rituals. On a damp weekend in June 1997, five months after the dedication of the stūpa, a small group of FWBO/NZ members led by the Friends of Tararu performed a ritual that involved relocating the Buddha statue from the base of the *pūriri* tree to the inside of the stūpa. The aim was to shift the focus away from the grove, "consolidate the spiritual focus" at Sudarshanaloka (*Tararu Transformer* 1997c, 1), and address the mishaps and hindrances that had occurred. The *Tararu Transformer* (1997c, 1) records the story, beginning with "On the full moon of June, also midwinter solstice, a keen bunch bundled against the chill to celebrate the growing of the light in a number of ways." It continues with a direct quote from Taranatha's speech.

> May all spirits of this place hear me. . . . It is nearly four years since we came here. At least some of us felt we were bringing the only true teaching to a wild place with no spiritual presence. I was one of those who came with more pride than sensitivity. Over the years you have made your

presence felt, usually gently and subtly—sometimes vigorously and unmistakably. You have led us to a sense of humility and reverence for you who inhabited this place long before we discovered it. Reverence too for this great tree and the land that it protects.

If through ignorance of your ways, or our own pride, we have offended, we ask your forgiveness. We come in the name of Metta, the love that extends to all beings without discrimination. Here in your place we aspire to develop that love—to know the potential for Enlightenment that lives in every being.

Now, with gratitude for your hospitality, we remove our symbol of Enlightenment and replace it with a shrine that will receive any offering that comes from reverence to Beauty, to Wisdom, to Compassion, in whatever form. We promise to guard this tree and this place and we ask your support and your help in our quest for the perfection of love and understanding. May all beings be happy! (*Tararu Transformer* 1997c, 1)

Ending his speech, Taranatha moved forward to the tree and picked up the statue. *Mitras* Andrea and Paul replaced it with a flattish log for a base and a dark, wedge-shaped stone as a centerpiece. Thus the grove remained a sacred space, but it was redefined as a shrine to the "pagan" spirits. A small procession took the statue the one hundred or so meters to the stūpa, where an Order member named Navachitta clambered through the access way below the eastern side of the stūpa to place the statue inside.

Taranatha addressed "the spirits of this place" in a way reminiscent of the *Ratana Sutta* excerpt quoted at the beginning of this chapter in seeking their help and support. Additionally, he interpreted aspects of the FWBO/NZ's experience of Sudarshanaloka in terms of his personal experience, while also articulating a collective memory of the place's history for those participating in the ritual. Three years later Taranatha reflected on the transformative period triggered by Denis's death.

The trees, the streams, the birds and the rocks and soil gently came alive. As I now see it, the spirits of the land sensed that we were becoming receptive to them and began to speak to us. So we changed from dominating to moving into partnership with the land, to restoring it where it had been ravaged in the past, and to developing our own spiritual places as part of that restoration. So that is Denis's true monument, the growing empathy with the spirits of the land, the whittling away of their mistrust born of their history with mankind and the restoration of their proper place in the Dharma (2000a).

The speech to the spirits was a highly charged moment. The subsequent relocation of the statue inside the stūpa marks the culmination of the critical conjuncture that is the central story of this book. In this chapter I discuss the trustees' intent, highlighted through this ritual of redress, to reconcile the preexisting energies in the land with their own aspirations for it. I revisit ideas I introduced at the outset: first, I illustrate the conjuncture to provide a framework for the stories of transformation that I recount in this book. Second, I return to the notion of transcultural religious bricolage, combining this with the idea that objects (such as the key symbolic landmarks of Sudarshanaloka) have social agency, to demonstrate the ways in which the land was redefined from a damaged ex-farm property to a sacred place for healing.

SOCIAL DRAMA AS REDEFINING PLACE

The ritual I have just described was a moment of what Victor Turner calls "social drama" (1986, 39). Turner is concerned with how social conflicts may mount towards a "crisis of the group's unity and continuity unless rapidly sealed off by redressive public action, consensually undertaken by the group's leaders, elders, or guardians." I would suggest that we understand conflict broadly, to include crises that appear to challenge a group's fundamental values, or other events that cause people to question whether they and their fellows have brought misfortune on themselves through some kind of moral or social transgression. Turner says that this "[r]edressive action is often ritualized" and can lead to a restoration of balance or radical restructuring. Barbara Myerhoff (1978, 32) names various forms of redressive action and identifies "definitional ceremonies," which do not so much rearrange society as make the group's shared understandings "unquestionable by being performed." Turner elaborates, describing these definitional ceremonies as means for a group to create its identity through "telling itself a story about itself" (1986, 40), allowing members to take stock of their situation.

Drawing on these ideas, I interpret the ritual involving the relocation of the Buddha statue as a definitional ceremony in the ways it evoked "the nature and strength of their social ties, the power of their symbols, the effectiveness of their religious traditions, and so forth." But it did more than this, bringing to a close a saga of misfortune, struggle, and uncertainty and formalizing discourses about a transformation in their cultural approach that had been gradually unfolding. In telling themselves a story about themselves, the participants recreated themselves as fundamentally different, in many respects, from the people they were when they embarked on their project.

Here, transformation of the land, as reflected in the new centrality of the completed stūpa, parallels the ideal of transformation of self and society at the heart of FWBO Buddhism. Thus this moment of redress was one that became an agent of social change, reorienting their style of interaction with the place to become more accommodating or inclusive of local spirits. This was a way they saw as being more in line with Buddhist practice, as set by the precedent of Padmasambhava (see chap. 4).

Still, the mythic and historical creations of those who would make or guide memory never fully achieve their object. Memories become collective, but the differences of perspectives and positioning of believers ensure that shared memory is never entirely unitary. Possibly this is more pronounced in a group of people who turned to the Dharma as adult members of a non-Buddhist society and with diverse understandings and knowledge of Buddhism. Those who heard the stories about the spirit presence in the *pūriri* grove, such as those Taranatha told, and were present at the redressive ritual share at least part of that collective memory. Later the *Tararu Transformer* and my own writing conveyed other aspects of the story.

When they shifted the Buddha statue from under the *pūriri* tree to the inside of the stūpa, the intention was to consolidate the role of the stūpa as the spiritual focal point in the land. Sue Thompson wrote in the Auckland Buddhist Centre's newsletter that "[t]he Pūriri grove is once again left to the tūīs and other local inhabitants, as it was before we came to the land, while the stūpa grows and grows as the embodiment of our highest aspirations and as the spiritual heart of Sudarshanaloka" (1997, n.p.).

Whether or not people consider the grove to be a Buddhist space, it is regarded as a sacred space, and the decision to remove the statue from beneath the tree did not mean that Buddhist rituals would no longer be performed there. Sue told me that she was concerned that when the retreat center is built, sounds from the buildings will impinge on the grove's peace, because the buildings will be too close to the *pūriri* grove. "It's a bit like a shrine room, you don't go wandering in there with a cup of tea." This would make it become what she called "a commonplace area, which is antithetical to our intentions" (2000).[1] Nagabodhi felt that conducting Buddhist rituals there was completely appropriate because "you only have to see the pūriri tree grove, to feel that . . . it's a ritual space. It's not just a place for kids to climb on, for people to go for strolls" (2000).

Following Taranatha's speech to the local spirits, the new Buddhist name Sudarshanaloka was formally bestowed on the property, with the unveiling of a small plaque. This had been fixed onto an old *tōtara* fencepost, a "symbol of past attempts to tame the land" (Taranatha 2002, 42), and it marked the edge of the proposed retreat center, only a few meters from the entrance to the *pūriri* grove. If one reads the act of naming as a way of claiming ownership (not something my interlocutors would agree with in this case, since they regard themselves as co-inhabitants with the spirits), then a degree of irony might be read into in their decision to rename the land so close to the place they had, only shortly before, returned to the nature spirits.

The relocation ritual revealed a moment in which the *pūriri* tree and stūpa were somehow separated into representations of a place helping Western Buddhists to "get in touch with their pagan roots" on the one hand and, on the other, a place of transformative power. The differentiation of these two sites, pagan and Buddhist, has created two interrelated loci through which people continue to explore their purposes and relationships with the land.

However, despite this relocation and the intention to leave the *pūriri* "to the tūīs," other *pūjās* have been performed there since the relocation ritual—for example, as part of the stūpa anniversary celebrations each year. At the stūpa anniversary and Parinirvana *pūjā* in 2000, for example, the trustees set up a temporary Buddhist shrine there. As a significant departure from previous *pūjās* in the grove, instead of making the offerings at this shrine under the tree, people walked in procession across the hillside to the stūpa and made offerings there.

The apparent contradiction in continuing to conduct devotional rituals at the *pūriri* tree, despite having separated it ritually from the imposition of Buddhist meanings, is not so pronounced on closer investigation. While there was a practical reason—the grove provides shelter—they had also considered other reasons. Taranatha told me that the spirits seem "less hostile now" and that "they take us in good faith, no bad feeling" (2000c). Indeed, the trustees did not so much relinquish the grove as redefine it in a way more deeply compatible both with Buddhist traditions around nature spirits and with their aspirations to create a place of healing.

A CONJUNCTURE AND IMAGINATIVE LANDMARKS

The *pūriri* tree, the *kauri* log, and the stūpa are located near each other at the heart of the maṇḍala of Sudarshanaloka. They are landmarks in the mundane sense because FWBO members orient themselves at Sudarshanaloka by reference to them, but they also can be understood through thinking about material culture. In writing about trees, Maurice Bloch adapts Lévi-Strauss's often-quoted phrase that animals are good "tools" to think with about society, and indeed any culturally significant object can be "good to think with" in this way (1998, 40). At Sudarshanaloka, the stūpa and the two trees, one living, one dead, are good to think with about transcultural religious bricolage in the Tararu Valley. With these landmarks sangha members can not only think about the inevitable tensions in their interactions with this physical place and its history and about the processes of indigenizing Buddhism at Sudarshanaloka, but can also take action through them.

The three landmarks can be considered key symbols, that is, vehicles for summarizing and elaborating cultural meaning (Ortner 1973, 1339).[2] But they are not simply symbolic, and as Igor Kopytoff (1986, 67) suggests, an approach that considers the biographies of symbolically important objects can elucidate facets that would otherwise remain obscure. This approach, he writes, is particularly useful "in situations of culture contact" because it allows us to follow how people culturally redefine and use things. Both the trees and the stūpa become foils for the ongoing, fluid process of "self-definition" of Sudarshanaloka. All three reference distinct phases in the history of the Tararu Valley, standing for and elaborating three phases of time and three clusters of ideas, which are in a process of interanimation (Basso 1996, 55; see below), that is, mutually animating each other. But they are also what Kent Ryden calls "imaginative landmarks" (1993, 40), superimposed, over time, as an "unseen layer of usage, memory and significance" onto the property. Prior meanings and usage, as well as the physical characteristics of the place itself, play into and impinge upon this invisible landscape.

Figure 6.1 shows the conjuncture that provides a framework for the stories that reference the landmarks. It shows the effects of layers of history and how chains of linked and disparate contexts and events, discussed in chapters 1–4, capped by the FWBO's arrival and members' subsequent experiences on the land, converge in the moment of crisis I discussed in chapter 4. From this, and interwoven out of prior circumstances, comes the creation of a narrative that, at least for a short time, renders oddly juxtaposed events into a coherent story or myth about why a stūpa was necessary (chaps. 5 and 6). Of course, the diagram simplifies the actual situation, as many of the "chains" are intermeshed long before they converge in the conjuncture: for example, the Indic tradition of spiritual questing provided the conditions for the quest of the person now mythologized as the Buddha, and one small offshoot of this chain of causality led to the development of the FWBO, which was brought to the Tararu Valley (table 6.1).

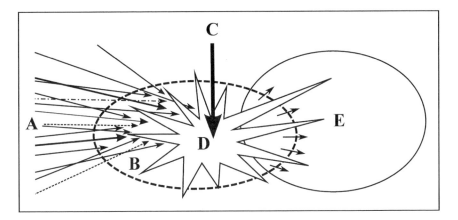

FIGURE 6.1 Conjuncture.
Note: the arrows (A) coming from the left each represent a "chain of causality" coming out of the past into the conjuncture (B) in which the project is taking place. An event (C) occurs that acts in the conjuncture as a catalyst (D). The parts that key actors interpret and integrate as a result of the catalyst become synthesized into what may briefly appear as a coherent whole (E), until new influences alter this.

TABLE 6.1
The Principal "Disparate Factors" in the Conjuncture

SOME KEY ELEMENTS OF THE CONJUNCTURE:

A *New Religious Movement* draws on a *2,500-year-old living tradition* (which itself both drew on and departed radically from earlier traditions) and attempts to *translate/adapt* it to the context of the time/place/people without compromising the essential teachings of the tradition.

The *time* is late modernity with its tendencies of *"globalization"* but also one of trying to work out locally specific identities and relationships in a postcolonial society; there are attempts to resist or transform aspects of this world.

The *place*, a newly acquired "block of land," has *layers of history*:

–a pre-European phase (romanticized);

–a phase of destruction after European arrival;

–the story unfolding into myth and a somewhat utopian vision for the future.

In members' discourses, the "elemental" forces in the land need to be befriended to make the "block of land" into a meaningful "place," a "spiritual home."

The people had backgrounds such as "city folk" and "pioneer farmer," which did not fit with what the land required of them, nor did it fit with their own Buddhist ideals.

THE *PŪRIRI, KAURI,* AND STŪPA

The *kauri* log was a reminder of harmful actions including their own, and, further, Satyananda had speculated that shifting the log to its site near the stūpa was connected to Denis's subsequent death (chap. 4).

Its charred trunk reminds Buddhists, too, of impermanence, which they recognize as central to their teachings. *Pūriri* and *kauri* are very different trees. While *kauri* are tall and straight, *pūriri* have a different kind of presence: more sinuous forms, bulging trunks, with limbs twisting and turning up through the bush toward the light. Their distinctive pale bark gives them a somewhat magical and animated appearance when encountered in the dimness of the forest. As one New Zealand poet writes,

> venerable puriri, / elephant eyed / digging massive / blunt-toed roots / into the dark earth
>
> venerable puriri, / your trunk puckered with anus-like hollows — / an ancient pillar / of earthiness
>
> venerable puriri, / lashed to the forest floor / with rata vines, / fountains of epiphytes / cascade from your branches
>
> venerable puriri, / having tied yourself in knots / to sustain your great weight / you now lean for support / against the sky (von Sturmer 2005).

The *pūriri* at Sudarshanaloka could also be read as representing, in contrast to the *kauri* log, the successful survival of a destructive episode in the valley. Taranatha prefers a more intuitive (and, I would add, Jungian) interpretation, telling me that he regards the *pūriri* as embodying the spirit of the land, while the stūpa represents "the energy we brought with us." For Taranatha, whose name translates as "protected by Tara" (Tara being a bodhisattva of compassion) or "protector of the qualities of Tara," this also means helping the forest goddess[3] by bringing her and other local spirits under the influence of the bodhisattva Green Tara. He also suggests that his response to the *pūriri* went back to the "myth of our own separation" from the placenta, from nature. We have cut ourselves off from our true nature and are trying to regain the feeling of being a part of the whole of existence.

The *kauri* log indexes this alienation from nature and its consequent destruction. Taranatha did not think it had been placed where it lay for symbolic reasons, but when he spoke about it as the "crown of one of the most noble trees of the hills — chopped down, mangled and burnt" (1999b), he was clearly making associations that echoed the critiques he had often voiced about human destruction of forests. The *kauri* log was lucid in its silent testament to the harm people have done to the land and an artifact of a way of life that FWBO members wish to leave behind, or transform. As a dead, unholy relic representing modern humanity's state of alienation that has led to death, desecration, and violation of the land, it was in some respects the conceptual opposite of the holy relics of Dhardo that animate the stūpa.

In a cultural sense, trees evoke complex responses and play diverse roles in human societies (Rival 1998). In New Zealand, their meanings vary widely across cultural and economic boundaries. In Māori tradition, these trees are descendants of the forest god Tane and should be respected and harvested only with due ritual. Economically, native trees are a valuable timber resource if harvested or, in protected areas, important natural capital for tourism. Needless to say, they also have great ecological value for the local and global environment. The *pūriri* tree, with its mysterious beauty, can provide an opportunity to celebrate the distinctiveness of the country's native bush.

For FWBO Buddhists, the stūpa represents human potential for overcoming conventional psychological limitations, drawing people into a future to which they aspire, and something that unifies and integrates. It is a material manifestation of the Buddhist mythic context, a symbol *and* agent of transformation, showing them a model for the integration of the five elements, present in the land, in the self, and in the world in general.

In tables 6.2, 6.3, and 6.4 I summarize some of the myriad meanings associated with each of the three landmarks. The three landmarks also connect the site and the present moment to three differently valued times (table 6.5). This is time sorted by meaning, and each time has its own, sometimes internally contradictory, cultural valences. The *pūriri* represents a remote archaic time, incorporating FWBO understandings of paganism and Māori spirituality;[4] the *kauri* log represents a more recent destructive era; and the stūpa represents the aspirations of Buddhists towards harmony and integration. The *pūriri* embodies the ancient time of pristine wilderness, yet also the raw, harsh aspects of life at the place: the mud, the harsh weather, and so forth. People also began to associate the *pūriri* tree both with a deep pagan past, one they saw as "natural" and harmonious but "pre-conscious" (Taranatha 1999b).

Both the *pūriri* and the *kauri* log represent what Sangharakshita calls the "Lower Evolution" (Subhuti 1994, 76ff; cf. S. Bell 1996, 101),[5] while the stūpa represents the potential for enlightenment, phrased as the "Higher Evolution of the individual." This term refers to a "creative" mode whereby the "self-aware individual can evolve his or her consciousness through many stages to transcendental consciousness and, finally, Enlightened consciousness itself" (Subhuti 1994, 79).

TABLE 6.2
Ideas Associated with *Pūriri* Tree

PŪRIRI TREE

Metaphorically:

-raw (as in "natural" or "elemental")

-"pagan"/"forest goddess," "local spirits"/"energies"

-"tree of life"

-"Bodhi tree"—sacred grove

-Green Tārā (a bodhisattva)

-"origins" of the land

Associated with:

-the bush and New Zealand and global discourses about nature conservation

-placenta tree for Māori?[1]

[1]For Māori the act of burying a placenta (*whenua*) links a baby to its land (also called *whenua*).

TABLE 6.3
Ideas Associated with *Kauri* Log

KAURI LOG

Metaphorically:

-"raw," flayed, damaged

A reminder of:

-unskillful actions: colonization/milling, mining, farming

-impermanence (of tree and of all beings)

Associated with:

-all relics from time of desecration

TABLE 6.4
Ideas Associated with the Sudarshanaloka Stūpa

SUDARSHANALOKA STŪPA

Metaphorically:

–enlightenment, self-transformation

–Dhardo Rimpoche

–cosmic center/axis

–Buddhist spiritual center (focal point of land)

The stūpa acts to:

–refine and integrate the energies in the land and in people

–localize Dhardo's charisma

–galvanize FWBO community and identity

Associated with:

–river mini-stūpas

–prayer flags

–shrine room

–the Buddha's body

–outer shrines of stūpa, five buddhas, five elements, etc.

TABLE 6.5
Time Period/Valence/Spiritual State

OBJECT	TIME	VALENCE	ENERGY
pūriri tree	"pagan" pre-European time	positive/ambivalent	unseparated from nature
kauri log	post-European settlement	negative	–desecration/destruction –alienation from nature
stūpa	–healing the past –universal Dharma –looking to the future	positive	integration of people and place

Keith Basso contends that "[a]s places animate the ideas and feelings of persons who attend to them, these same ideas and feelings animate the places on which attention has been bestowed" (1996, 55). This interanimation is an ongoing, mutual shaping of landscapes and the people who inhabit them. This occurs through the ways that "familiar places are experienced as inherently meaningful, their significance and value being found to reside in (and, it may seem, to emanate from) the form and arrangement of their observable characteristics" (1996, 55).

The interplay between the two "spiritual centers" of the land, one Buddhist and one "pagan," illuminates the inherent tensions in embedding Buddhism in the landscape. Considering the three landmarks together, they retell the trustees' quest to create a place of healing in the Tararu Valley. Each of the three landmarks represents stages in this quest, beginning with the *pūriri* grove embodying the original energy of the land, followed by the period of ignorance and destruction, resulting in the suffering and damage, symbolized by the *kauri* log. The stūpa then becomes a tool for transcending the earlier states while simultaneously integrating them.

REDEFINING PLACE THROUGH BRICOLAGE

I have already described how the FWBO makes self-conscious attempts to create a Western expression of Buddhism. Indeed, my book is a documentation of FWBO localizing strategies in New Zealand. Other FWBO groups take a similar approach: an Irish group revised the English-language parts of the FWBO *pūjā* to replace Indian imagery with self-consciously Gaelic and Celtic elements, and the center based in Mexico City combined Buddhist and Mexican elements for a celebration of the Mexican Day of the Dead festival, placing the traditional colorfully decorated sugar skulls commemorating deceased relations on their Buddhist shrine (Clear Vision 1997). Returning to the notions of bricolage and syncretism, I consider some of the eclectic sources of material objects at Sudarshanaloka and how these are part of an attempt to ritually create a sacred place.

Missionary religions that engaged in the creation of sacred places outside of their place of origin develop strategies to facilitate the establishment of their religion on new ground, including the creation of "elaborate visionary geographies in which the new homeland [has] as much a claim as did the original one" (Granoff and Shinohara 2003, 2). The sacred geographies of the earliest Buddhist sacred sites provide reference points for Buddhism around the world, including places that converts establish such as Sudarshanaloka. Applying the Sanskrit name of Sudarshanaloka creates a linguistic connection between the heartlands of the Buddha and the Tararu Valley.

Rather than recalling a distant homeland in a new and unfamiliar environment, at Sudarshanaloka the trustees re-imagined the *pūriri* as the Bodhi Tree under which the Buddha attained enlightenment, thus bringing the Buddhist homeland into theirs. In a similar act of superimposing Buddhism on the landscape, a rocky peak in the upper regions of the Tararu Valley, visible from various places on the property, was informally named "Vulture Peak,"[6] after the Buddhist sacred site in India where the Buddha was said to have imparted important teachings. This linking of local trees, peaks, and other sites with sacred sites and cosmology results in the creation of a Buddhist maṇḍala, an FWBO sacred geography in a new locale.

This basis of creatively redefining places through bricolage and eclecticism is evident in FWBO material culture at Sudarshanaloka, much as it is in the movement's foundational ideologies. I have already noted how placing a Buddha statue under the *pūriri* tree linked Sudarshanaloka to the all-important Bodhi Tree and that removing the statue recreated the tree both as a pagan enclave in the midst of a Buddhist realm and as a site for beginning to integrate the energies of the place with the ideals the Buddhists brought with them.

There are numerous other acts of redefining and recontextualizing the place, and these often do so in a bricolagic manner, drawing on whatever resources are at hand and using ritual to bring about the transformation. As I noted in chapter 5, the stūpa itself is based on an adapted design resembling Thai and Sinhalese bell-shaped stūpas and incorporating Indo-Tibetan cosmology into the ritual. Other material objects at Sudarshanaloka reflect yet other influences: the early promotional brochure for the retreat center described Hugh Tennent's architectural design as "contemporary, sustainable and site-appropriate with New Zealand and Japanese influences" (Sudarshanaloka n.d.). As mentioned in chapter 5, Tibetan-style prayer flags printed with mantras decorate the stūpa's surrounding space for special events, inspired by some prayer flags seen by an FWBO member traveling in Bhutan. The photograph albums show two kinds of objects associated with the Māori tradition of plaiting with *harakeke* (New Zealand flax). First, three *kete* (baskets) have been placed together to hold offerings of river stones at the stūpa site dedication ritual, referencing the traditional three baskets of knowledge in Māori tradition and the Buddhist *Tipiṭaka* (fig. 6.2). Second, three *putiputi harakeke* (plaited flax flowers) have been placed as offerings on the stūpa shrine (between the framed photograph of Dhardo Rimpoche on the left and the reclining Buddha statue on the right—see fig. 6.3). Another image shows the Amitābha shrine that was placed on the ground to the west of the stūpa. When the photograph was taken, the shrine held an interesting mixture of offerings: a red pool ball, a sheep's

FIGURE 6.2.
Three *kete* placed at center of stūpa site during site-warming ritual. (Photo
© Sudarshanaloka Trust.)

jawbone, beeswax candles, a painted stone, and an origami lotus as offerings to a
small, plaster Buddha (also red) sitting on a stone slab (fig. 6.4). A red ribbon that
had linked the shrine to the stūpa spire during the dedication event was wrapped
loosely around the rock.

A photograph of Satyananda hammering a post into a grassy paddock (not
reproduced here) shows an apparently familiar scene in the rural New Zealand
landscape, but not only does this gray-bearded, gumbooted[7] man have an adopted
Sanskrit name, he is actually putting in a stake to prepare the site for commence-
ment of the stūpa. A tall pole beside him had already acted as the focal point for
rituals to dedicate and prepare the site. Less than two years later, a visitor walking
into the same space encounters a very different place; a few more years pass and

FIGURE 6.3.
Shrine commemorating the Buddha's Parinirvana and Dhardo Rimpoche during stūpa anniversary celebration; "flowers" made from New Zealand Flax as offerings. (Photo © Sudarshanaloka Trust.)

FIGURE 6.4.
Improvised Amitābha shrine incorporating red offerings including a pool ball. (Photo © Sudarshanaloka Trust.)

the ground surrounding the stūpa has been landscaped, completing the transition from farm paddock to stūpa precinct.

Photographs in the Sudarshanaloka albums capture this process of redefinition, a transformation from commonplace things to sacred things. Prajñalila told me that they re-incorporate things into a "mythic" context, a sacred Buddhist place.

> We invented [rituals] as we went. It didn't have to be according to any prescribed format—we made them up. So again that creative response was sort of possible. And . . . there were skulls of old cows, from the pastoral time, and farming implements. . . . [T]he trees themselves, that were still standing, from the forestry, they all became elements in the ritual, or focus for ritual (1999).

Thus people picked out old bones and rusting machinery, displaying them in a way that both reminds viewers of the land's past and redefines them as reminders of

FIGURE 6.5.
Old farm harrow near the shrine room, reinterpreted as *nāgas* (serpent-like spirits).
(Photographed by S. McAra.)

Buddhist teachings. Ray told me that he saw the old farm harrow near the shrine room as *nāga*s, or serpent-like spirits (fig. 6.5). The informal shrine to Padmasambhava made use of animal bones found around the land,[8] evoking the transformation of energies in the land and in people as spiritual practitioners (fig. 6.6). An abandoned car, rusting away in a clearing sometimes used as a parking lot, was painted with green spirals and shapes of vegetation. An animal skull sat atop the car along with some bare branches from nearby scrub. While no one explicitly told me why they did this, for me this evoked the Buddhist teachings about impermanence, with an additional implication of the forces of nature reconquering machinery.

Prayer flags and colorful banners add a sacred dimension; the delicate fabrics printed with prayers against the backdrop of bush-clad hills created, or at least contributed to, the sense of being in a special place. This was something I noticed myself on my first visit to the land, prior to envisaging this research: the sound and sight of the fluttering banners somehow created an aura of something special and different about the place. The proposal to carve the old *kauri* log into a Buddha

FIGURE 6.6.
Informal shrine to Padmasambhava. (Photo © Sudarshanaloka Trust.)

statue continued this pattern of recreating meaning through the redefinition and transformation of things.

APPROPRIATION

All of these borrowed or appropriated objects are media for thinking about and en-acting the indigenization of Buddhism in new places, specifically Sudarshanaloka, New Zealand. The term "appropriation," referring to the processes of making some culturally "other" thing or idea one's own, can have problematic, dualistic conno-tations in postcolonial situations. Cross-cultural appropriation can be a survival and resistance strategy. Most of the anthropological literature on appropriation is concerned either with indigenous people's resistance to oppressive political and economic forces or the ways that dominant groups reinforce oppression of mar-ginalized peoples through appropriation. In anthropology, appropriation tends to have a positive valence when a dominated people accept an imposed religion and make it their own (see, e.g., Comaroff 1985, Wolf 2002). On the other hand, it can imply the arrogance of colonists who steal intellectual and cultural property:

in New Zealand, discussion of appropriation centers around the exploitation of Māori *taonga* (ancestral treasures) in the interests of tourism or a national identity, both transforming them into "airport kitsch" (J. Taylor 1998, 45), modern art, or an emblem of identity. The difference between the two appropriations is largely that the terrain on which it takes place is historically weighted in favor of those from the more powerful and wealthy West. The FWBO provides an instance of appropriation in a very different group: while many members belong to a relatively affluent and politically empowered social milieu, as a subgroup of Western society they challenge many of the assumptions, values, and practices of that material-istic and destructive society. Perhaps, then, these people are like Abu-Lughod's "Halfies" (1991, 137);[9] all are members, to a lesser or greater extent, both of a main-stream "Western" society *and* an alternative, convert Buddhist subculture guided by utopian visions. These two worlds are in some ways contradictory, and Sudar-shanaloka is a site for those contradictions to be explored and, possibly, integrated. I suggest that the FWBO's Buddhist appropriations should be recognized as an en-tangled mixture that itself carries out appropriations of its Others, while it also resists aspects of mainstream society.

Certainly, Sangharakshita's utopianist description of the New Society ex-presses a desire for a fundamentally different society, and members tie personal change to the ideal, envisaged society. In their choice of religion, committed FWBO members voluntarily render themselves as Other to the mainstream by living in single-sex FWBO communities, going on lengthy retreats, and, in some settings, living and working almost entirely within the FWBO social milieu (S. Bell 1996, 103). On the other hand, all maintain membership in some wider social networks, not being separated completely from the non-FWBO world.[10]

CREATING A NEW WORLD

In their often conscious efforts to create a Western form of Buddhism, members are agentive social actors. Just as Barbara Myerhoff (1978) wrote of a marginal community of old immigrant Jews from Eastern Europe, FWBO members display and perform their interpretations of themselves and in some respects become what they claim to be (Myerhoff 1986, 263). While the marginality of the FWBO is substantially different, not least in the degree of volition to members' apartness, there are parallels in the ways that performance and display of self and commu-nity create the body they seek to become. In adopting such a minority religion, they, too, have called upon "ingenuity, imagination and boldness" to enact their Buddhist context. To quote a particularly apposite passage from Myerhoff,

> The culture they had invented . . . was bricolage in the best sense—an assortment of symbols, customs, memories, and rituals, blending in a highly ecumenical spirit. . . . They knew that improvisation and invention were essential, but like all people they also needed to convince themselves that these solutions were proper, authentic, believable, and occasionally traditional (1986, 264).

The project of making an unfamiliar place into one that feels like home is important for many new immigrants, who attempt to make unfamiliar places resemble homelands through imaginative work. Karen Leonard describes how Japanese and Punjabi immigrants to California compared the landscape of their new home to that of their homelands and in doing so emphasized the few resemblances. This seeking out of such imagined parallels in the land helped them to shape their collective identities and ground them in the new country (1997, 118). Converts to a foreign religion who remain in their own homeland also undertake such imaginative exercises, but with an interesting twist. The creation of an antipodean Buddhist spiritual home at Sudarshanaloka is one such instance because they are cultivating a sense of connectedness and belonging to the locale, but rather than making an unfamiliar place resemble home, they are making a familiar place (albeit one with an uncanny atmosphere) exotic.

CREATING THE BEAUTIFUL VISION

Despite being shaped and sometimes constrained by their cultural origins, people have agency—in other words, they are actively involved in reshaping their cultural worlds. Culture is produced, invented, and revised through both conscious and unconscious human action, with invented tradition based on reifications of cultural practices or, sometimes, more conscious ideological manipulation or invention (Hobsbawm 1983). But culture is also a creative force, both shaping and being shaped by action (Nagel 1996, 72). It is a dynamic stream of being and becoming that is continually, creatively reshaped and renegotiated by its constituents and inseparable from them. All cultures are constructions that take elements from diverse sources and historical eras, combining images, words, and materials. They are created out of both life experience and the re-imaginings we all engage in.

At Sudarshanaloka, the trustees built a concrete structure, empowered it through relics, ritual, and stories, and called it a stūpa. This was another episode in the unfolding "Myth of Sudarshanaloka," the spiritual context in which they place their project. At Sudarshanaloka they have "[made] up an invisible world, watch[ed] themselves make it up and still believe in it so strongly that they can enter it" (Lansing n.d., apropos Bali, quoted in Myerhoff 1986, 284).[11] In this world they encountered unexpected forces, such as the nature spirits in the *pūriri* grove.

The ways that I have written about the critical conjuncture around which this myth centers risks freezing these stories in time, but time has already shown that the stories about Sudarshanaloka continue to arise, pass, and evolve. In the next chapter, then, I discuss some of what came to pass in the decade after the stūpa dedication and consider how this ethnography contributes to the notion of transculturality—in particular, a transcultural religious bricolage.

7   "Re-visioning" Place

I was staying at Sudarshanaloka for research in February 2000 when Taranatha, a visiting Dutch couple, and Satyananda decided to drive up to the stūpa after dinner to watch the sunset. I walked up the hill with Satyananda's dog and joined them standing on the scrubby piece of land where the retreat center was later to be built. The evening air was clear and still, with morepork calls sounding from time to time. Taranatha and Satyananda were chatting amicably as we watched the changing colors in the sky over the Firth of Thames. They reflected on the six years since they had first stood at the place they had designated as the retreat center site and speculated about what it might be like to stand in this very spot after the buildings are finished, saying they wanted to keep the view.

Then we turned around to look at the stūpa. The warm afterglow of the sunset stained the west side, while the east side was bathed in a cold, bluish light. One of the bronze rings in the spire was catching a radiant white light from the full moon rising above the high bush-clad hills at the top of the valley. From where we stood, though, we could not see the moon—it seemed instead as if the light shone from within the spire. During the day, the stūpa can look stark against the rugged surroundings, but at this moment it was beautiful, melting into the shifting colors of the dusk.

I began this book by raising a question about the stūpa. Given the characterization of the FWBO as resembling certain key aspects of Protestantism (Mellor 1991), why would they want to build a stūpa at Sudarshanaloka? Why did they change their priorities, since from the outset they intended to construct a purpose-built retreat center? In an ensuing chapter I raised the related question: given that the FWBO, in its own literature, proclaims itself a movement that seeks to jettison "cultural baggage" and return to the essence of Buddhism, how did they come to perform a ritual aimed at appeasing the local spirits?

After the crisis point I discussed in chapter 4, the trustees and Friends of Tararu began to articulate the notion that the project of building a retreat center needed to be preceded by the establishment of a harmonious relationship with existing conditions on the land. Denis's death and Vessantara's encounter with the local spirits highlighted the need to integrate the trustees' plans with the locale. The increased use of ritual, highlighted by the construction of the stūpa and relocation of the Buddha statue, provided an opportunity to bring their Buddhist ideals together with what they deemed to be the existing needs of the locale. Prajñalila said that it was as if "having *dared* to do such a spiritually significant thing on this piece of land, . . . and completed it despite all the set-backs that you could imagine," the "energy" of the place had indeed changed. In this book I have followed my interlocutors' stories about transforming and healing a damaged place, embarking on ritual activities and creating visual reminders of their transcendental ideals. All of this has become part of a process of linking meanings to things and place in order to rework them. The *pūriri* tree, *kauri* log, and stūpa all played a big part in this project of transformation.

REDEFINING THE LAND

The FWBO is a doubly or triply foreign arrival in the Tararu Valley. First, the ideologies of Buddhism carry material cultures and practices that are visibly different from either the Anglo-European or Māori strands of identity in New Zealand. Second, the forms of Buddhism practiced and taught in the FWBO entail a British Buddhist phenomenon taking hold in a small, countercultural sector of New Zealand society. Third, Pākehā New Zealanders, including those adopting Buddhism as their religion of choice, lack indigenous status in New Zealand, despite stories about being shaped by the land. Their interactions with the land and their discourses about those interactions seem to me to be a way of transforming a place with an uncomfortable and unsettling past into their own "land of beautiful vision."

This transformation was not all one way, however. The very material fabric of the valley, with its torrential downpours and flash floods, its 150-year history of destruction, and its key symbolic landmarks, have all been active players in the story of Sudarshanaloka. The valley's Buddhist trustees and the land have shaped one another in a process of interanimation, and this is something that FWBO/NZ members occasionally reflect on. At an Arts Day event at Sudarshanaloka in February 2000, Jayaghosa read an excerpt to a small FWBO audience from a classic allegorical story, *The Little Prince* (Saint-Exupéry 1944). The excerpt he read was the one where the fox "tames" the Little Prince, and after reading it he said of the project at Sudarshanaloka, "We set out to tame the land, but the land has actually tamed us."

The trustees and Friends of Tararu created, through a process of ritual and stories, two differently nuanced sites of meaning on the land: a sacred grove, home to the local spirits, and a Buddhist stūpa, a spiritual center proclaiming the universal Dharma. Their early placement of a Buddha statue beneath the pūriri tree created a place that referenced the sacred groves of ancient India. Later it was again redefined as a pagan grove dedicated to acknowledging the spirit energies or unseen forces inhabiting the land long before the Buddhists' arrival; once they had made this accommodation they then felt comfortable performing Buddhist rituals there.

The trustees' redefinition of the place is influenced by stories of nature spirits that Māori, Buddhists, and neo-pagans recognize, each in distinctive but sometimes overlapping ways. At the same time, however, the new relationships that these Buddhists build with these objects help them to reconcile their New Zealand (specifically Pākehā settler, and more generally Western) cultural backgrounds with Buddhism, transforming their collective enterprise into an increasingly Westernized and localized New Zealand expression of Buddhism.

The expression "transcultural religious bricolage" summarizes my discussion of how they undertook the work of redefining the property, converting it from a block of land saturated with a history of destruction into a Buddhist sacred place. They undertook to do this in a bricolagic fashion, combining a wide range of ideas and things and held together by their ideals. The stūpa, itself designed and dedicated in the manner of bricolage, played the most important role in "buddhifying" the landscape. The pūriri grove was more a difficult place to redefine and became the site for a ritual of redress. In the years following the stūpa dedication, the need to shift focus to fund-raising for the retreat center has led to what some people refer to as a "pragmatic" approach, although this time with a stronger intention to retain contact with the overall vision of Sudarshanaloka. Around 2000, the FWBO internationally and at Sudarshanaloka entered a time of "re-visioning" (a term Prajñalila used), that is, revisiting the basis of earlier decisions and reconsidering their goals and visions. Prajñalila reflected that at Sudarshanaloka they had become more conscious about what is involved in building a sangha and constructing the retreat center and had become closer to the land. What she was calling re-visioning was nonetheless contiguous with the idea of the centrality of the mythic dimension of Sudarshanaloka, with worldly matters like financial support still in the background.

A FLOOD

In January 2002 a flood that a government geologist described as a once-in-a-thousand-years event unleashed a "cataclysmic onslaught" on the valley (*Sudarshanaloka Newsletter* 2002, 4). Heavy rainfall in the large catchment area in the hills above turned the Tararu Creek into a raging torrent, scouring out the creek bed and completely wiping out a small creekside glade on the property where two caravans had stood as temporary accommodation. Throughout the valley, the torrent gouged massive chunks out of its banks, causing landslides that cut up the shingle road winding up the valley. The flood took with it a NZ$30,000 bridge that the FWBO members had installed across the creek only three years prior, leaving only broken concrete slabs and twisted metal girders. Many of those who had put so much of their energy and hopes into the place found this financially and emotionally draining. Ratnaketu recounts the flood and its aftermath by referring to the spirits that, in his interpretation of Indic mythology, control the elements.

> The Tararu Valley reminds me strongly of the Himalayan foothills that I recently visited in the Northeast of India. . . . Of course it's all on a different scale. Yet at Sudarshanaloka one finds the same Himalayan stillness, the same silence and solitude, the same atmosphere of awesome natural and supernatural forces. Wandering through Sudarshanaloka, as in Sikkim, one may chance upon some animistic shrine to local god or fairie or catch the murmur of mantra adrift in the trees. It's true, the Waihou and the Piako [Rivers] match not the Ganges or Brahmaputra, nor the Firth of Thames the Bay of Bengal, but mock not the Tararu dear friend—a nāga swims there that the Teesta [a tributary to the Brahmaputra running through Sikkim] would be proud to harbor. Twice this year our little creek flexed her muscles, twice reminded us that water rules rock. . . . In Indian mythology the great elements earth, water, fire, air and space are called bhūtas: spirits, whose material existence is the visible form of their more essential, living, nature. . . .
>
> Still it's an ill nāga that brings no good and, along with the reminder of impermanence, down in the stream, among the debris, the bhūta has deposited semi-precious stones quartz, jasper, iron pyrites, peacock ore and some say even gold and silver, so that as one walks along the riverbed a sparkling stream of stars bewitches the eye. Three huge rimu logs have been salvaged—perhaps they will be used on the retreat centre shrine. If so the beautiful colors of rimu and the sparkles of the stream will long remind us of 2002, long remind us of the power of nature and of the nāga that lies slumbering amongst the gold in Tararu's freshly made bed (Sudarshanaloka Newsletter 2002, 4, orthography lightly edited).

I take Ratnaketu's interpretation to be a cheerfully (rather than solemnly) poetic one and find no indication in his or others' accounts of the flood that it was a response by the spirits of the land specifically to the *Buddhists'* presence in the valley. This is a significant change from the stories recounted earlier, a change that suggests to me that their work of redefining and recontextualizing their relationship with the energies of the land had, in their estimation, succeeded.

Despite the loss of the bridge intended to provide all-weather access to the land, the trustees continued their plan to raise funds for the retreat center. From 2002 until 2006, there were two distinct periods of fund-raising,[1] and in early 2006 the target for the first of the three planned stages for the retreat center was reached. By April 2006, as I finish writing this account, the first stage of the construction is nearing completion. Jess, a volunteer who came from England after hearing about Sudarshanaloka, writes of her experience helping with the construction of the first stage.

> Early on, Kevin [another volunteer] put up prayer banners, and they seemed to proclaim that something of great importance was happening here. Soon after that, the beautiful rupa [Buddha statue] appeared, which has sat in our tea tent, calmly watching over us with a gentle smile. It has been important for the Buddhists on the team to keep in mind what we were building.
>
> To this end, when weather allowed we joined with others in the Sudarshanaloka community to hold evening pūjā at the site—they were magical. One in particular stands out: it was a calm, cold night at full moon. I remember looking up from the shrine, seeing the palms and ponga trees, silver in the moonlight, and such an exotic sight for me, and thinking "Pūjā out in the wild bush—not everyone gets to do this—it's a precious gift" (Sudarshanaloka Newsletter 2006).

The intention to imbue their work with ritual is being carried out: one Order member is helping to create specific rituals around the building project, and Satyananda has worked with the building team to ensure they have grounding in Sudarshanaloka's founding stories. There was, however, an interesting twist in one of these stories—that of the *kauri* log.

THE FATE OF THE *KAURI* LOG

Given the symbolic importance I have shown to be linked to landmarks such as the *kauri* log at Sudarshanaloka, one might expect that the aesthetic, financial, and utilitarian value attributed to *kauri* wood in wider New Zealand society was of less importance than the symbolic meanings with which the old *kauri* log had become imbued. Nonetheless, the question of the possible uses of the log arose again over the years. From the time it was first located and shifted, some members discussed the possibility of making use of its wood. Ajitasena, a Scots Order member and woodcarver who visited Sudarshanaloka in 1997, saw in the log a Buddha figure that he said he would like to "release" on a subsequent visit. The idea of carving it into a reminder of the human potential for spiritual awakening appealed to the concept of transforming the past destruction it indexed.

As it turned out, however, the log was destined for a significantly different use. Returning to Sudarshanaloka in 2003 after a year of absence, I was somewhat surprised to learn that the log had been sawn up into slabs, with only a few pieces left at the site where it had stood for some years, now shrouded under a tarpaulin. Some pieces were used to construct the shrine in the Thames Buddhist Centre; some were used for the counter of their shop, Lotus Realm; and other parts were turned into bowls and sold. Satyananda (2004) told me that some of the proceeds from the bowls went to the retreat center and some to the woodworkers.

I asked some FWBO people who had been involved with Sudarshanaloka about their responses to the log's fate. Sue Thompson expressed disappointment that the log had not been left there, saying she felt that my early research findings (McAra 2000) demonstrated the log's symbolic importance. Because he had also been involved with Sudarshanaloka, I e-mailed Michael Attwood (now Jayarava) in England to ask him if he had heard about the log being sawn up. He replied, "I hadn't heard this. It does surprise me a little. I hadn't heard of the idea of making a rupa out of it [either], but I had thought that it was going to be left alone as it had some 'spiritual' value—of an animistic sort I suppose. I guess some pragmatism has crept into the place" (2004b). Later he recalled, "[P]ersonally I would have cut it up right at the start, but there was a lot of talk about not doing that because it was special" (2004c). Prajñalila told me the initial moving of the log had been "unsettling" and that "we were deeply affected by the spirit" (2004), that is, it had powerful symbolic meanings for them, especially after Denis's death. While she thought that dispersing it into pieces did dilute its meaning, she noted that parts of it were used, or earmarked to be used, for Buddhist shrines. She also observed that one could not expect things to hold the same degree of significance over time, that the present era is a more pragmatic one. While reiterating that the place does have a strong effect on people, she also averred that she was happy for the meanings in things to be "rewritten—because the spirit is separate from the forms things take." She also reflected that in rewriting the meanings something can also be lost, and meanings can be degraded if the magic does not get transferred to something else.

What is interesting here is how they reconciled the dismantling of the log with the aspirations that motivated them in their wider project. The log had acquired a great deal of significance over time, and from that perspective dismantling it was the destruction of what for many had been an important memorial to the more dominating approach to the land taken in the past—the very approach that the trustees had talked so earnestly about transforming. But Satyananda told me that it had always been their intention to make use of the wood, and Prajñalila explained to me (2006) that the rituals they had performed "to heal and affirm an empathetic relation with the land" had transformed the log. Early on, she said, the log gave her the impression that "it would have kicked back" if they had touched it. The ritual had been necessary and "released" the wood for pragmatic purposes. Thus the decision to cut the log up may not have been simply a utilitarian turn but, depending on the spirit and awareness with which it was done, could have been in keeping with the ritual and mythic context. The fact that some of the wood has been used in the shrine of the Thames Buddhist Centre and several slabs are in storage for a similar purpose in the new retreat center suggests a continuity with the ways that they had engaged in a process of mythically and ritually healing the energy of "hurt" that they felt was present in the land.

REWEAVING THE VISION

Like the stories of spirits on the land, the stories about Sudarshanaloka continue to be rewoven, retold, and re-visioned. In making a Buddhist sacred place in the Tararu Valley, New Zealand, through talking about healing the land and through their engagement with such diverse material sources, the trustees and others who maintain a connection with Sudarshanaloka are both fashioning a new sense of themselves in line with their aspirations and redefining the place itself. Their stories are not fixed, as Prajñalila says.

> All exists in flux. Like a co-invention. As I appreciate more deeply what it means, I re-tell my "story," which is selectively understood by another depending on their views and experiences, disposition and inclination. And they adopt or not "their story" as a result. The story seems to be composed of fluid, a synthesis of these stories at any point in time—and out of time, too (2000b).

My own act of wrestling with ideas, images, and some of the stories of FWBO sangha members has helped me to make a "story" for myself, which I imagine that, being written, will feed back into the stories of those FWBO members who read this volume. My intention has been to outline the means by which a Buddhist group has redefined a place in ways that are more meaningful for them. Their stories are a way for the land and the people to interanimate one another (Basso 1996). I hope to have imbued my own version of these stories with something of a sense of the shifting and mutually animating characteristics these meanings have, rather than fixing them in concrete; thus I finish by imagining how even the most concrete of structures at Sudarshanaloka, the stūpa, can seem to be "composed of fluid."

After participating in a fund-raising concert in Thames in 2000, Sue Thompson and I stayed the night at Sudarshanaloka. To make the most of the short visit, I wanted to walk to the stūpa. It was around midnight when three of us left the house. It was a very still, peaceful night, and again the moon was full. We walked up the hill, drinking in the clear night air as we passed through groves of bush where the eerie light of glowworms lined the road. When we stood before the stūpa, the moon was directly above the spire, whose shadow fell onto the cupola. The three Perspex rings and bowl mounted on the pole near the top of the spire have hollow centers, and the moonlight passed right through this gap so that every detail of the spire was silhouetted on the cupola, reminding me of what Ray Taylor had told me.

When the moon's out, the stūpa . . . becomes a very different mirror for me. A very fluid, flowing, sort of mirror, and in glaring sunlight, it's quite a solid. . . . It takes on very different shapes, and different textures and forms. It's almost like it's living, really. It's like, especially on the full moon, it's so fluid that you could actually put your hand right through it (2000).

Appendix 1. FWBO Figures

Table A1 shows the listed place of residence for Western Buddhist Order members in thirteen countries compiled from the Order register for FWBO News and posted on the FWBO Web log (Jayarava 2006).

TABLE A1
Number of Western Buddhist Order Members and Country of Residence

COUNTRY	WESTERN BUDDHIST ORDER MEMBERS
United Kingdom	742
India	294
New Zealand	50
United States	48
Australia	36
Germany	31
Spain	29
Finland	15
Ireland	14
Sweden	14
Netherlands	13
Mexico	7
France	5
Total	1,298

Note: In addition to these figures, the following countries each have five or fewer Order members: Canada, Belgium, Italy, Estonia, Venezuela, Brazil, China (PRC), Nepal, Norway, Portugal, South Africa, Sri Lanka, Turkey (Jayarava 2006).

Appendix 2. The Five Precepts

This FWBO interpretation of the Five Precepts comes from the movement's Web site (FWBO 2005a).

1. Not killing or causing harm to other living beings. This is the fundamental ethical principle for Buddhism, and all the other precepts are elaborations of this. The precept implies acting non-violently wherever possible, and many Buddhists are vegetarian for this reason. The positive counterpart of this precept is love.
2. Not taking the not-given. Stealing is an obvious way in which one can harm others. One can also take advantage of people, exploit them, or manipulate them—all these can be seen as ways of taking the not-given. The positive counterpart of this precept is generosity.
3. Avoiding sexual misconduct. This precept has been interpreted in many ways over time, but essentially it means not causing harm to oneself or others in the area of sexual activity. The positive counterpart of this precept is contentment.
4. Avoiding false speech. Speech is the crucial element in our relations with others, and yet language is a slippery medium, and we often deceive ourselves or others without even realizing that this is what we are doing. Truthfulness, the positive counterpart of this precept, is therefore essential in an ethical life. But truthfulness is not enough, and in another list of precepts (the ten precepts or the ten kusala dharmas) no fewer than four speech precepts are mentioned, the others enjoining that our speech should be kindly, helpful, and harmonious.
5. Abstaining from drink and drugs that cloud the mind. The positive counterpart of this precept is mindfulness, or awareness. Mindfulness is a fundamental quality to be developed [on] the Buddha's path, and experience shows that taking intoxicating drink or drugs tends to run directly counter to this.

Notes

Introduction

1. Although some people in the Buddhist organization I am studying dislike the word "convert," I use it in a sociological sense to refer to people practicing a religion they adopted by choice; indeed, it has been widely used for discussing the Dalit conversion from Hinduism to Buddhism.

2. Although they owned the property for almost four years before adopting this name, for simplicity I use the name Sudarshanaloka throughout this book, except when quotations refer to "Tararu." Similarly, I use the Buddhist names of people who have become Order members and have thus taken Buddhist names before or during the time period I am discussing (up until 2000). With those who were ordained after 2000, I have retained their former name (e.g., Sue Thompson/Akasamati). To assist readers who find the Sanskrit and Pāli names of Western Buddhist Order (WBO) members difficult to follow, I include the names of key Order members from the book in the glossary.

3. There is no formal membership of the FWBO in that people can choose the manner of their association with the movement and do not sign up as formal members or pay membership fees. However, I use the term "member" in its sociological sense, as a way of referring to members of a group, as opposed to signed-up members of a club. Occasionally I use expressions such as "the FWBO represents itself as x." This is not intended to turn the organization or network into an entity with its own agency; rather, it is to avoid repeatedly spelling out such expressions as "key members of the FWBO represent the movement as x."

4. Pratt (1992) and others borrow the term "transculturation" from Cuban lawyer and public intellectual Fernando Ortiz.

5. Like most anthropologists, I use the term without the pejorative layer of meaning that a French speaker tells me the term *bricoleur* suggests.

6. Most anthropological studies of Buddhism have focused on small-scale community or nation-state settings in Buddhism's heartland areas. Such studies include Buddhism in Burma (Spiro 1970), Sri Lanka (e.g., Bartholomeusz 1994, Bond 1988, Carrithers 1983, Gombrich 1971), Thailand (Tambiah 1970), and Nepal (Ortner 1989). J. L. Taylor (1993) considers the relationship between "forest monks" and the nation-state in Thailand; Malalgoda (1976), Gombrich and Obeyesekere (1988), and Seneviratne (1999) discuss religious change in Sri Lanka, where Buddhism is a state religion. As Gellner (1990) notes, most anthropological literature on Buddhism focuses on Theravāda Buddhism as found in Sri

Lanka, Burma, Thailand, Laos, and Cambodia; his book addresses Mahāyāna Buddhism in an attempt to redress this imbalance, while Samuel (1993) focuses on Tibetan Buddhism.

7.   Chandler (2004) writes about modernization and globalization in the Foguangshan, an international Chinese Buddhist institution, and Covell (2005) discusses contemporary Japanese Temple Buddhism and its adaptations to modernity. With regard to studies of convert Buddhist movements, Kay (1997) compares the New Kadampa Tradition (Tibetan-based) and the Order of Buddhist Contemplatives (Zen-based) in Britain; Cadge (2005) compares immigrant and convert practitioners of Theravāda Buddhism; Rocha (2006) investigates the creolization of beliefs among Zen Buddhists of different backgrounds (Japanese Brazilians and upper middle-class Brazilians) in Brazil; and P. Moran (2004) explores the encounters of Western and Tibetan Buddhists in Kathmandu. The internationality of forms of Buddhism previously associated with a particular nation is a theme in Cate's (2003) study of the artwork in a Thai Buddhist temple completed in Wimbledon, England, in 1992.

8.   The guidelines for ethical research at The University of Auckland require fully informed consent from all research participants. In observing these requirements, I gave participant information sheets and consent forms to those I formally interviewed and ensured that the information about my research was also made available to the FWBO in the Auckland Buddhist Centre newsletter, *Kantaka*, and through a poster and personal communications with people at Sudarshanaloka. In circumstances in which I felt it was inappropriate or impractical to ask people to sign consent forms, I explained the research verbally. When the possibility of publishing the research arose I ensured that the key interlocutors were made aware of this and given an opportunity to comment. I explained the book manuscript to the Sudarshanaloka management committee in June 2005, and it met with unanimous approval.

9.   The word "Western" also runs into problems in that similar interpretations arise in places not conventionally considered "Western"—e.g., are "cosmopolitans" practicing Zen in places like Brazil (Rocha 2006) to be considered Western? Baumann and Prebish address this by defining it broadly, with reference to "non-Asian industrialized nation-states where Buddhist teachings, practices, people, and ideas have become established" (2002, 5).

10. Fields chooses the term "white Buddhist" because missionary Buddhism in the United States is largely white and middle class, itself problematic because it excludes many other ethnic groups, from African Americans to Hispanics. Alternative adjectives such as "convert," "elite," and "reformist" all have their particular complications.

1. A New Tradition

1.   In New Zealand, as well as in many other Western nations, Buddhist temples have acted as focal points for such communities. The linguistic and cultural difference from the host society results in what Fields (1998) refers to as "divided Dharma," where converts to Buddhism rarely mix with those born into the religion.

2.   There are at least two FWBO centers in Latin America (one in Mexico City, the other in Mérida, Venezuela), and Western Buddhist Order members are working more informally

in other parts of the world. I exclude the Indian wing of the FWBO from my discussion, since its history and trajectory diverges in many ways from the FWBO and would thus require a separate in-depth analysis.

3. I am aware that general discourse in the FWBO emphasizes that there is no formal membership in terms of people paying fees. I use the term "members" not in that sense, but in the neutral, sociological sense of members to mean people associated with a society or group.

4. For an introductory account of Buddhist thought and core teachings, see (inter alia) *Buddhist Thought* (Williams and Tribe 2000).

5. Ambedkar was the first politician in India to have come from the Dalit community, and he led the commission that drafted India's constitution (Subhuti 1994, 21). He publicly converted to Buddhism in 1956, along with around 400,000 followers, having concluded it was the best way out of the oppression of the Hindu caste system. Dalits have continued converting en masse, and the FWBO/TBMSG is one of several international Buddhist organizations participating in this phenomenon.

6. Right Livelihood is one of the eight aspects of the "Noble Eightfold Path." Baumann (2000) explores the FWBO's attempts to create an alternative, ethics-based economic system through what they refer to as Team-Based Right Livelihood enterprises. He suggests the FWBO approach entails a reevaluation of work as positive and beneficial, which parallels the Protestant notion of the "calling," but he also notes that the FWBO work ethic diverges from a Calvinist one with regard to religious motivation. Some of these businesses have become successful enough to provide financial support to the movement.

7. The reason for the FWBO's caution is that according to Sangharakshita, special preparation is necessary, and one's level of commitment must be deep, for the student to benefit from such practices. A contrasting view, held in many Tibetan-based Dharma centers around the world, is that such initiations should be offered widely in order that at least a few of the seeds sown might take root and flourish; in such a view, even if initiates do not maintain the tantric vows, they have received a "blessing" entailing a beneficial karmic imprint that will ripen in some future lifetime.

8. This text is named the *Bodhicaryāvatāra* (The bodhisattva's way of life), often spelled *Bodhicharyavatara* in FWBO literature.

9. They include a negative formulation and a corresponding positive aspiration—e.g., "abstaining from killing" corresponds to the positive aspiration to perform "deeds of loving kindness." For an emic explanation of the Ten Precepts observed in the Western Buddhist Order and the Five Precepts in the FWBO, see Subhuti's discussion in a chapter titled "The Fundamental Code of Ethics" (1994, 137). See also appendix 2.

10. The three-jewels image has become iconic in FWBO centers, with each jewel depicted as a teardrop shape in a triangular arrangement with a background of flames representing spiritual transformation. The symbol is emblazoned on the *kesas* that Order members wear at FWBO gatherings.

11. For instance, Batchelor (1994, 337–338) regards the FWBO as one of the most dynamic adaptations of Buddhism, while Green (1989) locates them midway between retaining tradition and conceding to the local worldview.

12. *Yāna* means "way" or "vehicle," with the *"tri"* suffix indicating "three." The Southern Transmission refers to the approach that historically has been found in regions such as South and Southeast Asia, and the Northern Transmission refers to regions from Nepal, Tibet, and China through to Japan and Taiwan. The Theravāda is the only surviving school of Pāli Buddhism (also known as Hinayāna or Southern Transmission), while Mahāyāna equates with the Northern Transmission and consists of numerous philosophical approaches. Both Zen and Vajrayāna can be regarded as Mahāyāna. See Williams and Tribe (2000) for more information.

13. He studied Neo-platonism and contends that as a Buddhist it is the most significant spiritual tradition in the West, comparable to Buddhism's significance in Asia (Subhuti 1994, 288).

14. The matter was debated openly in the movement, with many people expressing disgust. However, plenty of those who were critical of these events feel that in balance they benefit from their involvement with the movement and that things have moved on.

15. Namgyal Rimpoche was born in Toronto as Leslie George Dawson; he took ordination in the Burmese tradition as Anandabodhi and was based at the Hampstead Buddhist Vihara when Sangharakshita arrived there. According to Sangharakshita's memoirs of the time (2003), the two clashed. Anandabodhi later became involved in Tibetan Buddhism, hence the name change (see Dharma Fellowship 2005 for more information).

16. This problem of labels to designate different aspects of Buddhism is complex, and I do not attempt any solutions, preferring to emphasize the fluidity of all sociocultural labels. Sometimes the oversimplification is a result of the problem of finding simple and clear titles or keywords, as with the book *American Buddhism: Methods and Findings in Recent Scholarship* (Williams and Queen 1999), which gives a more diverse picture of issues in the study of Buddhism in the United States than the title implies.

17. Kuah-Pearce writes about "Reformist Buddhism" in Singapore. Adherents are mostly educated Singaporean Chinese elites. They not only react against aggressive Christian proselytization in Singapore, but also reject their inherited syncretistic blend of Buddhism, Taoism, and Confucianism, emphasizing a return to scriptural purity (2003, 10). Similarly, Sharf (1995, 228) describes the *vipassanā* revival in Southeast Asia and Zen in Japan as "twentieth-century Asian reform movements," arguing that "the privileging of experience" can be traced to these movements. He suggests that "[t]he laicized styles of Zen . . . might be called . . . 'Protestant Zen' in so far as they strive to rationalize Zen practice through minimizing the importance of the pietistic, ritualistic, and sacramental dimensions of practice in favor of an instrumental or goal-directed approach" (250).

18. Seneviratne (1999, 28–29) writes that Dharmapala was deeply, if not always, consciously influenced by this view in his colonial-era Christian schooling: the reformer "ex-

horted the Buddhists to give up the ritualism characteristic of rural peasant Buddhism and, instead, to cultivate morality and to infuse themselves with methodical and incessant activity rather than be content with the mere subsistence characteristic of peasant life." The parallels with Weber's analysis of the "Protestant ethic" and its contribution to the "spirit of capitalism," in which individuals have a "duty" to increase their wealth are striking (2002).

19. The FWBO employs the same consumerist metaphor, warning of the hazards of the "new spiritual supermarket of the West," saying that in such a situation probably every Buddhist tradition has been "taught inappropriately" (Subhuti 1994, 180–181).

20. By "knowledge," Howell means the always incomplete and fluid "cultural products of all kinds: artifacts, art, concepts, ideas, beliefs, values, practices" (1995, 165).

21. I use the term "insight" drawing on my interpretation of its Buddhist usage, which signifies an embodied, transformative understanding, while the kind of intellectual understanding referred to here is the academic mode of explaining the world. Intellectual understanding does not, for Buddhists, transform people as much as experiential insight.

22. The FWBO's own publishing house (Windhorse) issued his lengthy refutation.

23. At the time he wrote this, Vishvapani was working for the London-based FWBO Communications Office (the interface between the FWBO and the media).

2. Unplugging from the Grid

1. The Latin names of the species listed here are as follows: Common gorse: *Ulex europaeus*; Scotch Broom: *Cytisus scoparius*; Radiata pine: *Pinus radiata*. Of course, human activity and introduced fauna also damage the local environment.

2. Macrocarpa trees (*Cupressus macrocarpa*), because of their widespread use on New Zealand farms, have become an iconic part of the rural landscape.

3. In October 1995 it was incorporated pursuant to the Charitable Trusts Act 1957, and in December 2001 it was renamed "Sudarshanaloka Trust"; the criterion for joining was to have a close association with Sudarshanaloka. In late 2005 the trustees were Satyananda, Buddhadasa, Lokapala, Chris Stark, Nityajyoti, and Jayaghosa. Other configurations of people interested in Sudarshanaloka formed and reformed over the years.

4. The name that now applies to both the whole peninsula and a town on its west coast was named after the HMS *Coromandel*, a ship that brought the Rev. Samuel Marsden (1765–1838) on his second visit to the region, during which he established a Church of England–affiliated mission.

5. Various authors have explored the ways that the countercultural ideal of self-sufficiency that numerous people explored in the 1960s–1970s have largely been transformed in a return to urban, professional lifestyles (e.g., Agnew 2004, Miller 1999). In New Zealand, Larissa Webb (1999) documents such changes in one intentional community in the Coromandel, while Sargisson and Sargent (2004) survey a wide range of intentional communities, including some in the Coromandel.

6. The names of such retreat centers are interesting in themselves: Dharma Gaia Garden is a play on the Buddhist term *Dharmakāya* (the Dharma body of the Buddha) and Gaia, the Greek earth goddess who has been adopted by the ecological movement. Te Moata and Mana are both Māori names, despite the fact that there is little Māori involvement in Buddhist and New Age retreat centers in the region.

7. The application was made directly to the Thames and District Council, and besides the one opposition, four submissions supported the project. The details of the Buddhists' relationship with the local *iwi* requires further investigation.

8. This quote is from a Web log by a New Zealand journalist, Russell Brown, who accessed the sermon titled "Vipers of Religion" from the Destiny Church Web site. This church received media attention in New Zealand in 2004–2005 because of their opposition to a parliamentary bill on civil unions, which they decried as anti-family because it allowed rights similar to marriage for same-sex couples.

9. The newspaper report said that the objectors also argued "that the development is out of character with the rural surroundings, and will strain local infrastructure. 'It is also not culturally correct,' says Priscilla Kenna, one of the opponents. 'I'm a Christian and have lots of brothers and sisters in that area'"(Huo 1997).

10. Data gathering changed with the 1996 census, which allowed participants to mark affiliation with more than one ethnic group (U. Walker 2001, 6). The data in this section are from the census of population and dwellings in New Zealand, collected by Statistics New Zealand in 1991, 1996, and 2001. Secondary analysis came from the Christian Research Association of Aotearoa New Zealand (CRAANZ 2000). It should be noted, however, that four out of ten people (around one million) did not specify a religion in the 2001 census.

11. Of the minority religions, Islam shows the greatest intercensal increase (between 1996 and 2001, a 74 percent increase).

12. Many who engage in Buddhist-derived meditation practices such as *vipassanā*, a method well established in Theravādin societies, do not call themselves Buddhist. Indeed, some followers of other religions find Buddhist methods attractive—I have met a Dominican friar who practices *vipassanā* meditation.

13. I have not sought precision in numbers, because the list is not comprehensive: e.g., it omits Soka Gakkai International's four New Zealand centers, and I know of several other small sitting groups not listed there. The listing also repeats the same groups under different headings; further, affiliations are not always clear, so from the listing I could not determine exactly which listings are branches and which are main centers, etc.

14. For instance, when a women's refuge group set up a secondhand shop, Satyananda donated two truckloads of goods, and when a group of community welfare agencies (health, disabilities, counseling, etc.) established a center named Bowen House, the Buddhists were among the many community groups invited to provide blessing ceremonies.

15. There is also a move to increase awareness of ways in which the movement could reduce its ecological footprint (FWBO n.d.-e).

16. The concept of accruing merit, which can be used to seek a better material life in future rebirths to enhance spiritual powers or to be dedicated for the benefit all sentient beings, is widespread in more traditionalist approaches to Buddhism. In the FWBO, people often engage in the practice of "dedicating the merit" from any positive activity—e.g., at the conclusion of an individual meditation session or at the end of a retreat or *pūjā*. In its other forms the notion is rarely discussed in the FWBO except to say that they think the notion of acquiring anything, whether material or spiritual, simply for one's own personal benefit is not in keeping with their notion of altruistic spiritual practice.

17. The FWBO's system of spiritual friendship is their alternative to guru devotion, which they see as "open to abuse." In more traditional Tibetan Buddhism, progress on the spiritual path is deemed to be almost impossible without a guru (*lama*) or spiritual teacher (Capper 2002). However, Subhuti suggests it can lead to "confusion and damage" due to the exaggerated ideals that disciples come to hold about their guru. Ironically, several people have alleged experiencing sexual abuse by Order members who they had regarded as spiritual mentors (S. Bell 2002, FWBO n.d.-c).

18. The source of this is the *Upaddha Sutta* (in Samyutta Nikaya, XLV.2). The rhetorical emphasis on spiritual friendship is strong and is used to contrast the FWBO to other Buddhist groups. In a talk at the Auckland Buddhist Centre, one visiting U.K. Order member referred to the lack of emphasis on spiritual friendship in *other* Buddhist groups as "going for refuge to the two-and-a-half jewels," which provoked amused laughter from the audience.

19. Right Livelihood is one of the eight aspects of the "Noble Eightfold Path." Baumann (2000) explores the FWBO's attempts to create an alternative, ethics-based economic system through what they refer to as Team-Based Right Livelihood enterprises. He suggests the FWBO approach entails a reevaluation of work as positive and beneficial, which parallels the Protestant notion of the "calling," but he also notes that the FWBO work ethic diverges from a Calvinist one with regards to religious motivation.

20. The FWBO's engagement with a book discussing early Indian Buddhist social structures is noteworthy in that it shows an openness to responding to and engaging with academic research on Buddhism.

21. These points are (in brief) consuming less, consuming more wisely, going carbon neutral, creating and safeguarding havens for wildlife, and raising awareness (FWBO n.d.-a).

3. A Spiritual Home

1. The Buddhist flag was designed in Sri Lanka in the 1880s and later adopted by the World Fellowship of Buddhists. Various Buddhist organizations fly this flag, including FWBO centers, on occasion.

2. For a history of New Zealand's colonization from a Māori perspective, see R. Walker 2004. See King 2004 for a general history that attempts to address the problems of dispossession from a liberal Pākehā perspective (see also Belich 1996, 2001).

3. This translation is approximate; see Kawharu 2000.

4. Biculturalism is an ideological discourse that focuses on the ideal of an equal partnership between the two parties to the Treaty of Waitangi. People with politically conservative leanings in New Zealand often use the term "politically correct" to criticize ideas they associate with the Left.

5. HCC/FFNZ is an organization for the rural sector that appealed a Waitangi Tribunal ruling involving a claim lodged against the Crown in 1986 by the Ngai Tahu Māori Trust Board. Ngai Tahu is the largest Māori tribal group in the South Island.

6. Under international law, indigenous status refers to the "descendants of the inhabitants of a region at the time of colonization" (A. Bell 2004a, 133, citing the ILO Convention 169).

7. This Māori expression is often translated as "place to stand," i.e., the place one has the right to stand and be heard (Wakareo ā-ipurangi n.d.-c).

8. The original book (Hooper 1981) argues for the conservation of the remaining native forests of New Zealand.

9. British Buddhism and the New Age share Theosophy as a common ancestor (Cush 1996).

10. Harris cites the article "Stupa at Order Conference" in *Urthona* 12 (Winter 1999): 53.

4. Unsettling Place

1. Arguably, hunting is beneficial in that it reduces species that damage native flora and fauna, but even while recognizing that there is a need to control introduced species, Buddhists characterize as it as a destructive activity. The omnivorous brushtail possum (*Trichosurus vulpecula*) is an Australian marsupial, introduced to New Zealand in 1837 to establish a fur trade. The state-run Department of Conservation (DoC) estimates that there are seventy million possums in the country, and sadly they have become a major pest, threatening the survival of various native plants and bird life. It is impossible to eradicate them, but pest-control programs are run on a regular basis to "manage" them. Sudarshanaloka staff decided to participate in the program by hiring someone to lay poison pellets, a move that differs from many other Buddhist groups that attempt to avoid any kind of killing. The FWBO view was more akin to that of DoC, saying that while they regret having to kill the possums, it is necessary for the survival of the native ecosystem.

2. The expression "Wrong View" glosses a Buddhist term for ignorance of the true nature of reality. This ignorance leads to suffering.

3. The Māori and Latin names of the birds mentioned here are *tūī: Prosthemadera novaeseelandiae;* bellbird: *Anthornis melanura/korimako;* wood pigeon: *Hemiphaga novaeseelandiae novaeseelandiae/kereru* or *kukupa.*

4. The text that FWBO members use is reproduced in the epigraph of chapter 6.

5. The founding members of this trust were a couple (both *mitras*) who hoped to establish a residential community for like-minded families. This did not eventuate and the trust was later dissolved, although the original couple remains in residence.

6.   Buddhists recognize beings of six realms of existence: humans, gods, demi-gods, *pretas*, animals, and hell-dwellers. Some of the local spirits come into the category of the animal realm and some are *pretas*, while others as deities inhabit the god realm; however, FWBO members did not spell out these distinctions so I use the terms "spirit" and "deity" loosely to mean the unseen spirit forces that are said to inhabit certain locales and influence conditions therein. What I must point out is that local deities are not to be confused with the Tantric deities or deified bodhisattvas, since these awakened beings have transcended cyclic existence.

7.   He is referring to Cyclones Fergus and Drena, which brought storm-force winds and torrential rain to the North Island in December 1996 during the summer vacation period.

8.   While I have emphasized Sangharakshita's version of the story because it is the version upon which Satyananda is drawing, it is also documented in academic works; e.g., Matthew Kapstein discusses a text called *Testament of Ba* in which "the local deities and spirits of Tibet so obstructed the foundation of the temple at Samye [the first Buddhist temple in Tibet] that the intervention of occult power in the service of Buddhism was deemed essential." Consequently, Padmasambhava was summoned "in order to suppress and place under oath the restless demonic forces." (2000, 155–157).

9.   E.g., in July 2005 an Australian group affiliated with the Foundation for the Preservation of the Mahāyāna Tradition in which I have conducted research brought a statue of Padmasambhava to their retreat center because of his purported powers in overcoming obstacles to the success of a major construction project they are undertaking.

10.   While Snyder does not share the elder's optimism, he says that indeed staying still in a place does allow one to learn from it.

11.   With regard to how the environmentalist ethic is expressed at Sudarshanaloka, the brochure talks about the intention to work with "eco-friendly" materials, and "in line with Buddhist principles of non-violence . . . [using] environmentally empathetic materials, passive solar and wind power, compost toilets and bio-waste water systems."

5. The Stūpa Is Dhardo

1.   A Web site created by a New Zealand stūpa enthusiast, William Hursthouse, has links to some of these centers. See www.stupa.org.nz.

2.   Indo-Tibetan cosmology depicts cycles of time that last for sometimes billions of years and talks of four ages, the first being a golden age and subsequent ones entailing a progression of increased spiritual and physical deterioration. The fourth (current) is the most degenerate.

3.   I am unable to find the original source of this quote from Tarthang Tulku.

4.   The stūpa commemorated Geshe Ngawang Dhargyey, head of the Dhargyey Buddhist Centre. These two parties emphasized their "commonalities" such as a "high degree of spirituality in both cultures and their spiritual approach to nature—presumably in contrast to, and when compared with, western society" (217).

5. Snodgrass's approach to the stūpa's meaning is cosmological, lacking significant reference to what Trainor refers to as "the localization of authoritative religious presence" (Trainor 1997, 96).

6. Govinda (born Ernst Lothar Hoffman, 1895–1985) traveled several times to Tibet during the 1930s–1940s and claimed to have been initiated into the Gelugpa and other sects, although Lopez casts doubt upon his credentials (Lopez 1998, 59–62), also stating that Govinda's book on stūpas (1976) was based on mostly unreferenced Western scholarly sources.

7. Both of these architects had a personal connection to Buddhism and were interested in environmentally sustainable architecture. Tennent designed the Bodhiyanarama Buddhist Monastery near Wellington.

8. There are other configurations around the *dhyāni* buddhas, as well as controversies around the category, but this is beyond the scope of this book.

9. Further, just as the meeting house is regarded as the body of the tribe's ancestor, a stūpa represents the body of the Buddha—the spiritual ancestor of Buddhists.

10. Gell explains that he uses "idolatry" as a neutral term, distancing himself from the negative connotations the term has acquired because of historical Judeo-Christian and Islamic attitudes towards the use of images.

11. By the fifth anniversary of the stūpa (2002), the grounds around it were landscaped, and plaques were added to the stūpa. The first plaque, which faces you as you walk up the path towards the stūpa, bears the words "Dhardo Rimpoche 1917–1990." As you walk clockwise around the stūpa, the other three respective plaques say "Cherish the Doctrine," "Live United," and "Radiate Love." This is the motto of the school Dhardo Rimpoche established in Kalimpong. Sue Thompson undertook the landscape design.

6. Interanimation

1. Sacred places are made sacred partially through being conceptually and physically set apart from mundane things (Durkheim 1965). Further, in order for them to remain sacred, people must "perform" that place's sacredness through rituals, reverence, and restrained behavior, so mundane behaviors like chatting over a cup of tea feel inappropriate.

2. Similarly, Yalouri uses Ortner's concept of key symbols to interpret the Greek Acropolis as both a summarizing and elaborating symbol, because it condenses understandings about Greek identity, while at the same time these symbols provide a "means through which experiences, feelings, ideas, and actions are ordered" (2001, 192).

3. By this I understood Taranatha to be personifying the spirits of the *pūriri* grove as a goddess. In Buddhist cosmology, deities and spirits are "earthbound" like humans, that is, limited by causality and karma, so the Dharma can help them as it helps humans.

4. Perhaps pagan and Māori are conflated or associated because many Westerners impute some kind of essentialist "spirituality" to "indigenous people" as being "closer to nature" than Westerners.

5. The Lower Evolution should not be read in Darwinian or Spencerian terms. It is another way of describing the Buddhist idea of *saṃsāra* (cyclic conditionality), which leads to endless rebirths or cycles of growth and decay. On a personal level, this can mean operating in a "reactive" mode to the circumstances of life. It refers to the psychological and cultural levels of existence.

6. Vulture Peak is named after a rocky crag "where the Buddha used to stay when he wanted to get away from it all. . . . Symbolically speaking, the Vulture's Peak represents the summit of earthly existence. Go beyond it, and you're in the world of . . . the purely spiritual" (Sangharakshita 1993, 40–41).

7. Gumboots (also known as "wellies" or wellington boots, or galoshes) have come to be humorously regarded as a cultural icon referring to their use in rugged New Zealand farms and the outdoors in general.

8. Two Anglo followers of Tibetan Buddhism who saw this photograph hinted to me that it was inappropriate to make such an improvised shrine, especially outdoors and in the soil itself. Some Tibetan Buddhist teachers caution that putting holy objects such as Buddha statues and sacred texts directly on the ground is disrespectful.

9. By this Abu-Lughod means "people whose national or cultural identity is mixed by virtue of migration, overseas education, or parentage."

10. Those on the borders of the movement interact with the other members only part-time, to attend group meditation, retreats, and study groups, presumably at least enjoying the social contact, and who may or may not view the Dharma as providing tools to transform their lives.

11. I use this quote in the way Myerhoff uses it rather than the somewhat different sense in Lansing's published version in a chapter titled "The sounding of the texts" (Lansing 1983).

7. "Re-visioning" Place

1. In 2002 Sudarshanaloka contracted a professional fund-raising company to help them raise the NZ$1.5 million required for completing the retreat center facilities. This campaign did not raise the full amount and was abandoned. During 2005 Jacob Rawls (a *mitra* in ordination training) revived the fund-raising campaign and succeeded in raising the amount needed for the first stage of the construction in early 2006.

Glossary

Note: All non-English terms listed here are Sanskrit, unless otherwise specified. When listing both Pāli and Sanskrit terms, the Pāli term comes first.

Abhidhamma (Pāli): the third section of the *Tipiṭaka*, a philosophical treatise on states of mind.

Akṣobhya: one of the five *dhyāni* buddhas.

Akshobhya (Warren Atkins, ordained April 1969): established the first FWBO group to meet in New Zealand; no longer active in the Western Buddhist Order.

Amitābha: a bodhisattva associated with the color red; also a *dhyāni* buddha.

Amoghasiddhi: a bodhisattva and *dhyāni* buddha.

Anagarika: lit. "homeless one"; one who follows a celibate lifestyle devoted to the practice of the Dharma (in FWBO usage "Anagarika" is a title substituted for Dharmachari/ni when an Order member takes the additional vows). The Sanskrit forms are *anagārika* (masculine) and *anagārikā* (feminine).

ānāpāna sati (Pāli): mindfulness of breathing (meditation practice).

Aniketa (formerly Barbara Gill, 1927–2002): Order member and Anagarika. Ordained 1979; took Anagarika ceremony in 1987.

Aotearoa (Māori): Land of the Long White Cloud (New Zealand).

Attwood, Michael (b. 1966, ordained in 2005 as Jayarava): a *mitra* during the late 1990s.

Avalokiteśvara: the bodhisattva of compassion.

Bhante (Pāli): FWBO members use this to refer to Sangharakshita, meaning "teacher."

bhūta: variously translated as ghost, goblin, or "element" in the sense of the "five elements."

bodhi: enlightenment, used in reference to the "awakened" state this entails.

Bodhicaryāvatāra: a Mahāyāna text describing the bodhisattva ideal, attributed to Śāntideva.

bodhisattva: a buddha who has vowed to be reborn many times to help all beings attain enlightenment; sometimes, an emanation or deity manifesting a perfected archetypal quality, such as wisdom or compassion.

buddha: (i) the Buddha is the title given to the man who attained enlightenment and then taught other people to do so, and it is often translated as "awakened one." The Buddha is the first of the three jewels (see also dharma and sangha); (ii) a buddha is an awakened or enlightened being; (iii) see **dhyāni buddha/jina**.

Buddhadasa (b. 1943, ordained 1972): a senior Order member who was based at Sudarshanaloka for some years. Not to be confused with the Thai monk of the same name.

Buddhism: a broad term referring to the religion characterized by "devotion to 'the Buddha'" (Harvey 1990, 1), practice of the Dharma, and participation in sangha.

Buddhist: in the FWBO definition, anyone who goes for refuge to the three jewels.

Dalit: term used for the ex-untouchables of India.

dāna: generosity; donation (see also **koha**)

Denis: FWBO member from Wellington; involved with Sudarshanaloka until his death in 1995.

Dhardo Rimpoche (1917–1990): Tibetan lama of the Gelugpa lineage who lived in Kalimpong after China's invasion of Tibet. Dhardo was born in 1917, and after a monastic and tantric education in Tibet became abbot of a Tibetan monastery at Bodhgaya in India. He moved in 1954 to Kalimpong, near the India-Tibet border, where he founded a school for Tibetan refugee children, which he named the Indo-Tibetan Buddhist Cultural Institute (ITBCI). In the 1950s he imparted teachings to Sangharakshita, and several of Sangharakshita's disciples met Dhardo. Portions of Dhardo's cremation ashes have been interred in several FWBO stūpas, and the FWBO maintains contact with the ITBCI, assisting with financial support.

Dharma: the teachings of the Buddha that help one to reach enlightenment; also the ultimate truth, as conveyed in the teachings of the Buddha. The second of the three jewels (see also **Buddha** and **sangha**).

Dharma Gaia Centre for Mindful Living: a Buddhist center on the Coromandel Peninsula, associated with the Tiep Hien/Order of Interbeing established in 1964 by Vietnamese Zen monk Thich Nhat Hanh.

Dharmachari, Dharmacharini: the FWBO translates this word as "dharma-farer" and uses the word to refer to Order members. The masculine form is a gloss of the Sanskrit word *dharmacārin;* the feminine form with diacritics is *dharmacāriṇī.*

dhyāni buddhas: the five wisdom or meditation buddhas of Mahāyāna and Vajrayāna cosmology that FWBO members drew upon for the stūpa project. Also known as *jinas.*

enlightenment (cf. buddha; *bodhi; nirvāṇa*): the ultimate in spiritual awakening, resulting in the complete cessation of all suffering through spiritual realizations. Sangharakshita (1990, 209) describes it as a state of pure, clear, even radiant awareness, transcending subject/object duality. He adds that it entails "[a]wareness of things as they really are" and "a state of intense, profound, overflowing Love and Compassion." A standard definition is "a state of blissful illumination, cessation of karma generation, ending rebirth" (Lewis 1997, 320). Some interpretations construe *nirvāṇa* and *saṃsāra* to be mutually exclusive, while Nāgārjuna famously suggests that "[b]etween the two there is not the slightest bit of difference" (Williams 1989, 69, quoting *Madhyamakakārikā* 25: 19–20); thus *nirvāṇa* is "attainable here and now through the correct understanding of the here and now."

five buddhas: see *dhyāni buddhas.*

five elements, the: forms of "energy" present in the cosmos, with material and subtle levels, referred to as earth, water, fire, air, and ether. The stūpa incorporates them in its symbolism.

FPMT: the Foundation for the Preservation of the Mahāyāna Tradition is an international Tibetan Buddhist movement founded by Lamas Yeshe and Zopa Rimpoche in the 1970s. They have built stūpas at each of their three centers in New Zealand.

Friends: people who have learned to meditate with the FWBO and participate in FWBO events (always capitalized in FWBO usage).

Friends of Tararu team: a group of people who met regularly to be "friends to the land" and organize projects and events there. During the time of my research (1999–2000) this team included Sue Thompson, Punyasri, Averil Hunt, Prajñalila, Taranatha, and Satyananda.

FWBO: Friends of the Western Buddhist Order.

FWBO Tararu Trust: charitable trust set up by the FWBO/NZ to develop retreat facilities for the FWBO in Australasia at Sudarshanaloka. The Sudarshanaloka Trust replaced this in 2001.

GFR *mitras*: *mitras* who have asked for ordination into the Western Buddhist Order.

going for refuge (GFR): the central act in Buddhism, according to Sangharakshita, is to go for refuge to the three jewels, meaning that Buddhist aspirations are not just an interest or hobby, but rather an ever-increasingly integral aspect of one's life. It takes place on five different levels (Subhuti 1994, 92–94): *cultural* (cultural identity as a Buddhist); *provisional* (where one is aware of the possibility of GFR, as with *mitras*); *effective* (where one decides that the three jewels are central in one's life, a necessary stage for ordination into the Western Buddhist Order); *real*, also called "stream entry" (the "point of no return" on the path to enlightenment); *absolute* (buddhahood), "the point of full Enlightenment."

going forth: the quest for enlightenment.

Guhyaloka Retreat Centre: FWBO center in Spain; used for international men's ordination retreats.

Guhyasiddhi (Steven May, b. 1954, ordained 1985): An Auckland-based Western Buddhist Order member.

harakeke (Māori): New Zealand Flax (*Phormium tenax*), a plant whose long leaves provide good material for plaiting *kete* and making fiber cordage.

harmikā: the part of the stūpa just under the spire, wherein relics are placed.

Hinayāna: a polemical term for pre-Mahāyāna Buddhism; mainstream or Pāli Buddhism is more appropriate.

iwi (Māori): nation or people; often used in the sense of a tribal grouping; also means bone.

Jayaghosa (formerly David Rice, b. 1953, ordained 1997): the first male Order member to be ordained at Sudarshanaloka.

jina: another term for the *dhyāni* buddhas.

kaitiakitanga (Māori): stewardship (often used with regard to the land).

Kalimpong: town in the northern Indian Himalayas, near the borders of Nepal, Tibet, Bhutan, and Sikkim.

kalyāṇa mitratā: spiritual friendship.

Karaniya Mettā Sutta: a scripture describing *mettā*.

kauri (Māori): *Agathis australis*. A New Zealand native tree with straight and fine-grained timber. Because early European settlers logged them extensively, few old-growth *kauri* forests remain.

kesa (Japanese): strip of fabric that Order members wear around their necks on public occasions. It bears the emblem of the three jewels embroidered at each end. Anagarikas wear a yellow *kesa* (in reference to the saffron robe of Theravāda Buddhist monastics), and Dharmacari/nis wear a white one. Derived from *kāsāya* (Pāli), or robe.

kete (Māori): plaited bag or basket, often made from native plant fibers.

koha (Māori): gift or donation.

lama (Tibetan): spiritual teacher, in widespread use among Western Buddhists.

Mahamudra Centre for Universal Unity: a Buddhist center on the Coromandel Peninsula affiliated with the FPMT.

Mahāyāna: the Great Vehicle, as contrasted with Hinayāna.

Malini (b. 1949, ordained 1969): the seniormost Order member in New Zealand at the time of the stūpa dedication.

maṇḍala: circular diagram of the cosmos, with a center and four quarters with gateways. In Indic cosmology, it can be a diagram of the cosmos, represented in variant forms of a circle in a square, with four gateways, and a distinction between center and periphery.

mantra: "string of sound-symbols recited to concentrate and protect the mind," often as an invocation of a particular archetypal buddha (Vessantara 1993, 336).

mettā (Pāli): "the sort of love one feels for a friend, but carried to a very high pitch of intensity" (Sangharakshita, quoted in Subhuti 1994, 202). *Mettā* is "the basic positive emotion" (Subhuti 1994, 203), unconditional love for all beings including oneself, and it may be experienced as a sense of interconnectedness with all things.

mettā bhāvana: meditation practice to cultivate feelings of *mettā*.

mini-stūpa: a small stack of stones serving as a visual symbol of aspiration to the spiritual ideal of transcendence.

mitra: in FWBO parlance, Friends who have made a provisional commitment to the FWBO through a simple going-for-refuge ritual; the term is Sanskrit for "friend."

morepork: *Ninox novaeseelandiae*, New Zealand owl; *ruru* (Māori).

mythic context: a situation where every aspect of one's life is aligned to going for refuge.

nāga: nature spirit (in FWBO usage); in Indic mythology, the serpent-like spirits are guardians of treasure inhabiting bodies of water and associated with rain and fertility.

Nagabodhi (Terry Pilchick): senior Order member from Britain and president of the FWBO/NZ centers since 1992.

namo tassa bhagavato arahato sammā sambuddhasa (Pāli): a refrain found in many Pāli scriptures that honors the Buddha. It was chanted during the stūpa dedication procession.

Navachitta (b. 1952, ordained 1990): Auckland-based Order member.

navayāna ("new vehicle"): a term used by various reformist Buddhists; it has been applied to the Dalit conversion to Buddhism in India and some Western Buddhist approaches (Numrich 1999, 123).

new society, the: utopianist vision of the FWBO, "the ideal social setting for spiritual practice . . . environments in which people could meet all their material and social

needs, while also having the fullest possible support for spiritual development"
(Subhuti 1994, 221).

nirvāṇa: see **enlightenment**. This term refers to the cessation of suffering entailed by
becoming enlightened.

Order member: see **Western Buddhist Order member** ("Order member" is the
shorthand).

ordination: in FWBO usage, ordination entails the "formal expression of Effective Going
for Refuge," and ideally Order members are "simply individuals who are united in
their common Effective Going for Refuge" (Subhuti 1994, 126–127).

Parinirvāṇa: state beyond cyclic existence, where all suffering ceases, into which a
buddha enters at death.

Prajñalila (formerly Diane Quin, b. 1949, ordained in late 1999): a member of the
Friends of Tararu team during 1996–2000. She came from a farming family, has been
interested in Buddhism since the early 1980s, and studied social sciences at
university. After she encountered the FWBO she went to Britain and worked at
Windhorse Publications in Glasgow for three years. She returned to New Zealand
when she heard that the Tararu Valley property had been bought because she wanted
to be involved in the project and complete a Master of Fine Arts degree.

preta: hungry ghost, a kind of being inhabiting one of the six realms of existence in
Buddhist cosmology.

pūjā (lit. "worship"): in FWBO centers, a devotional ceremony in which participants
honor and make offerings to the Buddha. The FWBO's sevenfold *pūjā* (an hour-long
devotional ceremony performed at many FWBO gatherings) is based on a variety of
Sanskrit and Pāli sources in English translation; sometimes the *pūjā* will focus on a
different buddha or bodhisattva, and his or her mantra will be chanted during the
offering section.

Punyasri (b. 1946, ordained 1985): a Friends of Tararu team member based in Auckland
during the late 1990s.

pūriri (Māori): native tree of New Zealand, *Vitex lucens*.

putiputi harakeke (Māori): plaited ornamental flowers using leaves of New Zealand flax.

Ratana Sutta: Buddhist scripture in the *Sutta Nipata* II.1.

Ratnasambhava: a bodhisattva and *dhyāni* buddha.

refuge: see **going for refuge (GFR).**

retreat center: place for group meditation courses and intensive meditation practice.
Most retreats last from one weekend to a fortnight, but some ordination retreats last
up to four months.

rūpa: form, shape, figure (used in the FWBO to refer to a Buddha statue).

sabbe sattā sukhī hontu (Pāli): phrase meaning "May all beings be happy."

saṃsāra: cyclic existence, which is subject to the laws of conditionality and
impermanence.

sangha/*saṃgha*: spiritual community, the third of the three jewels. According to Subhuti
(1996b, 20), "everybody who goes for refuge, regardless of their circumstances, is a
member of the Spiritual Community," and "[g]oing for Refuge is the unifying
principle of the Buddhist sangha" (105). See also **Buddha** and **Dharma.**

Sangharakshita: founder of the FWBO, b. 1925 in England as Dennis Lingwood to working-class parents. From 1947 to 1964 he lived in India, where he became a monk, living in Kalimpong for fourteen years. He founded the FWBO in London in 1967 and the Western Buddhist Order in 1968.

Satyananda (b. 1951, ordained 1984): resident of Sudarshanaloka; has played various key roles there and for the Lotus Realm business in Thames. He is also the men's *Mitra* Convenor for Australasia and has held key roles in the Friends of Tararu team and Sudarshanaloka Trust.

Shraddha Trust: land-holding trust established on 75 hectares (185 acres) across the valley from Sudarshanaloka in 1997.

siddhi: at the mundane level, *siddhi*s are magical powers or attainments, although the supreme *siddhi* is buddhahood itself (Samuel 2005, 75).

solitary (retreat) hut: small cabin for individual, solitary retreat. One "goes on solitary" for days, weeks, months, or even years in order to pursue intensive spiritual practice.

spiritual community: FWBO community that aspires to the transcendental ideal of Enlightenment.

stūpa: Buddhist monument containing relics.

Subhuti (formerly Alex Kennedy, b. 1947 ordained in 1973): A senior Order member in Britain.

Sudarshanaloka: translated by FWBO members as "land of beautiful vision," the name given to the FWBO retreat center on the Coromandel Peninsula.

Sudarshanaloka Trust: established in December 2001, the FWBO Tararu Trust was renamed "Sudarshanaloka Trust," with the main purpose of keeping in touch with the overall vision of Sudarshanaloka, similar to the role that the Friends of Tararu team had played. The Sudarshanaloka Trust delegated the management of Sudarshanaloka to a small committee that oversees various projects such as building and fund-raising. Thus the tasks of keeping in touch with the overall spiritual vision and the practical management issues were now partly differentiated. Some of the new developments incorporated the mythic context in new ways, drawing on developments in the British FWBO.

Sutta/sūtra: scripture deriving from the discourses of the Buddha and key disciples.

tangata whenua (Māori): the "people of the land" (usually used in reference to the local Māori tribe affiliated with a particular region); see also **whenua.**

tantric (from tantra): another name for the esoteric practices of the Vajrayāna.

taonga (Māori): treasured possession, ancestral treasure, anything of special value; may be imbued with spiritual ancestral essence.

tapu (Māori): ceremonial restriction (Wakareo ā-ipurangi n.d.-a); sometimes glossed as "sacred."

Tārā: a female bodhisattva associated with compassion; there is a White Tārā and a Green Tārā and many other emanations.

Taranatha (b. 1929, ordained 1992): grew up on a Taranaki farm. He lives in the men's community, Saranadipa, in Auckland, and was a Friends of Tararu team member during the research period; a trustee of Sudarshanaloka.

Tararu (Māori): the name of the valley where Sudarshanaloka is situated and formerly applied to the FWBO property. FWBO members have noted that it sounds much like the name of the bodhisattva, Tārā.

Taylor, Ray (b. 1954, ordained 2003 as Kuladasa): a *mitra* who lived at Sudarshanaloka during 2000.

TBMSG: Trailokya Bauddha Mahasangha Sahayak Gana, the Indian wing of the FWBO, founded in 1978. Subhuti (1994, 25) provides the translation of TBMSG as "The Community of Helpers of the Buddhist Order of the Three Worlds," saying this alludes to "both the three worlds of Buddhist cosmology and to the First, Second and Third Worlds of modern politics."

Team-Based Right Livelihood enterprise: FWBO businesses that aim to create a working environment in line with Buddhist ethics.

Theravāda: the school of Buddhism based on the Pāli canon. See also **Hinayana.**

Thompson, Sue (b. 1962, ordained in 2004 as Akasamati): English GFR *mitra* living in Auckland, involved in the Friends of Tararu and later the Sudarshanaloka Trust.

three jewels, the (*triratna*, three refuges, triple gem, triple refuge, etc.): the Buddha, the Dharma, and the sangha.

tikanga Māori (Māori): Māori customary values and practices (Wakareo ā-ipurangi n.d.-b).

tino rangatiratanga (Māori): self-determination or sovereignty.

Tipiṭaka/Tripiṭaka: the Three Baskets of the Pāli canon (a collection of texts incorporating the *Vinaya*, *Suttas*, and *Abhidhamma*).

tōtara (Māori): *Podocarpus totara*, a native New Zealand tree.

triyāna: three vehicles, referring to Hinayāna, Mahāyāna, and Vajrayāna.

tūī (Māori): *Prosthemadera novaeseelandiae*, a native New Zealand songbird.

tūrangawaewae (Māori): lit. "place to stand," i.e., a permanent place where you have the right to stand and be heard (Wakareo ā-ipurangi n.d.-c).

Urthona: title of FWBO arts magazine, with its name deriving from a mythical figure in William Blake's writing.

Vairocana: a *dhyāni* buddha.

Vajrasattva: a buddha/bodhisattva associated with purification.

Vajrayāna: esoteric sect of the Mahāyāna.

Vessantara (b. 1950 in England, ordained in 1974): a senior Order member who visited Sudarshanaloka in 1994 and 1996.

Vihāra (Pāli): monastery or abode.

vinaya: monastic discipline.

vipassanā (Pāli): insight, a term used for a school of meditation.

Wangapeka Retreat Centre: established in 1975 by students of Namgyal Rimpoche in the South Island. Its stūpa /pagoda was built in 1983.

Western Buddhist Order: the organization, founded in 1968 as the central body of the FWBO, consisting of all Order members.

Western Buddhist Order member (Order member): person ordained into the Western Buddhist Order in both private and public ceremonies, initiated into a visualization practice, and given a Buddhist name.

whenua (Māori): land, country; also placenta.

Windhorse Publications: the FWBO publishing house, based in Birmingham, U.K.

Windhorse Trading: the largest of the FWBO Team-Based Right Livelihood businesses, operating from Britain.

yakkha (Pāli): a kind of supernatural being.

Sources Cited

Abu-Lughod, L. 1991. Writing against culture. In *Recapturing anthropology: Working in the present*, ed. R. G. Fox. Santa Fe, N.M.: School of American Research Press, 137–162.

Agnew, Eleanor. 2004. *Back from the land: How young Americans went to nature in the 1970s, and why they came back.* Chicago: Ivan R. Dee.

Almond, P. C. 1988. *The British discovery of Buddhism.* Cambridge: Cambridge University Press.

Aloka. 1994. *The refuge tree as mythic context.* Padmaloka retreat centre, U.K.: Padmaloka Books, 1994.

Anderson, Benedict. 1983. *Imagined communities: Reflections on the origin and spread of nationalism.* London: Verso.

———. 1991. *Imagined communities: Reflections on the origin and spread of nationalism.* Rev. ed. London: Verso.

Aniketa. 1999. A path with art. *Tararu Transformer,* Winter: 4.

Appadurai, Arjun. 1995. The production of locality. In *Counterworks: Managing the diversity of knowledge,* ed. R. Fardon. London: Routledge, 204–225.

Attwood, Michael. 2004a. Personal communication, 18 September.

———. 2004b. Personal communication, 19 September.

———. 2004c. Personal communication, 22 September.

Austin-Broos, Diane. 2003. The anthropology of conversion: An introduction. In *The anthropology of religious conversion,* ed. A. Buckser and S. D. Glazier. Lanham, Md.: Rowman and Littlefield, 1–12.

Barnes, Gina. 1999. Buddhist landscapes of East Asia. In *Archaeologies of landscape: Contemporary perspectives,* ed. W. Ashmore and A. B. Knapp. Malden, Mass.: Blackwell, 103–123.

Bartholomeusz, Tessa. 1994. *Women under the Bo tree: Buddhist nuns in Sri Lanka.* Cambridge: Cambridge University Press.

———. 1998. Spiritual wealth and neo-orientalism. *Journal of Ecumenical Studies* 35 (1): 19–33.

Basso, Keith H. 1996. Wisdom sits in places: Notes on a western Apache landscape. In *Senses of Place,* ed. S. Feld and K. H. Basso. Santa Fe, N.M.: School of American Research Press, 53–90.

Batchelor, S. 1994. *The awakening of the West: The encounter of Buddhism and Western culture.* Berkeley: Parallax.

Batten, Juliet. 2005. *Celebrating the southern seasons: Rituals for Aotearoa.* Rev. ed. Auckland: Random House New Zealand.

Baumann, Martin. 1997a. Culture contact and valuation: Early German Buddhists and the creation of a "Buddhism in Protestant Shape." *Numen* 44: 270–295.

———. 1997b. The Dharma has come West: A survey of recent studies and sources. *Journal of Buddhist Ethics* 4: 194–211.

———. 2000. Work as Dharma practice: Right Livelihood cooperatives in the FWBO. In *Engaged Buddhism in the West*, ed. C. S. Queen. Boston: Wisdom Publications, 372–393.

———. 2001. Global Buddhism: Developmental periods, regional histories, and a new analytical perspective. *Journal of Global Buddhism* 2: 1–43.

———. 2002a. Buddhism in Europe: Past, present, prospects. In *Westward Dharma: Buddhism beyond Asia*, ed. C. S. Prebish and M. Baumann. Berkeley: University of California Press, 85–105.

———. 2002b. Protective amulets and awareness techniques, or how to make sense of Buddhism in the West. In *Westward Dharma: Buddhism beyond Asia*, ed. C. S. Prebish and M. Baumann. Berkeley: University of California Press, 51–65.

Baumann, Martin, and Charles S. Prebish. 2002. Introduction. In *Westward Dharma: Buddhism beyond Asia*, ed. C. S. Prebish and M. Baumann. Berkeley: University of California Press, 1–13.

Belich, James. 1996. *Making peoples: A history of the New Zealanders: From Polynesian settlement to the end of the nineteenth century.* Auckland: Penguin.

———. 2001. *Paradise reforged: A history of the New Zealanders from the 1880s to the year 2000.* Auckland: Penguin.

Bell, Avril. 2004a. "Half-castes" and "White natives": The politics of Maori-Pakeha hybrid identities. In *Cultural studies in Aotearoa New Zealand: Identity, space and place*, ed. C. Bell and S. Matthewman. South Melbourne, Vic.: Oxford University Press, xiv, 298.

Bell, Sandra. 1991. Buddhism in Britain: Development and adaptation. Unpublished Ph.D., University of Durham.

———. 1996. Change and identity in the Friends of the Western Buddhist Order. *Scottish Journal of Religious Studies* 17 (2): 87–107.

———. 1998. "Crazy wisdom," charisma, and the transmission of Buddhism in the United States. *Nova Religio* 2 (1): 55–75.

———. 2000. A survey of engaged Buddhism in Britain. In *Engaged Buddhism in the West*, ed. C. S. Queen. Boston: Wisdom Publications, 397–422.

———. 2002. Scandals in emerging Western Buddhism. In *Westward Dharma: Buddhism beyond Asia*, ed. C. S. Prebish and M. Baumann. Berkeley: University of California Press, 230–242.

Bergin, Helen, and Susan Smith, eds. 2004. *Land and place: Spiritualities from Aotearoa New Zealand: He whenua, he wahi.* Auckland: Accent Publications.

Bloch, Maurice. 1998. Why trees, too, are good to think with: Towards an anthropology of the meaning of life. In *The social life of trees: Anthropological perspectives on tree symbolism*, ed. L. Rival. Oxford: Berg, 39–55.

Bluck, Robert. 2004. Buddhism and ethnicity in Britain: The 2001 census data [research article]. *Journal of Global Buddhism* 5: 90–96.

Bond, G. D. 1988. *The Buddhist revival in Sri Lanka: Religious tradition, reinterpretation and response.* Columbia: University of South Carolina Press.

Bouma, Gary D. 1997. The settlement of Islam in Australia. *Social Compass* 44 (1): 71–82.

Brettell, Caroline. 1993. Introduction: Fieldwork, text, and audience. In *When they read what we write: The politics of ethnography*, ed. C. Brettell. Westport, Conn.: Bergin & Harvey, 1–24.

Brown, Russell. 2005. Incipient Moonbats (Web log) [online]. Available at http://publicaddress.net/default,1959.sm#post1959. [Accessed 24 March 2005.]

Buddhadasa. 2006. Personal communication, February.

———. 2005. Alchemy in the spiritual life (FWBO Sangha Day talk at Auckland Buddhist Centre), 13 November.

Buddhafield. 2005. Buddhafield retreats 2005 [online]. Available at www.buddhafield .com/allretreats.html. [Accessed 13 July 2005.]

BuddhaNet. 2005. BuddhaNet's New Zealand Buddhist directory [online]. Available at www.buddhanet.net/nzealand.htm. [Accessed 4 April 2006.]

Bunting, Madeleine. 1997. The dark side of enlightenment. *The Guardian*, 27 October.

Cadge, Wendy. 2005. *Heartwood: The first generation of Theravada Buddhism in America*. *Morality & Society* series. Chicago: University of Chicago Press.

Campbell, Colin. 1999. The Easternisation of the West. In *New religious movements: Challenge and response*, ed. B. Wilson and J. Cresswell. London: Routledge, 35–48.

Campbell, J. 1968. *The hero with a thousand faces*. 2nd ed. Princeton, N.J.: Princeton University Press.

Campbell, J., and B. Moyers. 1988. *The power of myth*. New York: Doubleday.

Campbell, Joseph, and Antony Van Couvering. 1997. *The mythic dimension: Selected essays 1959–1987*. 1st ed. San Francisco: HarperSanFrancisco.

Capper, Daniel. 2002. *Guru devotion and the American Buddhist experience: Studies in religion and society*, vol. 57. Lewiston, N.Y.: Edwin Mellen Press.

Carrithers, Michael. 1983. *The forest monks of Sri Lanka: An anthropological and historical study*. Oxford: Oxford University Press.

Cate, Sandra. 2003. *Making merit, making art: A Thai temple in Wimbledon*. Honolulu: University of Hawai'i Press.

Chandler, Stuart. 2004. *Establishing a Pure Land on Earth: The Foguang Buddhist perspective on modernization and globalization. Topics in Contemporary Buddhism*. Honolulu: University of Hawai'i Press.

Chasteau, Monique, and Rachel Furdas. 1990. Pioneers in a new country. *Dakini: The FWBO's Buddhist Magazine for Women* 5: 9–10.

Chintamani. 1999. Stupa at Order conference. *Urthona: A Journal for Rousing the Imagination* 12 (Winter): 53.

———. 2001. A contemplation of the Green Man *Urthona: A Journal for Rousing the Imagination*, Spirit of Place 16 (Autumn): 27–28.

Christian Research Association Aotearoa New Zealand (CRAANZ). 2000. *The religion question: Findings from the 1996 census*. Auckland: Christian Research Association Aotearoa New Zealand.

Clear Vision. 1997. FWBO Britain, newsreel 12 [videotape].

Clifford, James. 1986. Introduction: Partial truths. In *Writing culture: The poetics and politics of ethnography*, ed. J. Clifford and G. E. Marcus. Berkeley: University of California Press, 1–26.

Comaroff, Jean. 1985. *Body of power, spirit of resistance: The culture and history of a South African people.* Chicago: University of Chicago Press.

Covell, Stephen Grover. 2005. *Japanese temple Buddhism: Worldliness in a religion of renunciation. Topics in Contemporary Buddhism.* Honolulu: University of Hawai'i Press.

Croucher, Paul. 1989. *A history of Buddhism in Australia 1848–1988.* Kensington, NSW: New South Wales University Press.

Cush, Denise. 1996. British Buddhism and the New Age. *Journal of Contemporary Religion* 11 (2): 195–208.

Dant, Tim. 1999. *Material culture in the social world: Values, activities, lifestyles.* Buckingham, U.K.: Open University Press.

Darlington, Susan. 2003. Practical spirituality and community forests: Monks, ritual and radical conservatism in Thailand. In *Nature in the global south: Environmental projects in South and Southeast Asia*, ed. P. R. Greenough and A. L. Tsing. Durham, N.C.: Duke University Press, 347–366.

Day, David, ed. 1998. *Australian identities.* Melbourne: Australian Scholarly Publishing.

DeCaroli, Robert. 2004. *Haunting the Buddha: Indian popular religions and the formation of Buddhism.* New York: Oxford University.

Dharma Fellowship. 2005. Biographies: The venerable Kyabje Namgyal Rinpoche [online]. Available at www.dharmafellowship.org/biographies/contemporarymasters/kyabje-namgyal.htm. [Accessed 21 August 2006.]

Dominy, Michèle D. 1990. New Zealand's Waitangi Tribunal: Cultural politics of an anthropology of the high country. *Anthropology Today* 6 (2): 11–15.

Durkheim, Emile. 1965. *The elementary forms of the religious life.* Glencoe, Ill.: The Free Press. [First published 1915.]

Ellemor, Heidi. 2003. White skin, black heart? The politics of belonging and Native title in Australia. *Social & Cultural Geography* 4 (2): 233–252.

Fields, Rick. 1998. Divided dharma: White Buddhists, ethnic Buddhists, and racism. In *The faces of Buddhism in America*, ed. C. S. Prebish and K. K. Tanaka. Berkeley: University of California Press, 196–206.

Fleras, Augie, and Paul Spoonley. 1999. *Recalling Aotearoa: Indigenous politics and ethnic relations in New Zealand.* Auckland: Oxford University Press.

FPMT flyer. n.d. Invitation to Mahamudra stupa dedication [2000].

Friedman, J. 1992. The past in the future: History and the politics of identity. *American Anthropologist* 94 (4): 837–859.

FWBO. 2005a. Buddhist ethics [online]. Available at www.fwbo.org/buddhism/ethics.html. [Accessed 11 April 2006.]

———. 2005b. Contacts [online]. Available at www.fwbo.org/contacts.html. [Accessed 11 April 2006.]

———. n.d.-a. The five-point eco-action agenda. PS Buddhist Ecopractice Web site [online]. Available at www.ecopractice.fwbo.org/5point.htm. [Accessed 23 February 2006.]

———. n.d.-b. Friends of the Western Buddhist Order [online]. Available at www.fwbo.org/. [Accessed 21 April 2005.]

———. n.d.-c. The FWBO files—A short statement [online]. Available at www.fwbo.org/criticism_statement.html. [Accessed 23 January 2006.]

———. n.d.-d. A network of friendships [online]. Available at www.fwbo.org/friendship.html. [Accessed 21 April 2005.]

———. n.d.-e. PS Buddhist ecopractice Web site [online]. Available at www.ecopractice.fwbo.org/home.htm. [Accessed 18 September 2004.]

FWBO Files. n.d. Homepage of the FWBO files [online]. Available at www.fwbo-files.com. [Accessed 13 March 2005.]

Gell, Alfred. 1998. Art and agency. Oxford: Clarendon Press.

Gellner, David N. 1990. Introduction: What is the anthropology of Buddhism about? Journal of the Anthropological Society of Oxford 21 (Special Issue: Anthropology of Buddhism): 95–112.

Gill, Andrea. 1997. Opening to Tara. Tararu Transformer: 2.

Gombrich, R. F. 1971. Precept and practice: Traditional Buddhism in the rural highlands of Ceylon. Oxford: Clarendon Press.

Gombrich, Richard, and Gananath Obeyesekere. 1988. Buddhism transformed: Religious change in Sri Lanka. Princeton, N.J.: Princeton University Press.

Govinda, Lama. 1960. Foundations of Tibetan mysticism. London: Rider & Co.

———. 1976. Psycho-cosmic symbolism of the Buddhist stupa. Emeryville, Calif.: Dharma Publications.

Granoff, P. E., and Koichi Shinohara. 2003. Introduction: Pilgrims, patrons and place: Localizing sanctity in Asian religions. In Asian religions and society. Vancouver, B.C.: University of British Columbia Press; London: Eurospan, 1–14.

Green, Deidre. 1989. Buddhism in Britain: Skilful means or selling out? In Religion, State, and Society in Modern Britain, ed. P. Badham. Texts and Studies in Religion, vol. 43. Lewiston, N.Y: E. Mellen Press, 277–291.

Grubb, Fiona. 2005. Jade and belonging: Making a social landscape of belonging on the West Coast. SITES, New Series 2 (1): 186–211.

Guhyaloka Buddhist Retreat Centre. Home page [online]. n.d. Available at www.guhyaloka.com/. [Accessed 12 July 2005.]

Guhyasiddhi. 2005. Hidden talents [interview]. Sangha Scene (Auckland Buddhist Centre Newsletter): 12.

Gupta, Akhil, and James Ferguson. 1992. Beyond "culture": Space, identity, and the politics of difference. Cultural Anthropology 7 (10): 6–23.

———. 1997. Discipline and practice: "The Field" as site, method, and location in anthropology. In Anthropological locations: Boundaries and grounds of a field science, ed. A. Gupta and J. Ferguson. Berkeley: University of California Press, 1–46.

Guy, Camille. 1997. Buddhists' faith symbol perches among the possums. New Zealand Herald, Monday, 17 February.

Harris, Ian. 1995. Buddhist environmental ethics and detraditionalization: The case of EcoBuddhism. Religion 25: 199–211.

———. 2002. A "Commodius Vicus of Recirculation": Buddhism, art, and modernity. In Westward dharma: Buddhism beyond Asia, ed. C. S. Prebish and M. Baumann. Berkeley: University of California Press, 365–382.

Harvey, Peter. 1990. *An introduction to Buddhism: Teachings, history and practices.* Cambridge: Cambridge University Press.

Hobsbawm, Eric. 1983. Introduction: Inventing traditions. In *The invention of tradition, past and present publications,* ed. E. Hobsbawm and T. Ranger. Cambridge: Cambridge University Press.

Holt, John. 1991. Protestant Buddhism? *Religious Studies Review* 17 (4): 307–312.

Hooper, Peter. 1981. *Our forests ourselves.* Dunedin, N.Z.: McIndoe.

Howard, Alan, and Jeannette Marie Mageo. 1996. Introduction. In *Spirits in culture, history and mind,* ed. J. M. Mageo and A. Howard. New York: Routledge, 1–10.

Howell, Signe. 1995. Whose knowledge and whose power? A new perspective on cultural diffusion. In *Counterworks: Managing the diversity of knowledge,* ed. R. Fardon. London: Routledge, 164–181.

Huo, Jianqiang Raymond. 1997. Planned temple "not health risk." *The New Zealand Herald,* 28 July.

Jayaghosa. 2000a. Personal communication, 3 July.

———. 2000b. Personal communication, 25 July.

Jayarava. 2006. Where is the FWBO? [online]. Available at www.fwbo.blogspot.com/ 2006/03/where-is-fwbo.html. [Accessed 11 April 2006.]

Kamalashila. 2001. Buddhafield—A new going forth. Madhyamavani [online]. Available at http://madhyamavani.fwbo.org/4/ buddhafield.html. [Accessed 3 May 2005.]

Kapstein, Matthew T. 2000. *The Tibetan assimilation of Buddhism: Conversion, contestation, and memory.* Oxford: Oxford University Press.

Karaniya Mettā Sutta [The discourse on loving-kindness]. 1999. Trans. Piyadassi Thera. Sutta Nipata I.8 [online]. Buddhist Publication Society. Available at www.accessto insight.org/canon/sutta/khuddaka/ khp/khp-b.html. [Accessed 20 May 2005.]

Karenza. 2000. Personal communication, 13 February.

Kawharu, Merata. 2000. *Kaitiakitanga:* A Maori anthropological perspective of the Maori socio-environmental ethic of resource management. *Journal of the Polynesian Society* 110 (4): 349–370.

Kay, David. 1997. The New Kadampa Tradition and the continuity of Tibetan Buddhism in transition. *Journal of Contemporary Religion* 12 (3): 277–293.

———. 2004. *Tibetan and Zen Buddhism in Britain: Transplantation, development and adaptation.* New York: RoutledgeCurzon.

Kennelly, Paul, and Andrea Gill. 1997. Stupa dedication. *Tararu Transformer* (May): 1.

Kenrick, J., and J. Lewis. 2004. Indigenous peoples rights and the politics of the term indigenous. *Anthropology Today* 20 (2): 4–9.

Khadro, Yeshe. 1995. From Catholic farm girl to Buddhist nun. In *From utopian dreaming to communal reality,* ed. B. Metcalf. Sydney: University of New South Wales Press, 115–126.

King, Michael. 1985. *Being Pakeha: An encounter with New Zealand and the Maori renaissance.* Auckland: Hodder and Stoughton.

———. 1999. *Being Pakeha now: Reflections and recollections of a white native.* Auckland: Penguin Books.

———. 2004. *The Penguin history of New Zealand.* Auckland: Penguin Books.

Kolig, Erich. 1997. Recycling charisma and the sacralization of the landscape: A Buddhist stupa in Dunedin, New Zealand. *Baessler-Archiv* 45: 201–221.

Kopytoff, Igor. 1986. The cultural biography of things: Commoditization as process. In *The social life of things: Commodities in a cultural perspective*, ed. A. Appadurai. Cambridge: Cambridge University Press, 64–91.

Kuah-Pearce, Khun Eng. 2003. *State, society, and religious engineering: Towards a reformist Buddhism in Singapore*. Singapore: Eastern Universities Press.

Kulananda. 1992. Protestant Buddhism. *Religion* 22 (1): 101–103.

Kunzang, Ani. n.d. Untitled section in article titled "The stupa project: Three perspectives." [In online Dunedin Buddhist Centre Newsletter.] Available at http://dbc.dharmakara.net. [Accessed 13 September 2002.]

Kurtz, Lester. 1995. *Gods in the global village: The world's religions in sociological perspective.* Thousand Oaks, Calif.: Pine Forge Press.

Lansing, John Stephen. 1983. *The three worlds of Bali.* New York: Praeger.

Leonard, Karen. 1997. Finding one's own place: Asian landscapes re-visioned in rural California. In *Culture, power, place: Explorations in critical anthropology*, ed. A. Gupta and J. Ferguson. Durham, N.C.: Duke University Press, 118–136.

Levine, Stephen. 1990. Untitled commentary in debate on cultural politics in New Zealand. *Anthropology Today* 6 (3): 4–6.

Lévi-Strauss, Claude. 1966. *The savage mind.* Chicago: University of Chicago Press.

Lewis, Todd. 1997. Buddhist communities: Historical precedents and ethnographic paradigms. In *Anthropology of religion: A handbook*, ed. S. D. Glazier. Westport, Conn.: Greenwood Press, 319–368.

Liu, James H. 2005. History and identity: A system of checks and balances for Aotearoa/New Zealand. In *New Zealand identities: Departures and destination*, ed. J. H. Liu et al. Wellington: Victoria University Press, 69–87.

Lopez, Donald S., Jr., ed. 1995a. *Curators of the Buddha: The study of Buddhism under colonialism.* Chicago: University of Chicago Press.

———. 1995b. Introduction. In *Curators of the Buddha: The study of Buddhism under colonialism*, ed. D. S. Lopez. Chicago: University of Chicago Press, 1–29.

———. 1998. *Prisoners of Shangri-La: Tibetan Buddhism and the West.* Chicago: University of Chicago Press.

MacCormack, C. P., and M. Strathern, eds. 1980. *Nature, culture, and gender.* Cambridge: Cambridge University Press.

Malalgoda, Kitsiri. 1976. *Buddhism in Sinhalese society, 1750–1900: A study of religious revival and change.* Berkeley: University of California Press.

Malini. 1997a. Adding the ashes. *Tararu Transformer* (May): 2.

———. 1997b. Dhardo's eyes. *Tararu Transformer* (September): 4.

Malinowski, B. 1953 [1922]. *Argonauts of the western Pacific.* New York: E. P. Dutton.

Matsudo, Yukio. 2000. Buddhist views on ritual practice: Protestant character of modern Buddhist movements. *Buddhist-Christian Studies* 20: 59–69.

McAra, Sally Ann. 2000. "The land of the stupa and sacred puriri": Creating Buddhism in the Tararu Valley, New Zealand. Unpublished master's thesis, University of Auckland.

McLean, Robyn. 2001. Bay has no welcome for local Buddhists. *Sunday Star Times*, 11 November.

Mellor, Philip A. 1989. The cultural translation of Buddhism: Problems of theory and method arising in the study of Buddhism in England. Unpublished PhD diss., University of Manchester.

———. 1991. Protestant Buddhism? The cultural translation of Buddhism in England. *Religion* 21 (1): 73–93.

———. 1992. The FWBO and tradition: A reply to Dharmachari Kulananda. *Religion* 22 (1): 104–107.

Metraux, Daniel Alfred. 2001. *The international expansion of a modern Buddhist movement: The Soka Gakkai in Southeast Asia and Australia.* Lanham, Md.: University Press of America.

Mikaere, Ani. 2004. Are we all New Zealanders now? A Māori response to the Pākehā quest for indigeneity. Bruce Jesson Memorial Lecture 2004 [online]. Available at www.brucejesson.com/lecture2004.htm. [Accessed 30 March 2006.]

Miller, Timothy. 1999. *The 60s communes: Hippies and beyond.* Syracuse, N.Y.: Syracuse University Press.

Mills, Martin A. 2003. *Identity, ritual and state in Tibetan Buddhism: The foundations of authority in Gelukpa monasticism.* London: RoutledgeCurzon.

Moran, Anthony. 2002. As Australia decolonizes: Indigenizing settler nationalism and the challenges of settler/indigenous relations. *Ethnicity and Racial Studies* 25 (6): 1013–1042.

Moran, Peter Kevin. 2004. *Buddhism observed: Travellers, exiles and Tibetan dharma in Kathmandu.* Anthropology of Asia. London: Routledge.

Morrison, Robert G. 1997. *Nietzsche and Buddhism: A study in nihilism and ironic affinities.* Oxford: Oxford University Press.

Mus, Paul. 1998. *Barabudur: Sketch of a history of Buddhism based on archaeological criticism of the texts.* New Delhi: Indira Gandhi National Centre for the Arts; Sterling Publishers.

Myerhoff, Barbara. 1978. *Number our days.* New York: Simon and Schuster.

———. 1986. "Life not death in Venice": Its second life. In *The anthropology of experience*, ed. V. W. Turner and E. M. Bruner. Urbana: University of Illinois Press, 261–286.

Nagabodhi. 2000. Interview with S. McAra, 15 February.

Nagel, Joane. 1996. *American Indian ethnic renewal: Red power and the resurgence of identity and culture.* New York: Oxford University Press.

Narayan, Kirin. 1993. How native is a "native" anthropologist? *American Anthropologist* 95 (3): 671–686.

Neich, Roger. 1994. *Painted histories.* Auckland: Auckland University Press.

New Zealand Association of Social Anthropologists (NZASA). 1990. Untitled commentary in debate on cultural politics in New Zealand. *Anthropology Today* 6 (3): 3–4.

New Zealand Herald. 2001. Monastery plan not welcome. *Weekend Herald*, 3–4 November.

Northcote, Jeremy. 2004. Objectivity and the supernormal: The limitations of bracketing approaches in providing neutral accounts of supernormal claims. *Journal of Contemporary Religion* 19 (1): 85–98.

Numrich, Paul David. 1999. Local inter-Buddhist associations in North America. In *American Buddhism: Methods and findings in recent scholarship, Curzon critical studies in Buddhism*, ed. D. R. Williams and C. Queen. Richmond, Surrey: Curzon, 117–142.

Obeyesekere, Gananath. 1970. Religious symbolism and political change in Ceylon. *Modern Ceylon Studies* 1 (1): 43–63.

Okely, Judith. 1996. Introduction. In *Own or Other Culture*. London: Routledge, 1–21.

Ortner, Sherry B. 1973. On key symbols. *American Anthropologist* 75:1338–1346.

———. 1989. *High religion: A cultural and political history of sherpa Buddhism*. Princeton, N.J.: Princeton University Press.

———. 1990. Patterns of history: Cultural schemas in the foundings of Sherpa religious institutions. In *Culture through time: Anthropological approaches*, ed. E. Ohnuki Tierney. Stanford, Calif.: Stanford University Press, 57–93.

———. 1999. Thick resistance: Death and the cultural construction of agency in Himalayan mountaineering. In *The fate of "culture": Geertz and beyond*, ed. S. B. Ortner. Berkeley: University of California Press, 136–163.

Park, Geoff. 2004. Whenua: The ecology of placental connection. *Urthona: A Journal for Rousing the Imagination*, Visions of the sacred earth and mythic landscapes 20.

Parr, Christopher. 2000. Inquiring into theosophical interests in Buddhism in New Zealand, since 1884. *Theosophy in New Zealand* (June): 9–14.

Pearce, Susan M. 1997. Foreword: Words and things. In *Experiencing material culture in the Western world*, ed. S. M. Pearce. Leicester: Leicester University Press, 1–10.

Pike, Sarah M. 2001. *Earthly bodies, magical selves: Contemporary pagans and the search for community*. Berkeley: University of California Press.

Potton, Craig. 1995. *Tongariro: A sacred gift*. Nelson, N.Z.: Craig Potton Publishing.

Prajñalila. 1999. Interview with S. McAra, 20 August.

———. 2000a. Interview with S. McAra, 22 June.

———. 2000b. Personal communication, October. [Handwritten comments on an early draft of this book.]

———. 2004. Personal communication, 23 September.

———. 2006. Personal communication, 30 April.

Pratt, Mary Louise. 1992. *Imperial eyes: Travel writing and transculturation*. London: Routledge.

Prebish, Charles S. 1979. *American Buddhism*. North Scituate, Mass.: Duxbury Press.

———. 1999. The academic study of Buddhism in America: The silent *sangha*. In *American Buddhism: Methods and findings in recent scholarship, Curzon critical studies in Buddhism*, ed. D. R. Williams and C. Queen. Richmond, Surrey: Curzon, 183–214.

Prebish, Charles S., and Martin Baumann, eds. 2002. *Westward dharma: Buddhism beyond Asia*. Berkeley: University of California Press.

Prebish, Charles S., and Kenneth K. Tanaka, eds. 1998. *The faces of Buddhism in America*. Berkeley: University of California Press.

Prothero, Stephen. 1995. Henry Steel Olcott and "Protestant Buddhism." *Journal of the American Academy of Religion* 63 (2): 281–302.

Purna. 1997. Untitled subsection of article titled "The stupa is now the Buddha." *Tararu Transformer* (May): 3.

Queen, Christopher S., Charles S. Prebish, and Damien Keown, eds. 2003. *Action Dharma: New studies in engaged Buddhism. RoutledgeCurzon critical studies in Buddhism.* New York: RoutledgeCurzon.

Quin, Diane, and Sue Thompson. 1999. On the Dharma road [videotape]. Auckland: Unitec.

Rambach, Pierre. 1979. *The art of Japanese tantrism.* Geneva: Skira.

Ratana Sutta [The jewel discourse]. 1999. Trans. Piyadassi Thera. Sutta Nipata II.1 ʹ [online]. Buddhist Publication Society. Available at www.accesstoinsight.org/canon/sutta/khuddaka/suttanipata/snp2-01a.html. [Accessed 11 July 2005.]

———. 2000. Translation supplied by Taranatha, August.

Ray, Reginald. 1994. *Buddhist saints in India: A study in Buddhist values and orientations.* Oxford: Oxford University Press.

Ritchie, James E. 1992. *Becoming bicultural.* Wellington: Huia Publishers; Daphne Brasell Associates Press.

Rival, Laura, ed. 1998. *The social life of trees: Anthropological perspectives on tree symbolism. Materializing Culture* series. Oxford: Berg.

Rocha, Cristina. 2006. *Zen in Brazil: The quest for cosmopolitan modernity. Topics in Contemporary Buddhism.* Honolulu: University of Hawai'i Press.

Roof, Wade Clark. 1999. *Spiritual marketplace: Babyboomers and the remaking of American religion.* Princeton, N.J.: Princeton University Press.

Rountree, Kathryn. 2004. *Embracing the witch and the goddess: Feminist ritual-makers in New Zealand.* London: Routledge.

Ryden, K. 1993. *Mapping the invisible landscape: Folklore, writing, and the sense of place.* Iowa City: University of Iowa Press.

Sahlins, Marshall. 1981. *Historical metaphors and mythical realities: Structure in the early history of the Sandwich Islands kingdom.* Ann Arbor: University of Michigan Press.

Said, E. W. 1978. *Orientalism: Western conceptions of the Orient.* Harmondsworth: Penguin.

Saint-Exupéry, Antoine de. 1944. *The little prince.* London: William Heinemann.

Samuel, Geoffrey. 1993. *Civilized shamans: Buddhism in Tibetan societies.* Washington, D.C.: Smithsonian Institution Press.

———. 2004. *Tantric revisionings: New understandings of Tibetan Buddhism and Indian religion.* Burlington, Vt.: Ashgate.

———. 2005. Tibetan Tantra as a form of shamanism. In *Tantric revisionings: New understandings of Tibetan Buddhism and Indian religion.* Burlington, Vt.: Ashgate, 72–93.

Sangharakshita. 1990. *A guide to the Buddhist path.* Glasgow: Windhorse.

———. 1992a. *Buddhism and the West: The integration of Buddhism into Western society.* Glasgow: Windhorse.

———. 1992b. *The FWBO and "Protestant Buddhism": An affirmation and a protest.* Glasgow: Windhorse Publications.

———. 1993. *The drama of cosmic enlightenment: Parables, myths, and symbols of the White Lotus Sutra.* Glasgow: Windhorse.

——. 1996a. *Buddhism for today—and tomorrow.* Birmingham, U.K.: Windhorse Publications.

——. 1996b. *Tibetan Buddhism: An introduction.* Birmingham, U.K.: Windhorse Publications.

——. 2003. *Moving against the stream: The birth of a new Buddhist movement.* Birmingham, U.K.: Windhorse.

Sargisson, Lucy, and Lyman Tower Sargent. 2004. *Living in utopia: New Zealand's intentional communities.* Aldershot, Eng.: Ashgate.

Satyagandhi. 2001. Spirit of place (editorial). *Urthona: A Journal for Rousing the Imagination,* Spirit of place (16): 3.

Satyananda. 1997. [In interview with Anne Reich.] A vision transformed into reality. *Sydney Buddhist Centre Newsletter* (Autumn): 2–5.

——. 1999a. At last, resource consent. *Tararu Transformer* (Winter): 11.

——. 1999b. Audiotaped talk at the FWBO's North London Buddhist Centre.

——. 2004. Personal communication, 9 August.

Seneviratne, H. L. 1999. *The work of kings: The new Buddhism in Sri Lanka.* Chicago: University of Chicago Press.

Sharf, Robert. 1995. Buddhist modernism and the rhetoric of meditative experience. *Numen* 42: 228–283.

Shaw, Rosalind, and Charles Stewart. 1994. Introduction: Problematizing syncretism. In *Syncretism/anti-syncretism: The politics of religious synthesis,* ed. C. Stewart and R. Shaw. London: Routledge, 1–26.

Snodgrass, Adrian. 1985. *The symbolism of the stupa. Studies on Southeast Asia.* Ithaca, N.Y.: Cornell University Southeast Asia Program.

Snyder, Gary. 1990. *The practice of the wild: Essays.* San Francisco: North Point Press.

——. 1995. *A place in space: Ethics, aesthetics, and watersheds: New and selected prose.* Washington, D.C.: Counterpoint.

Snyder, Gary, Bruce Woods, and Dane Schoonmaker. 1985. Gary Snyder talks about bioregionalism. *Utne Reader* 2 (1): 115–117.

Spiro, Melford E. 1967. *Burmese supernaturalism: A study in the explanation and reduction of suffering.* Englewood Cliffs, N.J.: Prentice-Hall.

——. 1970. *Buddhism and society: A great tradition and its Burmese vicissitudes.* 1st ed. New York: Harper & Row.

Spuler, Michelle. 2002. The development of Buddhism in Australia and New Zealand. In *Westward dharma: Buddhism beyond Asia,* ed. C. S. Prebish and M. Baumann. Berkeley: University of California Press, 139–151.

Statistics New Zealand. 2005. 2001 census of population and dwellings—cultural diversity tables. Table 16: Religious affiliation (total responses) by sex, for the census usually resident population count, 1991, 1996 and 2001 [CulturalTable16.xls] [online]. Available at www.stats.govt.nz/census/cultural-diversity-tables. [Accessed 15 October 2005.]

Stewart, Charles. 1999. Syncretism and its synonyms: Reflections on cultural mixture. *Diacritics* 29 (3): 40–62.

Stewart, Charles, and Rosalind Shaw. 1994. Introduction: Problematizing syncretism. In

Syncretism/anti-syncretism: The Politics of religious synthesis, ed. C. Stewart and R. Shaw. London: Routledge, 1–26.

Strain, Charles R. 1999. The Pacific Buddha's wild practice: Gary Snyder's environmental ethic. In *American Buddhism: Methods and findings in recent scholarship, Curzon critical studies in Buddhism*, ed. D. R. Williams and C. Queen. Richmond, Surrey: Curzon, 143–167.

Stromberg, Peter G. 1993. *Language and self-transformation: A study of the Christian conversion narrative*. Cambridge, Eng.: Cambridge University Press.

Stutchbury, Elisabeth. 1994. Perceptions of landscape in Karzha: "Sacred" geography and the Tibetan system of "geomancy." *The Tibet Journal* 19 (4): 59–102.

Subhuti. 1983. *Buddhism for today: A portrait of a new Buddhist movement*. Salisbury, Wiltshire: Element Books, in association with the Friends of the Western Buddhist Order.

———. 1994. *Sangharakshita: A new voice in the Buddhist tradition*. Birmingham, U.K.: Windhorse Publications.

———. 1996a. Picking up the threads of sangha. *Dharma Life* 1: 16–62.

———. 1996b. *Unity and diversity: The sangha, past, present, and future*. Padmaloka Retreat Centre, U.K.: Padmaloka Books.

———. n.d. Subhuti explores freedom and responsibility within the Western Buddhist Order [online]. Available at www.fwbo.org/articles/freedom_in_theorder.html. [Accessed 8 November 2005].

Sudarshanaloka Buddhist Retreat Centre. n.d. An invitation to participate in the building of the retreat centre project. [Brochure written by Prajñalila and Friends of Tararu, ca. 1998.]

Sudarshanaloka Newsletter. 2002. Of water and rock. *Sudarshanaloka Buddhist Retreat Centre [untitled newsletter]*, August: 4.

———. 2006. Jess's newsletter bit. *New Retreat Centre Newsletter* 8 (May): 1–2.

Tacey, David J. 1995. *Edge of the sacred: Transformation in Australia*. North Blackburn, Vic.: HarperCollins.

Tambiah, Stanley Jeyaraja. 1970. *Buddhism and the spirit cults of Northeast Thailand: A study in charisma, hagiography, sectarianism, and millenial Buddhism. Cambridge Studies in Anthropology*, vol. 49. Cambridge: Cambridge University Press.

Tanczos, Nandor. 2004. Tangata whenua, tangata tiriti: Opinion piece [online]. Available at www.greens.org.nz/searchdocs/other7291.html. [Accessed 20 April 2006.]

Taranatha. 1997. [Subsection of] "The Friends of Tararu ask 'Why do I come to Sudarshanaloka?'" *Tararu Transformer* (September): 2–3.

———. 1999a. Interview with S. McAra, 27 August.

———. 1999b. Personal communication, 22 October.

———. 2000a. Script for Arts Day talk on community at Sudarshanaloka, 12 February.

———. 2000b. Personal communication, 3 August.

———. 2000c. Personal communication, 13 November.

———. 2002. Presence minded. *Dharma Life: Buddhism for Today: Cultural Encounters* 18: 38–43.

———. 2006. *Steps to happiness: Travelling from depression and addiction to the Buddhist path*. Birmingham, U.K.: Windhorse.

Tararu Transformer. 1995. Denis' inspiration. September: 1.

———. 1996. The stupa project. March: 1.

———. 1997a. The deed of purchase. September: 2.

———. 1997b. First meeting. September: 5.

———. 1997c. Under the puriri. September: 1.

———. 1999. Open the Dharma road. Winter: 5.

Taylor, J. L. 1993. *Forest monks and the nation-state: An anthropological and historical study in northeastern Thailand.* Singapore: Institute of Southeast Asian Studies.

Taylor, John. 1998. *Consuming identity: Modernity and tourism in New Zealand. Research in Anthropology and Linguistics,* vol. 2. Auckland: Department of Anthropology, The University of Auckland.

Taylor, Ray. 2000. Interview with S. McAra, 12 January.

Taylor, Ruth. 2002. Locals curse plans by "noisy" monks. *West Weekly Community Newspapers,* 27 February.

Thomas, Nicholas. 1995. Kiss the baby goodbye: *Kowhaiwhai* and aesthetics in Aotearoa New Zealand. *Critical Inquiry* 22 (Autumn): 90–121.

Thompson, Sue. 1996a. A stupa at Tararu. *Kantaka, Auckland Buddhist Centre Newsletter* (Winter): 3.

———. 1996b. Sue speaks on ritual. *Tararu Transformer* (August): 1.

———. 1997. Place of beautiful vision. *Kantaka, Auckland Buddhist Centre Newsletter* (August): n.p.

———. 2000. Personal communication, 30 October.

Trainor, Kevin. 1997. *Relics, ritual and representation in the Theravada tradition of Sri Lanka: Rematerializing the Sri Lankan Theravada tradition.* Cambridge: Cambridge University Press.

Turner, V. W. 1967. *The forest of symbols: Aspects of Ndembu ritual.* London: Cornell University Press.

Turner, Victor. 1986. Dewey, Dilthey, and drama: An essay in the anthropology of experience. In *The Anthropology of Experience,* ed. V. W. Turner and E. M. Bruner. Urbana: University of Illinois Press, 33–44.

Tweed, Thomas A. 1999. Night-stand Buddhists and other creatures: Sympathizers, adherents, and the study of religion. In *American Buddhism: Methods and findings in recent scholarship, Curzon critical studies in Buddhism,* ed. D. R. Williams and C. Queen. Richmond, Surrey: Curzon, 71–90.

———. 2000 [1992]. *The American encounter with Buddhism, 1844–1912: Victorian culture & the limits of dissent.* Chapel Hill: University of North Carolina Press.

Upaddha Sutta [online]. In *Samyutta Nikaya* 45.2, trans. Thanissaro Bhikkhu. Available at www.accesstoinsight.org/canon/sutta/samyutta/sn45-002.html. [Accessed 21 April 2005.]

Van Dyke, Mary. 1997. Grids and serpents: A Tibetan formulation ritual in Switzerland. In *Constructing Tibetan culture: Contemporary perspectives,* ed. F. J. Korom. St-Hyacinthe, Quebec: World Heritage Press, 178–227.

Vessantara. 1993. *Meeting the buddhas: A guide to buddhas, bodhisattvas, and tantric deities.* Birmingham, U.K.: Windhorse.

———. 2000. Personal communication, 24 July.

Viradhammo, Ajahn. 1996. Buddhism. In *Religions of New Zealanders*, ed. P. Donovan. Palmerston North, N.Z.: Dunmore Press, 33–47.

Vishvapani. 1994. Buddhism and the New Age. Western Buddhist review: 1 [online]. Available at www.westernbuddhistreview.com/vol1/new_age.html. [Accessed 12 July 2005.]

———. 2000. Personal communication, 14 July.

———. 2001. Testing articles of faith. *Dharma Life: Buddhism for Today* 17: 46–50.

———. n.d. Perceptions of the FWBO in British Buddhism. *Western Buddhist Review,* 13.

Vishvapani and Cittapala. 1999. A comment on the "refutation" of the "response" to the "FWBO files" [online]. FWBO Communications Office. Available at http://response .fwbo.org/refutationcomment.html. [Accessed 6 December 2005.]

Viveka. 2002. A world of difference. *Dharma Life* 18: 24–27.

von Sturmer, Richard. 2005. *Suchness: Zen poetry and prose.* Wellington: HeadworX.

Waitangi Tribunal. n.d. Waitangi Tribunal: About us [online]. Available at www.waitaing-tribunal.govt.nz/about/waitangitribunal/. [Accessed 13 July 2005.]

Wakareo ā-ipurangi. n.d.-a. "Tapu," reference WR-WWC.11448 and 11449. Māori-English Lexicon [online]. Available at www.reotupu.co.nz.ezproxy.auckland.ac.nz/ wakareo/. [Accessed 12 July 2005.]

———. n.d.-b. "Tikanga Māori," reference WR-CL.112. Māori-English Lexicon/Māori Custom Law Lexicon [online]. Available at www.reotupu.co.nz.ezproxy.auckland .ac.nz/wakareo/. [Accessed 20 April 2006.]

———. n.d.-c. "Tūrangawaewae," reference WR-CL.122. Māori-English Lexicon/Māori Custom Law Lexicon [online]. Available at www.reotupu.co.nz.ezproxy. auckland.ac.nz/wakareo/. [Accessed 20 April 2006.]

Walker, Ranginui. 2004. *Ka whawhai tonu matou: Struggle without end.* Rev. ed. Auckland: Penguin.

Walker, Ute. 2001. A question of ethnicity . . . one word, different people, many perceptions: The perspectives of groups other than Maori, Pacific Peoples and New Zealand Europeans: Review of the "Measurement of Ethnicity in Official Statistics Perspectives" paper for consultation. New Zealand Federation of Ethnic Councils Inc. for Statistics, New Zealand.

Waterhouse, Helen. 1997. *Buddhism in Bath: Adaptation and authority. Monograph Series: Community Religions Project.* Leeds, U.K.: Department of Theology and Religious Studies, University of Leeds.

Webb, Larisa Ingrid. 1999. Living together? Change and continuity of a New Zealand intentional community. Unpublished MA thesis, University of Auckland.

Weber, Max. 2002 [1904–1905]. *The Protestant ethic and the spirit of capitalism.* Trans. Stephen Kalberg. Los Angeles: Roxbury.

Welsch, Wolfgang. 1999. Transculturality: The puzzling form of cultures today. In *Spaces of culture: City, nation, world, theory, culture and society,* ed. M. Featherstone and S. Lash. London: Sage, 194–213.

Williams, Duncan Ryuken, and Christopher Queen, eds. 1999. *American Buddhism: Methods and findings in recent scholarship, Curzon critical studies in Buddhism.* Richmond, Surrey: Curzon.

Williams, Paul. 1989. *Mahayana Buddhism: The doctrinal foundations. Library of religious beliefs and practices.* London: Routledge.

Williams, Paul, and Anthony Tribe. 2000. *Buddhist thought: A complete introduction to the Indian tradition.* London: Routledge.

Wolf, Eric. 2002. The Virgin of Guadalupe: A Mexican national symbol. In *A reader in the anthropology of religion,* ed. M. Lambek. Malden, Mass.: Blackwell, 168–174.

Wuthnow, Robert, and Wendy Cadge. 2004. Buddhists and Buddhism in the United States: The scope of influence. *Journal for the Scientific Study of Religion* 43 (3): 361–378.

Yalouri, Eleana. 2001. *The Acropolis: Global fame, local claim. Materializing Culture* series. Oxford: Berg.

Young, Audrey. 2004. Pakeha are indigenous too: Mallard. *The New Zealand Herald,* 29 July.

Index

Page numbers in **boldface** indicate illustrations.

About the Author

Sally McAra received her master's degree with First Class Honors in social anthropology at The University of Auckland, where she is completing her doctorate in anthropology, conducting research into the cross-cultural translation of Buddhism in Bendigo, Australia. Related interests include settler identity, meaning of place, and the vernacularization of world religions. She has also published articles on Māori material culture.

Production Notes for McAra/*Land of Beautiful Vision*

Cover design by Santos Barbasa Jr.

Text design by Elsa Carl with text in Goudy Old Style and display in Hiroshige

Text composition by Tseng Information Systems, Inc.

Printing and binding by The Maple-Vail Manufacturing Group

Printed on 60 lb. Glatfelter Offset, 420 ppi